The Gluten-Free Italian Vegetarian Kitchen

Cookbooks by Donna Klein

The Mediterranean Vegan Kitchen

The PDQ (Pretty Darn Quick) Vegetarian Cookbook

Vegan Italiano

The Gluten-Free Vegetarian Kitchen

The Tropical Vegan Kitchen

Supermarket Vegan

The Chinese Vegan Kitchen

The Gluten-Free Italian Vegetarian Kitchen

THE GLUTEN-FREE
Italian Vegetarian Kitchen

More Than 225 Meat-Free, Wheat-Free,
and Gluten-Free Recipes
for Delicious and Nutritious Italian Dishes

Donna Klein

A PERIGEE BOOK

A PERIGEE BOOK
Published by the Penguin Group
Penguin Group (USA) LLC
375 Hudson Street, New York, New York 10014

USA • Canada • UK • Ireland • Australia • New Zealand • India • South Africa • China

penguin.com

A Penguin Random House Company

Library of Congress Cataloging-in-Publication Data

Klein, Donna (Donna M.).
The gluten-free Italian vegetarian kitchen : more than
225 meat-free, wheat-free, and gluten-free recipes for delicious
and nutritious italian dishes / Donna Klein.
p.   cm.
ISBN 978-0-399-16616-7 (paperback)
1. Gluten-free diet—Recipes.   2. Wheat-free diet—Recipes.
3. Vegetarian cooking.   4. Cooking, Italian.   1. Title.
RM237.86.K642   2014   2014010299
641.5'638—dc23

First edition: September 2014

PRINTED IN THE UNITED STATES OF AMERICA

10   9   8   7   6   5   4   3   2   1

Text design by Kristin del Rosario

The recipes contained in this book are to be followed exactly as written. The publisher is not
responsible for your specific health or allergy needs that may require medical supervision.
The publisher is not responsible for any adverse reactions to the recipes contained in this book.

While the author has made every effort to provide accurate telephone numbers, Internet addresses,
and other contact information at the time of publication, neither the publisher nor the author assumes
any responsibility for errors, or for changes that occur after publication. Further, the publisher does not have
any control over and does not assume any responsibility for author or third-party websites or their content.

Most Perigee books are available at special quantity discounts for bulk purchases for sales promotions,
premiums, fund-raising, or educational use. Special books, or book excerpts, can also be created
to fit specific needs. For details, write: Special.Markets@us.penguingroup.com.

To

Sts. Benedict and Anselm

and the Monastic Community of St. Anselm's Abbey, Washington, DC,

for exhorting me to listen with the ear of my heart

ACKNOWLEDGMENTS

As always, many thanks to the following: my literary agent, Linda Konner; my publisher, John Duff, and the staff and crew at Perigee Books/Penguin Random House; my family, namely my daughters, Emma and Sarah; and my dogs, Trevor and Cooper. With their continuing support and presence in my life, writing my eighth cookbook was a pleasure.

Sincere thanks to the Rt. Rev. Dom James Wiseman, OSB, abbot of St. Anselm's Abbey, Washington, DC, for warmly welcoming me as an oblate of St. Benedict on Epiphany Sunday, January 5, 2014.

Special thanks to the oblates of St. Anselm's Abbey, a congenial group of predominately laypeople affiliated with the monastery, whose embodiment of Benedictine hospitality helped set the tone of this book.

Heartfelt thanks to Abbot Aidan Shea, our previous oblate director, and to Dom Boniface Von Nell, our current guide, for providing spiritual nourishment on the way home.

CONTENTS

PROVIDENCE IS PROLOGUE

When I put my seventh book to bed, I presumed it would be my last. After all, there are seven days in the week, the seventh being the day of rest; seven deadly sins, the seventh sometimes listed as the sin of gluttony (These are all cookbooks, mind you, with a combined total of more than 1,600 recipes!); and seven sacraments, the seventh known in my childhood as the Last Rites—all signs forecasting retirement at the very least. But before the ink on *The Chinese Vegan Kitchen* was barely dry, Providence began hinting "not so fast . . ." On the first Sunday of November 2012, I was received as a novice oblate of St. Anselm's Abbey in Washington, DC. Before my blessing, I was handed a copy of *The Rule of St. Benedict* and noted with delight our shared publisher, Penguin. An individual familiar with the acknowledgment of St. Francis in one of my previous books, *Vegan Italiano*, blithely suggested that, for the sake of Benedictine balance, I write a new cookbook and dedicate it to my "other" favorite Italian saint. I replied that I had no chance—my publisher would never consider another Italian cookbook written by the same author, especially an author who is not even Italian. Besides, one was enough. Three days later, I opened an email from my publisher asking if I would be interested in writing an Italian cookbook for my gluten-free readers who were missing their pasta and pizza. On November 1, 2013, the Feast of All Saints, I submitted the manuscript for *The Gluten-Free Italian Vegetarian Kitchen*, dedicated to Sts. Benedict and Anselm and the Monastic Community of St. Anselm's Abbey. With number eight—a numeral associated with resurrection and renewal—officially published, I am pleased to proclaim with a bow to Providence that number seven was, blessedly, not my last.

I would like to think that St. Benedict approves of this cookbook. Though not explicitly vegetarian, *The Rule* is intrinsically peaceful and forbids monks (other than the sick) to eat the meat of "four-footed animals" and, in some stricter traditions, fowl and fish. Though uniformity in diet is desirable, St. Benedict allows for individual weaknesses by providing his monks with two kinds of cooked food from which to choose, and adding a third dish of fruit and fresh vegetables when available. In further demonstration of *The Rule*'s flexibility, particularly where nourishment of the body is concerned, St. Benedict essentially gives the abbot the authority, when deemed necessary, to change the diet. Back in the day of St. Benedict, the menu was hardly gluten-free—far from it. According to *The Rule*, a generous pound of bread was assigned to each monk to accompany his meals throughout the day. Though celiac disease was first described in the second century, before St. Benedict's time, it wasn't until the late nineteenth century that dietary changes were used as a medical treatment. In any case, had St. Benedict been cognizant of the disease and its treatment, I can easily envision the saint rising before dawn to bake a gluten-free loaf in a designated gluten-free oven to provide an afflicted brother with his dose of daily bread.

The same loving-kindness St. Benedict displays toward his fellow monks is extended to those outside the monastery in the form of hospitality, a pillar of *The Rule*. In chapter 53, St. Benedict stipulates that all guests "should be received as if they were Christ" and directs his monks to set aside a separate kitchen for the abbot and his guests. Moreover, he assigns two monks each year who are competent cooks to oversee the kitchen to ensure that guests are well served. This Benedictine open-door policy is actually a direct act of obedience to the command from Scripture, which exhorts us to practice hospitality, as there are some who have "entertained angels unawares" (Hebrews 13:2). Indeed, in Genesis, chapter 18, Abraham and Sarah share their finest food and drink with three supernatural beings in the guise of men—but not before Abraham has duly provided water for washing their feet. Ultimately, the visitors not only confirm that Sarah (at age eighty-nine!) would soon become the mother of Isaac and that Abraham (at age ninety-nine!) would soon become the father of Israel, but affirm that, in the fullness of time, Abraham would become no less than the father in faith of the whole world. Clearly, a good host is blessed by the guests.

As my guest throughout this cookbook, may you be blessed with good gluten-free recipes. May we each be blessed moment to moment with food ever new from the Host of the eternal banquet.

Pax,

DONNA MARIE MICHAELA KLEIN, oblate OSB

The Benefits of a Gluten-Free Diet

Gluten-free diets are continuing to make headlines these days. Approximately one in 130 Americans have celiac disease, an autoimmune disease that causes gluten intake to damage the small intestine and interfere with the absorption of vital nutrients—completely eliminating gluten from their diet will heal existing intestinal damage, restore nutrient absorption, and prevent further damage. An additional 6 percent (about 18 million people) are classified with gluten-intolerance, experiencing symptoms such as bloated stomachs, intestinal problems, and headaches when eating gluten-containing foods, while not displaying damage to their small intestines—going gluten-free will eliminate these unpleasant effects almost immediately. It's been estimated that up to one-third of the population has milder forms of gluten-intolerance, while many people who can physically tolerate gluten report increased energy after a meal when the gluten has been cut out or reduced—they often report decreased waistlines to boot. Not surprisingly, according to marketing statistics, about 25 percent of the U.S. population at any given time are either trying to limit or completely omit gluten from their diets.

Gluten-Free Vegetarian Eating, Italian Style

For lovers of Italian cuisine—and who doesn't love pizza or pasta?—the good news is that saying good-bye to gluten doesn't have to mean saying good-bye to your favorite Italian foods. While you will have to give up traditionally prepared wheat-based breads and pastas, thanks to the burgeoning gluten-free market, there is a treasure trove of delicious gluten-free flour substitutes available for making outstanding homemade breads, pizzas, and focaccia. Happily, most major supermarkets now carry packaged gluten-free pastas—whole-grain brown rice fusilli and quinoa linguine, to name a few—that taste remarkably like the original. Moreover, wheat is not king throughout all of Italy; rather, in northern Italian kitchens, rice and corn reign supreme, triumphant in an impressive array of creamy risotto and hearty polenta dishes, which are naturally gluten-free. For vegetarians on a gluten-free diet, eggs, cheeses, and other dairy products can be an excellent means of adding extra protein; these ingredients find their way into frittatas, stratas, tortas, casseroles, breads, cakes, and other culinary delights. Most promising of all, especially for those following a plant-based, or vegan, diet, is the wide variety of vegetables, fruits, nuts, seeds, beans, and legumes that are incorporated into just about every Italian meal, from appetizers to desserts, each offering testimony to the intrinsic healthfulness of the world-acclaimed Mediterranean diet and gluten-free eating.

The Lowdown on Gluten

Gluten is a protein composite of gliadin and glutenin that is commonly found in many grass-related grains—namely, wheat, barley, rye, and spelt. By several accounts, Buddhist vegetarian monks discovered gluten in seventh-century China. While kneading wheat flour with water to make a dough, they noticed that the starch washed off and all that remained was an elastic, rubbery mass—gluten. Indeed, it is gluten that gives elasticity to breads and bounce to cakes—without it, baked products often lose their chewy texture as well. Fortunately, while there are glutens in rice, corn, and other grains, they lack the lethal combo of gliadin and glutenin and are blessedly benign. Oats, unfortunately, are typically treated as an exception—though technically gluten-free, due to their high risk of cross-contamination with grains containing harmful glutens, they are generally not recommended for those with celiac disease.

Cereals and Grains That Contain Gluten

Barley

Oats* (due to cross-contamination)

Rye

Spelt

Wheat

Gluten-Free "Safe" Grains, Flours, Starches, and Related Foods

Almond flour/meal (and all nut flours/meals)

Amaranth flour

Arrowroot powder

Buckwheat flour and buckwheat groats/kasha

Carob flour

Cassava flour and starch (see tapioca and yucca flour)

Chestnut flour (and all nut flours)

Chickpea flour/garbanzo bean flour/besan flour/gram flour
  (and all bean flours and starches)

Cornmeal, corn flour, corn grits, polenta, masa, and cornstarch

Finger millet (Ragi)

Flaxseed and flaxseed flour/meal (see linseed)

Job's tears/Chinese pearl barley and flour

Linseed and linseed flour/meal

Millet and millet flour

Montina (Indian rice grass)

Potato flour and starch

Quinoa and quinoa flour

Rice flour

Sago flour and starch

Sorghum flour

Soy flour (and all bean flours and starches)

Tapioca flour and starch (see cassava and yucca flour)

---

* Several companies now produce 100-percent-pure oats specifically for the gluten-free market; they are labeled gluten-free. It is strongly recommended that those with celiac disease check with their health-care professional before consuming oats or oat products of any kind.

Taro flour and powder

Teff and Teff flour

Wild rice

Yucca flour and starch (see cassava and tapioca flour)

Xanthan gum

Yeast (fresh and dried)

"Unsafe" Grains, Starches, and Related Products

All of the foods and food labeling terms below refer to wheat, barley, malt, rye, spelt, oats (due to cross-contamination), and related products that indicate or strongly suggest the presence of gluten and must be avoided by those on a gluten-free diet.

Barley starch

Binder

Bran

Bromated flour

Bulgur (cracked wheat)

Cereal protein

Couscous

Dextrin (unless derived from corn, potato, arrowroot, rice, or tapioca)

Durum wheat/durum wheat flour

Einkorn

Emmer

Emulsifier

Enriched flour

Farina

Flour (unless made with pure rice flour, corn flour, potato flour, or soy flour)

Gluten flour

Graham flour (not to be confused with gram flour, made from gluten-free chickpeas)

Hydrolyzed plant protein (HPP) (unless derived from soy or corn)

Hydrolyzed vegetable protein (HVP) (unless derived from soy or corn)

Kamut

Malt or malt flavoring (unless derived from corn)

Malted barley

Maltose

Matzoh/matzo

Modified food starch (unless arrowroot, corn, potato, or tapioca)

Natural flavoring

Oat bran

Oat germ

Oatmeal (rolled oats)

Pearl barley (not to be confused with Chinese pearl barley, a term for gluten-free Job's tears)

Phosphated flour

Plain flour

Rusk

Rye starch

Self-rising flour

Semolina

Stabilizer

Starch (unless arrowroot, corn, potato, or tapioca)

Thickener

Triticale (a grain crossbred from wheat and rye)

Vegetable gum (except carob bean gum, locust bean gum, cellulose gum, guar gum, gum arabic, gum aracia, gum tragacanth, or xanthan gum)

Vegetable starch

Wheat bran

Wheat germ

Wheat meal

Wheat rusk

Wheat starch

White flour

"Sneaky" Sources of Gluten

Baking powder (may contain wheat starch as a moisture-absorption agent)

Beer, lager, stout, and ale (all made from grains; some gluten-free beers, made using sorghum, are available)

Bouillon cubes and powder, canned broths and soups (especially creamed varieties)

Breakfast beverages (such as Ovaltine)

Cereals (including cornflakes)

Cheese: cream, cottage, and ricotta cheeses (especially reduced-fat varieties); shredded and crumbled (may contain flour to prevent clumping); veined cheese such as Gorgonzola, Roquefort, and blue cheese

Cheese spreads and processed cheese foods

Chili powder (may contain flour to prevent clumping)

Coffees, flavored

Communion wafers

Corn tortillas (may also contain wheat flour)

Curry powder (may contain flour to prevent clumping)

Dried fruits (may be dusted with flour to prevent sticking)

French fries, frozen (flour may be present to keep them white)

Hard candy

Ice cream and frozen yogurt (especially reduced-fat varieties)

Jelly beans

Licorice

Margarine and butter spreads

Mustard powder

Mustard, prepared, and ketchup

Nondairy creamers

Nuts, dry-roasted

Potato and tortilla chips, flavored

Salad dressings and mayonnaise (especially reduced-fat or light varieties)

Seasoning mixes

Sour cream (especially reduced-fat or light varieties)

Soy sauce

Tamari sauce (while many brands are gluten-free, some may contain small amounts of wheat)

Teriyaki sauce

Vanilla extract and other flavorings

White pepper (may be bulked with flour)

Yogurt (especially reduced-fat or flavored varieties)

Note: The labels on all processed and canned foods should be checked carefully before each use. What might be safe one time might not be the next, as manufacturers tend to change their products periodically. When in doubt, contact the manufacturer directly.

Glossary of Gluten-Free Specialty Ingredients

While most of the ingredients called for in this book's recipes are readily found in traditional supermarkets, cooking (baking, in particular) without wheat requires alternative grains, flours, starches, and related products, several of which are available primarily in health food and specialty stores. For the recipes in this book, you will need the following gluten-free specialty ingredients, some of which are also available in well-stocked supermarkets.

ALMOND FLOUR (ALMOND MEAL): Ground from sweet almonds, almond flour is generally made with blanched almonds (no skin) and has a finer consistency than almond meal, which is often made with unblanched almonds; interchangeable in most recipes.

AMARANTH FLOUR: Ground from the seed of the ancient amaranth plant, with a high moisture content and slightly sweet, nut-like flavor.

BROWN ARBORIO RICE: Short-grain rice used for risotto from which only the hull has been removed; has a creamy, slightly chewy, nut-like flavor.

BROWN RICE FLOUR: Ground form of long-grain brown rice, with a slightly nut-like flavor.

BUCKWHEAT GROATS (KASHA): The triangular seeds of a flowering plant related to rhubarb; in roasted or toasted form, the groats are typically known as kasha.

CHESTNUT FLOUR: A sweet, mellow flour ground from chestnuts, with a comparatively low fat content and light texture as a nut flour; expensive.

CHICKPEA FLOUR (GARBANZO BEAN, BESAN, OR GRAM FLOUR): Ground from dried chickpeas, with an earthy, bean-like flavor; very nutritious and high in protein. Flour ground from roasted dried chickpeas known as besan or gram flour in Asian markets.

JOB'S TEARS (COIXSEED, JOBI, YI YI REN, CHINESE PEARL BARLEY): Seed of ancient annual grass native to southeast Asia, with a taste and texture similar to barley, but unrelated; unhulled wild seeds used as beads for making rosaries and jewelry; available in Asian markets.

MILLET: One of the earliest cultivated grains, originating in China nearly 5,000 years ago, the tiny raw seeds are well known as birdseed; cooked food-grade millet has a distinctive, sweet flavor, similar to bulgur wheat or couscous, but is unrelated; good source of protein, fiber, and essential amino acids.

POTATO STARCH (POTATO STARCH FLOUR): A light, neutral-tasting starch commercially prepared from cooked potatoes that are washed of all fibers until only the starch remains; not to be confused with potato flour, which has a much heavier texture and distinctive potato flavor.

QUINOA: Seed of an ancient pseudocereal (rather than true cereal, or grain) native to South America, with a mild, nut-like flavor and chewy texture; a complete protein source containing all nine essential amino acids; high in fiber, iron, and calcium.

SORGHUM FLOUR: Ground from sorghum grain, a drought-tolerant cereal grain similar to millet, and the third most prevalent food crop worldwide; the sweet white variety of flour, with its light color and mild taste, is preferred in baking.

SOY FLOUR: Ground from raw soybeans, with a mild, nut-like flavor; a complete protein source containing all nine essential amino acids; a good source of fiber, iron, calcium, magnesium, and phosphorus.

SWEET RICE FLOUR: Ground from glutinous, or sticky, rice, with more starch than the regular brown and white rice flours; excellent thickener and binder; imparts a lighter, less grainy texture to baked goods when used in combination with regular rice flours; cannot be substituted for regular rice flours.

TAPIOCA FLOUR (TAPIOCA STARCH): A powdery substance ground from the root of the cassava plant, with a light texture and slightly sweet flavor; adds lightness and spring to gluten-free breads.

XANTHAN GUM: A corn-based, fermented natural gum used in foods as a binder, thickener, gelling agent, and stabilizer; essential in many gluten-free baking recipes.

About the Nutritional Numbers

All of the nutritional analyses in this book were compiled using MasterCook Deluxe 4.06 software from SierraHome. As certain ingredients (sorghum flour, Job's tears) were unknown to the software at the time of compilation, substitutes of equivalent caloric and nutritional value were used in their place. All of the recipes using broth have been analyzed using low-sodium canned vegetable broth. All of the recipes using rinsed and drained canned beans have been analyzed using freshly cooked dried beans. Unless salt is listed as a measured ingredient (versus to taste, with no preceding suggested measurement) in the recipe, or unless otherwise indicated, no salt has been included in the analysis; this applies to other seasonings (black pepper, cayenne, etc.) as well. None of the recipes' optional ingredients, unless otherwise indicated, has been included in the nutritional analyses. If there is a choice of two or more ingredients in a recipe (for example, skim milk or rice milk), the first ingredient has been used in the analysis. Likewise, if there is a choice in the amounts of a particular ingredient in a recipe (for example, 2 to 3 tablespoons gluten-free freshly shredded Parmesan cheese, plus additional, to serve), the first amount has been used in the analysis. If there is a range in the number of servings a recipe yields (for example, 4 to 6 servings), the analysis has been based on the first amount.

What Do the Terms Mean?

Dairy-free: Contains eggs, but no dairy products.

Egg-free: Contains dairy products, but no eggs.

Lacto-ovo: Contains dairy products and eggs.

Dairy-free, Egg-free: Contains honey, but no dairy products or eggs.

Vegan: No animal products, including honey, are used in the recipe,
   although optional ingredients may contain dairy products or eggs.

Low-carb: Contains 20 grams or less of carbohydrates per serving.

ONE

Appetizers

Appetizers are a must-have at any Italian get-together. Antipasti, which literally means "before the meal," are meant to stimulate the appetite and prep the stomach for the feast to come—indeed, no serious Italian cook would even think of serving a simple supper without one or two offerings of these delectable little dishes. Fortunately, for those with celiac disease, gluten intolerance, and wheat allergies, many authentic antipasti are already gluten-free—for notable exceptions such as bruschetta, the wide availability of gluten-free breads and flours makes healthy adaptation a breeze. From hot Artichoke Bottoms with Creamy Spinach Florentine to cold skinny roll-ups of marinated Zucchini Carpaccio, whether you're hosting a formal cocktail hour, casual Super Bowl party, or something in between, the following gluten-free appetizers will strike a warm and welcoming note of hospitality.

Cannellini Bean Dip with Basil (vegan/low-carb)

Bruschetta with Caponata (vegan/low-carb)

Artichoke Bottoms with Creamy Spinach Florentine (egg-free/low-carb)

Butternut Squash, Spinach, and Gorgonzola Polenta Canapés (egg-free/low-carb)

Artichoke, Grape Tomato, and Basil Spears (vegan/low-carb)

Tomato-Olive Bruschetta (vegan/low-carb)

Classic Bruschetta with Tomatoes and Basil (dairy-free/low-carb)

Celery Stuffed with Herbed Goat Cheese (egg-free/low-carb)

Italian Chickpea Flour Pancake (vegan/low-carb)

Italian Egg Salad in Lettuce Cups (dairy-free/low-carb)

Polenta Crostini with Sun-Dried Tomato-Basil Pesto (vegan/low-carb)

Herbed Parmesan Crackers (lacto-ovo/low-carb)

Italian-Style Lima Bean Dip (vegan/low-carb)

Roasted Chickpeas with Rosemary (vegan/low-carb)

Grilled White Eggplant in Balsamic Vinaigrette (vegan/low-carb)

Sweet and Sour Eggplant (vegan/low-carb)

Portobello Mushrooms Stuffed with Artichokes and Roasted Red Peppers (vegan/low-carb)

Beefsteak Tomato Caprese Canapés (egg-free/low-carb)

Potato Skins with Mozzarella Cheese and Pizza Sauce (egg-free/low-carb)

Endive Leaves Stuffed with Gorgonzola, Cranberries, and Pecans (lacto-ovo/low-carb)

Crispy Kale Chips (vegan/low-carb)

Stuffed Mushrooms with Asiago Cheese and Basil (lacto-ovo/low-carb)

Spiced Toasted Pistachios (vegan/low-carb)

Baked Risotto Balls (vegan/low-carb)

Slow-Roasted Herbed Tomatoes (vegan/low-carb)

Sun-Dried Tomato and Green Onion Dip (lacto-ovo/low-carb)

Lemon-Pesto Dip with Raw Vegetables (lacto-ovo/low-carb)

Zucchini Carpaccio (vegan/low-carb)

Cannellini Bean Dip with Basil

(VEGAN/LOW-CARB)

Serve this creamy dip with crunchy fresh vegetables, or spread over gluten-free flatbreads or crackers, namely Herbed Parmesan Crackers, page 21. It's also a fine topping for baked potatoes.

MAKES ABOUT 1¼ CUPS, TO SERVE 5 TO 6

1 (15-ounce) can cannellini or other white
    beans, rinsed and drained
2 tablespoons extra-virgin olive oil
1 to 2 tablespoons fresh lemon juice, or
    more, to taste
2 to 3 cloves garlic, finely chopped
¼ teaspoon coarse salt, or to taste
¼ cup finely chopped fresh basil
Paprika (optional)

In a food processor fitted with the knife blade, process the beans, oil, lemon juice, garlic, and salt until smooth and pureed. Transfer to a small bowl and add the basil, stirring well to combine. Sprinkle with the paprika, if using, and serve at room temperature. Dip can be stored in the refrigerator, covered, up to 3 days before returning to room temperature and serving.

PER SERVING (per ¼ cup, or ⅕ of recipe): Calories 126; Protein 5g; Total Fat 6g; Sat Fat 1g; Cholesterol 0mg; Carbohydrate 14g; Dietary Fiber 3g; Sodium 98mg

Variation

For Cannellini Bean Dip with Parsley and Red Onion, replace the basil with finely chopped fresh flat-leaf parsley and garnish with 1 to 2 tablespoons chopped red onion in lieu of the optional paprika.

Bruschetta with Caponata

(VEGAN/LOW-CARB)

Caponata, a sweet and sour eggplant appetizer, can be found in most supermarkets next to the olives. Though optional, a garnish of fragrant toasted pine nuts and fresh basil will prevent even your most discerning guests from guessing that the caponata came out of a jar. The recommended Gluten-Free Brown Ciabatta Bread on page 83 is vegan; though equally delicious on Gluten-Free Italian Bread, page 86, note that the latter contains egg whites.

MAKES 10 APPETIZERS

1 (7.5-ounce) jar gluten-free caponata
    (about 1 cup)
2 tablespoons finely chopped fresh basil
½ loaf Gluten-Free Brown Ciabatta Bread,
    page 83, cut into about 10 (⅜-inch thick)
    slices, toasted until nicely browned, or
    about 4 ounces of other gluten-free Italian-
    style bread
1 garlic clove, halved
Toasted pine nuts, for garnish (optional)
Shredded fresh basil, for garnish (optional)

In a small bowl, mix the caponata and chopped basil until thoroughly combined. Rub the toasted bread slices on one side with the flat sides of the garlic halves. Top the garlic-rubbed side of each slice with about 1½ tablespoons of the caponata. Garnish with the pine nuts and shredded basil, if using, and serve at room temperature.

PER SERVING (per appetizer): Calories 54; Protein 2g; Total Fat 2g; Sat Fat 0g; Cholesterol 0mg; Carbohydrate 7g; Dietary Fiber 1g; Sodium 112mg

Artichoke Bottoms with Creamy Spinach Florentine

(EGG-FREE/LOW-CARB)

The luscious creamed spinach filling can be made a day ahead before assembling and baking these elegant dinner party appetizers. For a vegan option, use soy creamer in lieu of the half-and-half.

MAKES 15 TO 18 APPETIZERS

¼ cup plus 1 tablespoon water, divided
½ tablespoon cornstarch
1 (10-ounce) bag ready-washed spinach
⅓ cup half-and-half or soy creamer
Salt and freshly ground black pepper, to taste
Pinch ground nutmeg, or more to taste
3 (14-ounce) cans artichoke bottoms (about 15 to 18 pieces), rinsed, drained, and patted dry with paper towels

Preheat the oven to 350F (175C). In a small container, stir together 1 tablespoon water and the cornstarch until smooth; set aside.

In a medium deep-sided nonstick skillet with a lid, bring half the spinach and the remaining ¼ cup of water to a boil over medium-high heat. Reduce the heat, cover, and simmer until the spinach begins to wilt, stirring and tossing a few times, about 2 minutes. Add the remaining spinach, cover, and simmer until all the spinach is wilted, stirring and tossing a few times, 2 to 3 minutes. Uncover and increase the heat to medium-high; cook, stirring and breaking up the spinach with the edge of a spatula, until most of the liquid has evaporated and the spinach is greatly reduced in volume. Reduce the heat to medium and add the half-and-half, salt, pepper, nutmeg, and cornstarch mixture. Cook, stirring, until thickened and bubbly, about

3 minutes. Remove from heat and let cool a few minutes. (At this point, completely cooled creamed spinach can be covered and refrigerated up to 1 day before continuing with the recipe.)

Place the artichoke bottoms on an ungreased baking sheet and fill each with about 1 tablespoon of the creamed spinach. Bake 10 minutes (15 minutes, if creamed spinach has been refrigerated), or until heated through. Serve at once.

PER SERVING (per appetizer, or ¹⁄₁₅ of recipe): **Calories 51; Protein 3g; Total Fat 1g; Sat Fat 1g; Cholesterol 3mg; Carbohydrate 7g; Dietary Fiber 4g; Sodium 528mg**

Butternut Squash, Spinach, and Gorgonzola Polenta Canapés

(EGG-FREE/LOW-CARB)

These sophisticated appetizers also make a fine first course or side dish for 4 to 6, or dinner for 3. For easy entertaining, the canapés can be assembled 24 hours before baking.

MAKES 12 CANAPÉS

1 (18-ounce) tube cooked polenta, cut into 12 rounds, about ½-inch thick
1½ tablespoons plus 1 teaspoon extra-virgin olive oil, divided
¼ cup plus 2 tablespoons gluten-free crumbled Gorgonzola cheese, divided
1 tablespoon fresh lemon juice
Salt and freshly ground black pepper, to taste
10 ounces peeled and seeded butternut squash, cut into ½-inch cubes (about 1½ cups)
¼ small red onion (about 1 ounce), sliced into thin half-rounds

2 ounces fresh baby spinach (about 2½ cups), coarsely chopped

6 grape tomatoes, halved

Preheat oven to broil; position oven rack 6 to 8 inches from heat source. Lightly oil a baking sheet and set aside.

Arrange the polenta slices in a single layer on the prepared baking sheet and brush the tops evenly with the 1 teaspoon of oil; set aside. In a large bowl, mash together the ¼ cup cheese, lemon juice, salt, and pepper; set aside.

Broil the polenta until tops are beginning to brown, about 5 minutes. Remove baking sheet from the oven and set aside. Preheat the oven to 350F (175C).

In a large bowl, toss the squash and onion with the remaining 1½ tablespoons oil and salt and pepper to taste until thoroughly coated. Place in a single layer on an ungreased rimmed baking sheet. Roast until squash is tender and browned and onion is caramelized, about 35 to 40 minutes, stirring a few times. Remove baking sheet from oven and add the spinach, tossing with a spatula to wilt the spinach. Immediately transfer the hot squash mixture to the cheese mixture in the bowl; toss well to combine.

Top the polenta rounds with equal amounts of the squash-spinach-cheese mixture. Sprinkle evenly with remaining 2 tablespoons cheese (½ teaspoon per canapé). Garnish with a grape tomato half (at this point, completely cooled canapés can be stored, covered, in the refrigerator up to 24 hours before returning to room temperature and continuing with the recipe). Bake on the center oven rack until canapés are hot and cheese is melted, about 5 minutes (a few minutes longer if previously refrigerated). Serve at once.

PER SERVING (per appetizer): Calories 72; Protein 2g; Total Fat 3g; Sat Fat 1g; Cholesterol 3mg; Carbohydrate 9g; Dietary Fiber 1g; Sodium 64mg

Artichoke, Grape Tomato, and Basil Spears

(VEGAN/LOW-CARB)

This no-cook, virtually instant appetizer is always dependable and delicious.

MAKES 12 APPETIZERS

12 marinated artichoke heart quarters (from about a 6-ounce jar), drained

12 small fresh basil leaves or 6 medium to large fresh basil leaves, torn in half

12 small grape or cherry tomatoes

Salt, preferably the coarse variety, and freshly ground black pepper

¼ cup gluten-free reduced-fat balsamic vinaigrette

Alternate an artichoke quarter, basil leaf, and tomato on each of 12 wooden picks. Arrange in a single layer on a serving plate and season lightly with salt and pepper. Drizzle evenly with the vinaigrette, turning to thoroughly coat. Serve at room temperature.

PER SERVING (per appetizer): Calories 16; Protein 1g; Total Fat 1g; Sat Fat 1g; Cholesterol 0mg; Carbohydrate 3g; Dietary Fiber 1g; Sodium 54mg

Tomato-Olive Bruschetta

(VEGAN/LOW-CARB)

If you don't have time to bake the Gluten-Free Brown Ciabatta Bread on page 83, any ready-made gluten-free ciabatta, Italian bread, or French bread can be used as a base for this tasty topping—just make sure it's egg-free and dairy-free if your goal is to create vegan appetizers. While the Gluten-Free Italian Bread on page 86 is an ideal foundation, it contains egg whites.

ABOUT 10 APPETIZERS

> 6 ounces plum tomatoes (about 2 medium), finely chopped
>
> 2 tablespoons finely chopped kalamata or other good-quality black olives
>
> 2 tablespoons chopped fresh flat-leaf parsley
>
> 1 tablespoon extra-virgin olive oil
>
> ½ tablespoon red wine vinegar
>
> 1 large clove garlic, finely chopped, plus 1 large clove garlic, halved
>
> Salt, preferably the coarse variety, and freshly ground black pepper, to taste
>
> ½ loaf Gluten-Free Brown Ciabatta Bread, page 83, cut into about 10 (³/₈-inch thick) slices, toasted until nicely browned, or about 4 ounces of other gluten-free Italian-style bread

In a small bowl, combine the tomatoes, olives, parsley, oil, vinegar, chopped garlic, salt, and pepper; toss gently to combine. Set aside to let the flavors blend, about 10 minutes; toss again.

Rub the toasted ciabatta bread on one side with the flat sides of the halved garlic. Spoon about 1½ tablespoons of the tomato mixture on the garlic-rubbed side of each slice. Serve at room temperature.

PER SERVING (per appetizer): Calories 65; Protein 1g; Total Fat 4g; Sat Fat 0g; Cholesterol 0mg; Carbohydrate 7g; Dietary Fiber 1g; Sodium 115mg

Classic Bruschetta with Tomatoes and Basil

(DAIRY-FREE/LOW-CARB)

No Italian cookbook would be complete without a recipe for this perennial favorite. For a vegan alternative, prepare with Gluten-Free Brown Ciabatta Bread, page 83.

MAKES 8 SERVINGS

> 2 medium vine-ripened tomatoes (12 ounces total), seeded and finely chopped
>
> 2 tablespoons finely chopped fresh basil
>
> 1 tablespoon extra-virgin olive oil
>
> ½ teaspoon balsamic vinegar
>
> Salt, preferably the coarse variety, and freshly ground black pepper, to taste
>
> 8 (½-inch thick) pieces Gluten-Free Italian Bread, page 86 (about ¼ recipe, or ½ loaf), well toasted, or about 4 ounces other gluten-free Italian-style bread
>
> 1 large clove garlic, halved

In a medium bowl, toss the tomatoes, basil, oil, vinegar, salt, and pepper gently yet thoroughly to combine. Set aside about 10 minutes to allow the flavors to blend; toss gently again.

Rub one side of the toasted bread with the flat sides of the garlic halves. Top each garlic-rubbed side with about 1½ tablespoons of the tomato mixture. Serve at room temperature.

PER SERVING (per appetizer): Calories 69; Protein 2g; Total Fat 3g; Sat Fat 1g; Cholesterol 0mg; Carbohydrate 9g; Dietary Fiber 1g; Sodium 91mg

Celery Stuffed with Herbed Goat Cheese

(EGG-FREE/LOW-CARB)

Tangy goat cheese and fragrant fresh herbs dress up celery stalks in fine style.

MAKES 8 SERVINGS

4 ounces creamy goat cheese

4 ounces gluten-free Neufchâtel cream cheese, cut into chunks, at room temperature

4 tablespoons chopped fresh basil, thyme, oregano, rosemary, and/or sage leaves

Salt and freshly ground black pepper, to taste

1 bunch celery, separated into stalks, washed, trimmed, strings removed, if desired, and patted dry with paper towels

In a medium bowl, mix together the goat cheese, cream cheese, herbs, salt, and pepper until thoroughly blended. Spread the mixture evenly into the celery stalks. Cut into bite-size pieces. Transfer to a platter, cover, and refrigerate for 1 hour, or overnight. Serve chilled.

PER SERVING (⅛ of recipe): Calories 102; Protein 6g; Total Fat 8g; Sat Fat 6g; Cholesterol 26mg; Carbohydrate 1g; Dietary Fiber 0g; Sodium 110mg

Italian Chickpea Flour Pancake

(VEGAN/LOW-CARB)

Farinata, a thin pancake made exclusively with chickpea flour, is the Ligurian counterpart to Nicoise socca. I like mine sprinkled with rosemary and coarse salt—feel free to substitute with your favorite toppings. For an interesting and tasty thin-crust pizza, see the variation, below.

MAKES 6 TO 8 SERVINGS

1½ cups water

1½ cups chickpea flour

2 tablespoons extra-virgin olive oil, divided

½ teaspoon garlic salt

Freshly ground black pepper, to taste

1 tablespoon dried rosemary leaves (optional)

Coarse salt (optional)

In a medium bowl, whisk together the water and flour; cover and refrigerate 2 hours or overnight. Return to room temperature before proceeding.

Preheat oven to 475F (245C). Grease a standard-size baking sheet with 1 tablespoon oil.

Stir the garlic salt, pepper, and remaining 1 tablespoon of oil into the batter (batter should be pancake-like in consistency; if too thick, stir in a tablespoon or so of water). Pour the batter evenly onto the prepared baking sheet. Sprinkle with the rosemary and coarse salt, if using. Bake 10 minutes, or until lightly browned and set. Cut into wedges and serve at once.

PER SERVING: Calories 122; Protein 4g; Total Fat 5g; Sat Fat 1g; Cholesterol 0mg; Carbohydrate 10g; Dietary Fiber 5g; Sodium 176mg

Variation

To make Chickpea Flour Pancake Cheese Pizza, omit the optional rosemary and coarse salt. Spread ½ to ¾ cup gluten-free pizza sauce evenly over the cooked chickpea pancake; sprinkle evenly with 1 to 1½ cups gluten-free shredded mozzarella cheese. Sprinkle lightly with dried oregano and additional garlic salt. Return to oven and bake an additional 3 to 5 minutes, or until cheese is melted. Cut into wedges and serve at once.

Italian Egg Salad in Lettuce Cups

(DAIRY-FREE/LOW-CARB)

Serve this creamy, mayonnaise-less egg salad in hollowed-out tomatoes or artichoke bottoms, as well, or spoon onto cucumber rounds or Herbed Parmesan Crackers, page 21. For a fabulous egg salad sandwich, spread between two pieces of Olive Bread with Rosemary, page 85.

MAKES 4 TO 6 SERVINGS

¼ cup finely chopped red onion

3 tablespoons extra-virgin olive oil

2 tablespoons finely chopped fresh flat-leaf parsley

¼ teaspoon salt, or to taste

Freshly ground black pepper, to taste

4 large eggs, hard-cooked, still warm, peeled and halved lengthwise (see Cook's Tip, on the right)

Assorted radicchio, Belgian endive, and/or butter lettuce cups, to serve

In a medium bowl, mix together the onion, oil, parsley, salt, and pepper until thoroughly combined. Separate the egg yolks and whites. Add the yolks to the bowl; mash in with a fork until mixture is creamy. Coarsely chop the whites and add to the bowl, stirring well to combine. Allow to come to room temperature. (At this point, egg salad can be covered and refrigerated up to 2 days before serving chilled). Spoon into lettuce cups and serve.

PER SERVING (without lettuce cups): Calories 168; Protein 6g; Total Fat 15g; Sat Fat 3g; Cholesterol 213mg; Carbohydrate 2g; Dietary Fiber 0g; Sodium 198mg

Cook's Tip

To hard-cook eggs, place eggs (at room temperature) in a medium saucepan with water to cover. Bring to a boil over medium-high heat. Remove from heat, cover, and let stand for 22 minutes. If using at room temperature in the recipe, drain and plunge in an ice-water bath and let cool completely. If using warm in the recipe, drain and rinse under cold-running water until cool enough to handle; proceed as directed in the recipe.

Polenta Crostini with Sun-Dried Tomato-Basil Pesto

(VEGAN/LOW-CARB)

Incredibly easy to make, these mouthwatering crostini are always a crowd-pleaser.

MAKES 18 APPETIZERS

1 (18-ounce) 6-inch tube cooked polenta, cut into 18 rounds, about ⅓-inch thick

½ tablespoon extra-virgin olive oil

Sun-Dried Tomato-Basil Pesto, page 102

Shredded fresh basil, for garnish (optional)

Preheat the oven to broil; position oven rack 6 to 8 inches from heat source. Lightly oil a baking sheet.

Arrange the polenta slices in a single layer on the prepared baking sheet and brush evenly with the oil. Broil until lightly browned, about 5 minutes, turning the baking sheet as necessary to promote even browning. Remove from oven and immediately top with equal amounts (about a scant ½ tablespoon) of the pesto. Return briefly to the oven and broil until just heated, about 1 minute. Garnish with the shredded basil, if using. Serve warm or at room temperature.

Variation

To make Polenta Crostini with Caponata, prepare the polenta as directed in the recipe. Replace the Sun-Dried Tomato-Basil Pesto with 1 (7.5-ounce) jar gluten-free caponata. Add 2 tablespoons finely chopped fresh basil to the caponata. Top each broiled polenta slice with equal amounts of the caponata-basil mixture. Heat briefly under the broiler. Garnish with toasted pine nuts and shredded basil, if desired. Serve warm or at room temperature.

Herbed Parmesan Crackers

(LACTO-OVO/LOW-CARB)

These fragrant crackers are delicious on their own or spread with your favorite bruschetta topping, egg salad, or dip. Feel free to vary the selected dried herbs according to your own tastes, or to complement a favorite topping. For best results, use finely grated, not freshly shredded, Parmesan cheese; if using a commercially prepared variety, check the label to ensure that it's gluten-free.

MAKES 18 TO 24 SMALL CRACKERS OR 8 TO 12 LARGE CRACKERS

    ¼ cup gluten-free all-purpose flour
    ¼ cup grated gluten-free Parmesan cheese
    2 tablespoons dried parsley flakes
    ½ teaspoon sugar
    ¼ teaspoon dried rosemary leaves, crushed
    ¼ teaspoon dried thyme leaves
    ¼ teaspoon dried oregano
    ¼ teaspoon garlic salt

⅛ teaspoon freshly ground black pepper
2 egg whites
1 tablespoon extra-virgin olive oil

Preheat oven to 300F (150C). Lightly oil a large baking sheet and set aside.

In a small bowl, whisk together the dry ingredients until thoroughly blended. In a medium mixing bowl, using an electric mixer on medium speed, beat the egg whites until foamy. Add the oil and beat on high speed until the mixture is thick and creamy. With a spoon, gradually add the dry mixture to the egg white mixture, stirring until thoroughly combined.

For smaller crackers: Drop the batter by level ½ tablespoons onto the prepared baking sheet, leaving a 2-inch space in between each. Spread the batter slightly with the back of the spoon to form 1½- to 2-inch circles. For larger crackers: Drop the batter by level tablespoons onto the prepared baking sheet, leaving a 2-inch space between each. Spread the batter slightly with the back of the spoon to form 3- to 3½-inch circles. Bake about 15 to 18 minutes for smaller crackers, or 18 to 20 minutes for larger crackers, or until golden brown.

Let cool on the baking sheet 5 minutes before transferring the crackers to a wire rack to cool completely. Serve at room temperature. Completely cooled crackers can be stored in an airtight tin at room temperature up to 1 day for optimal freshness. Re-crisp in a warm oven (about 200F/95C) for 5 to 10 minutes, if necessary.

Italian-Style Lima Bean Dip

(VEGAN/LOW-CARB)

This simple yet delicious fiber-rich dip is a tasty alternative to hummus. Spread on gluten-free whole-grain breads and crackers, it forms a complete protein.

MAKES 8 SERVINGS

2 cups frozen lima beans

½ cup low-sodium vegetable broth

2 large cloves garlic, coarsely chopped

½ teaspoon salt, or to taste

2 tablespoons extra-virgin olive oil

1 to 2 tablespoons fresh lemon juice, or to taste

Freshly ground black pepper, to taste

Chopped red onion and/or assorted olives (optional)

In a medium saucepan, combine the beans, broth, garlic, and salt; bring to a boil over medium-high heat. Reduce the heat to low, cover, and simmer 15 minutes, or until beans are tender, stirring occasionally.

Transfer lima bean mixture and oil to a food processor fitted with the knife blade, or to a blender; process or blend until smooth yet slightly chunky. Transfer to a serving bowl and add the lemon juice and pepper, to taste, stirring well to combine. Garnish with the onion and/or olives, if using, and serve at room temperature. Alternatively, cover and refrigerate up to 3 days before serving chilled, or returning to room temperature.

PER SERVING: Calories 89; Protein 4g; Total Fat 4g; Sat Fat 1g; Cholesterol 0mg; Carbohydrate 11g; Dietary Fiber 2g; Sodium 182mg

Roasted Chickpeas with Rosemary

(VEGAN/LOW-CARB)

These crunchy chickpeas are as addictive as nuts—happily, they're lower in fat and calories and contain even more fiber.

MAKES 8 SERVINGS

2 (15-ounce) cans chickpeas, rinsed and drained

2 tablespoons extra-virgin olive oil

1 tablespoon dried rosemary leaves

1 teaspoon coarse salt

Preheat oven to 375F (190C).

In a medium bowl, toss together the chickpeas, oil, rosemary, and coarse salt until thoroughly combined. Arrange in a single layer on a large baking sheet with sides. Bake 1 hour, or until chickpeas are browned and crunchy through the center, stirring and turning halfway through cooking time. Let cool to room temperature before serving. Completely cooled chickpeas can be stored in an airtight container up to 2 weeks.

PER SERVING: Calories 132; Protein 6g; Total Fat 5g; Sat Fat 1g; Cholesterol 0mg; Carbohydrate 17g; Dietary Fiber 2g; Sodium 240mg

Grilled White Eggplant in Balsamic Vinaigrette

(VEGAN/LOW-CARB)

These succulent strips of marinated white eggplant are a wonderful addition to any antipasti platter. Because of its typically firmer flesh and skin, the white variety is a better

grilling choice than its purple counterpart. While you can certainly use the latter, salting for 30 minutes in a colander, and then rinsing away any bitter juices, is highly recommended before proceeding with the following recipe.

MAKES 4 SERVINGS

1 (1-pound) white eggplant, trimmed and cut into ½-inch-thick rounds

1 tablespoon extra-virgin olive oil

Salt, preferably the coarse variety, and freshly ground black pepper, to taste

½ cup gluten-free reduced-fat balsamic vinaigrette

Place the eggplant slices between paper towels and press lightly to release some of their moisture.

Heat a nonstick grill pan with grids over medium-high heat. Brush the eggplant evenly on both sides with the oil. Working in batches, as necessary, grill the eggplant until browned and tender, about 2 to 3 minutes per side. Transfer grilled eggplant to a baking sheet with sides and season with salt and pepper.

When all eggplant has been grilled and seasoned, cut into 1-inch-wide strips and transfer to a shallow bowl. Add the vinaigrette and toss gently to thoroughly coat. Arrange eggplant in a single layer, cover, and marinate a minimum of 3 hours, or overnight. Serve chilled, or return to room temperature.

PER SERVING: Calories 85; Protein 1g; Total Fat 7g; Sat Fat 1g; Cholesterol 0mg; Carbohydrate 7g; Dietary Fiber 2g; Sodium 239mg

Sweet and Sour Eggplant

(VEGAN/LOW-CARB)

Sweet and sour dishes were a hallmark of medieval Italian cuisine—petonciane in agrodolce, a forerunner of caponata, is one of the oldest and most delicious. Serve the eggplant alone as an appetizer, or toss with rice as a main course.

MAKES 4 SERVINGS

1 medium eggplant (about 12 ounces), peeled, cut into 1-inch cubes

Table salt

2½ tablespoons extra-virgin olive oil

1 stalk celery, chopped

¼ cup water

2½ tablespoons red wine vinegar

1 tablespoon tomato paste

1 tablespoon sugar

Salt and freshly ground black pepper, to taste

Sprinkle eggplant with salt and set in a colander to drain for 30 minutes. Rinse the eggplant under cold-running water and drain well between paper towels.

In a large nonstick skillet, heat the oil over medium-high heat. Add the eggplant and cook, stirring, until lightly browned, about 5 minutes. Reduce the heat to medium and add the celery; cook, stirring, 1 minute. Reduce the heat to medium-low and add the water, vinegar, tomato paste, sugar, salt, and pepper; cook, stirring, until liquids are greatly reduced and thickened, about 3 minutes. Serve at room temperature.

PER SERVING: Calories 111; Protein 1g; Total Fat 9g; Sat Fat 1g; Cholesterol 0mg; Carbohydrate 9g; Dietary Fiber 2g; Sodium 43mg

Portobello Mushrooms Stuffed with Artichokes and Roasted Red Peppers

(VEGAN/LOW-CARB)

For an elegant first course for four, present these tangy stuffed mushrooms on small serving plates coated with marinara sauce. For a cozy dinner for two, serve on a bed of rice or polenta. The filling also makes an excellent topping for bruschetta and crostini.

MAKES 4 SERVINGS

1 (7-ounce) jar roasted red bell peppers, drained and coarsely chopped, drained again

1 (6-ounce) jar marinated artichoke hearts, drained and chopped, drained again

2 tablespoons gluten-free reduced-fat Italian dressing

1 tablespoon plus 1 teaspoon extra-virgin olive oil, divided

1 teaspoon balsamic vinegar

1 large clove garlic, finely chopped

½ teaspoon dried oregano

Salt and freshly ground black pepper, to taste

4 large Portobello mushroom caps, about 2 ounces each

2 tablespoons gluten-free, egg-free, dairy-free Italian-seasoned dry bread crumbs

Preheat oven to broil. Lightly oil a baking sheet with a rim and set aside.

In a small bowl, toss together the red peppers, artichokes, dressing, ½ tablespoon oil, vinegar, garlic, oregano, salt, and black pepper. Set aside to let flavors blend, about 10 minutes; toss again.

Rub the undersides of the mushrooms with ½ tablespoon oil; season on all sides with salt and pepper. Place on the prepared baking sheet, stem-side down. Broil 4 to 6 inches from heating element 3 to 4 minutes, or until lightly browned and sizzling. Remove from oven and turn over; carefully drain any juices from baking sheet. (Do not turn off oven.)

Position oven rack 6 to 8 inches from heating element.

Fill the mushroom caps with equal amounts of the artichoke mixture (about ¼ cup). Sprinkle each with ½ tablespoon of the bread crumbs; drizzle with ¼ teaspoon of the remaining oil. Broil about 2 minutes, or until lightly browned and heated through, turning the baking sheet to promote even browning. Serve warm or at room temperature.

PER SERVING: Calories 112; Protein 4g; Total Fat 6g; Sat Fat 1g; Cholesterol 0mg; Carbohydrate 14g; Dietary Fiber 4g; Sodium 202mg

Beefsteak Tomato Caprese Canapés

(EGG-FREE/LOW-CARB)

I enjoyed this scrumptious, no-fuss appetizer at a friend's house on the Jersey shore the summer I was compiling recipes for this book. While no tomato in the world tastes better than a Jersey beefsteak in July, any good-quality large vine- or field-ripened variety can be substituted.

Thanks, Rob—this one's for you.

MAKES ABOUT 24 CANAPÉS, TO SERVE 4

24 (¼-inch-thick) slices ripe Jersey beefsteak tomatoes (about 2 large, 8 ounces each)

Salt, preferably fine sea salt, and freshly ground black pepper, to taste

12 large thin slices (about ¼ pound) deli-style mozzarella cheese, cut in half crosswise, or 24 small thin slices

2 tablespoons chopped fresh basil

About 2 tablespoons extra-virgin olive oil

On a large serving platter, arrange the tomato slices in a single layer; sprinkle lightly with salt and pepper. Top each with a piece of cheese, then sprinkle evenly with the basil. Drizzle each canapé with equal amounts of the oil (about ¼ teaspoon). Serve at once.

PER SERVING (per one appetizer, or ¹/₂₄ of recipe): Calories 29; Protein 1g; Total Fat 2g; Sat Fat 1g; Cholesterol 4mg; Carbohydrate 1g; Dietary Fiber 0g; Sodium 21mg

Variation

To make Insalata Caprese, substitute the deli-style mozzarella cheese with about ¾ pound of fresh mozzarella, sliced into 24 rounds, and the chopped basil with 24 whole basil leaves. Increase the oil to 4 tablespoons and whisk with 2 tablespoons of balsamic vinegar, salt, and pepper. On a large serving platter, arrange the tomatoes, basil leaves, and mozzarella in an overlapping circular fashion; drizzle evenly with the vinaigrette and serve at once.

Potato Skins with Mozzarella Cheese and Pizza Sauce

(EGG-FREE/LOW-CARB)

If you like potatoes and pizza, you'll love these crispy double-duty potato skins. For a vegan option, omit the cheese—they'll still taste delicious.

MAKES 8 APPETIZERS

4 large russet potatoes (about 8 ounces each), scrubbed

1 tablespoon canola oil

Garlic salt, to taste

Freshly ground black pepper, to taste

1 cup prepared gluten-free pizza sauce

¾ cup gluten-free shredded part-skim mozzarella cheese

Dried oregano, to taste

Preheat oven to 425F (220C). Prick the potatoes with the tines of a fork and bake for 1 hour, or until tender. Remove from the oven and set aside to cool slightly. (Do not turn off oven.)

When the potatoes are cool enough to handle, cut in half lengthwise and, using a spoon, scoop out and discard most of the flesh (or reserve to thicken soups, etc.), so that the shells are about ¼-inch thick. Brush the outside of the shells evenly with the oil. Sprinkle the insides lightly with garlic salt and pepper. Transfer the shells to an ungreased baking sheet and spoon 2 tablespoons of pizza sauce inside each shell. Sprinkle 1½ tablespoons of cheese over the sauce, then sprinkle lightly with oregano and garlic salt. Bake for 10 to 12 minutes, or until the outsides of the shells are crisp and golden and the cheese is melted. Serve at once.

PER SERVING: Calories 133; Protein 5g; Total Fat 5g; Sat Fat 2g; Cholesterol 6mg; Carbohydrate 19g; Dietary Fiber 1g; Sodium 258mg

Endive Leaves Stuffed with Gorgonzola, Cranberries, and Pecans

(LACTO-OVO/LOW-CARB)

This easy yet elegant appetizer provides a festive, tangy touch to any winter holiday gathering. The recipe easily doubles to serve eight. For an egg-free dish, use a vegan mayonnaise or substitute with an additional tablespoon of cream cheese.

MAKES 8 OR 9 APPETIZERS (ABOUT 4 SERVINGS)

> 4 ounces crumbled gluten-free Gorgonzola
> cheese
> 1 tablespoon gluten-free Neufchâtel cream
> cheese, softened
> 1 tablespoon gluten-free light mayonnaise
> 1 tablespoon whole dried cranberries,
> chopped
> Freshly ground black pepper, to taste
> 1 head Belgian endive, separated into leaves
> (about 8 or 9)
> 2 tablespoons chopped pecans or walnuts,
> toasted, if desired

In a small bowl, mix together the Gorgonzola, cream cheese, mayonnaise, cranberries, and pepper with a fork until thoroughly blended. Fill the leaves with equal amounts of the cheese mixture. Sprinkle with equal amounts of the pecans. Serve at once.

PER SERVING (per appetizer, or ⅛ of recipe): Calories 79; Protein 4g; Total Fat 6g; Sat Fat 3g; Cholesterol 12mg; Carbohydrate 3g; Dietary Fiber 2g; Sodium 225mg

Crispy Kale Chips

(VEGAN/LOW-CARB)

A healthful, low-carb alternative to potato chips, these swift and simple kale chips never last long in my household—a good thing, as they should be consumed shortly after baking for best results. I use Trader Joe's prewashed bagged kale for added ease and convenience.

MAKES 4 TO 6 SERVINGS

> 1 (10-ounce) bag prewashed and trimmed
> kale, or 1 (1-pound) bunch kale, washed
> and patted completely dry with paper
> towels, thick stems and ribs removed, cut
> into 2-inch pieces
> 2 tablespoons extra-virgin olive oil
> Sea salt, to taste

Preheat oven to 275F (135C). Lightly oil 2 large rimmed baking sheets and set aside.

Place the kale in a large bowl and toss with the oil. Sprinkle lightly with the salt and toss again, using your fingers to evenly coat each piece. Divide the kale equally among the prepared baking sheets. Working with 1 baking sheet at a time, bake until kale is crisp, 15 to 20 minutes, turning with a large spatula halfway through cooking. Repeat with remaining baking sheet. Let cool completely before serving at room temperature. For best results, consume within a few hours.

Leftovers can be refrigerated, covered, overnight before re-crisping in a warm oven (about 200F/95C) for 5 to 10 minutes.

PER SERVING (with ¼ teaspoon salt): Calories 95; Protein 2g; Total Fat 7g; Sat Fat 1g; Cholesterol 0mg; Carbohydrate 7g; Dietary Fiber 0g; Sodium 164mg

Stuffed Mushrooms with Asiago Cheese and Basil

(LACTO-OVO/LOW-CARB)

This elegant appetizer can be made with cultivated white mushrooms in lieu of the cremini variety, if desired. For easy entertaining, the prebaked and filled mushrooms can be held at room temperature up to 1 hour before popping in the oven for the final 10 minutes and serving. For an egg-free version, use a vegan mayonnaise.

MAKES 24 APPETIZERS; SERVES 6

24 cremini mushrooms, washed and stemmed
¾ cup gluten-free shredded Asiago cheese
½ cup gluten-free reduced-fat mayonnaise
Salt and freshly ground black pepper, to taste
¼ cup finely chopped fresh basil
12 small cherry or grape tomatoes, halved

Preheat oven to 375F (190C). Lightly grease a standard baking sheet with sides.

Place the mushrooms, gill-sides up, on the prepared baking sheet and bake 10 minutes. Remove baking sheet from oven; carefully drain off any accumulated liquids. Set baking sheet aside.

In a small bowl, mash together the cheese, mayonnaise, salt, and pepper until thoroughly blended. Add the basil, stirring well to thoroughly combine. Fill each mushroom with equal portions (about 1 heaping teaspoonful) of the cheese mixture; top with a tomato half. Return baking sheet to oven and bake an additional 8 to 10 minutes, or until hot and lightly browned. Let cool a few minutes before serving warm.

PER SERVING (per piece): Calories 49; Protein 3g; Total Fat 3g; Sat Fat 2g; Cholesterol 8mg; Carbohydrate 3g; Dietary Fiber 1g; Sodium 117mg

Spiced Toasted Pistachios

(VEGAN/LOW-CARB)

If you can catch shelled pistachios on sale, the purchase is well worth the time saved on otherwise shelling the labor-intensive, yet ultra-delicious, green nut. For a savory appetizer, use the lesser amount of sugar and spice. For a sublime dessert, use the greater amount and coarsely chop and mix the toasted nuts into slightly softened vanilla ice cream or nondairy frozen dessert to create "homemade" pistachio ice cream, or stir into Whipped Ricotta with Honey, page 221.

MAKES 2 CUPS, OR 8 TO 12 SERVINGS

1 to 2 teaspoons sugar
1 to 2 teaspoons ground cinnamon
⅛ to ¼ teaspoon ground nutmeg
2 cups shelled roasted and salted pistachio nuts, skins rubbed off, as necessary

In a small bowl, combine the sugar, cinnamon, and nutmeg; set aside.

In a medium heavy-bottomed skillet over medium heat, toast the nuts until golden, stirring occasionally, about 5 minutes. Lift the skillet off the heat and immediately add the sugar-spice mixture, stirring well to thoroughly coat. Immediately transfer to a baking sheet, spread in a single layer, and cool to room temperature.

Completely cooled nuts can be stored in an airtight container at room temperature up to 1 week for optimal freshness.

PER SERVING (per ¼ cup): Calories 187; Protein 7g; Total Fat 16g; Sat Fat 2g; Cholesterol 0mg; Carbohydrate 9g; Dietary Fiber 4g; Sodium 2mg

Baked Risotto Balls

(VEGAN/LOW-CARB)

These delectable little rice balls, commonly known as *arancini*, are an excellent way to use up leftover risotto. This baked variation is no less crunchy—and far less greasy—than the standard deep-fried version. To ensure a vegan dish, check that the gluten-free bread crumbs are also egg-free and dairy-free as well. For an attractive first-course presentation, serve atop marinara sauce and garnish with a sprig of fresh basil.

MAKES 8 RICE BALLS

> ¼ cup gluten-free Italian-seasoned bread crumbs (preferably egg-free and dairy-free), plus additional, as necessary (see Cook's Tip, on the right)
>
> 1 packed cup leftover Microwave Cabbage Risotto with Basil (page 125), well-chilled, or other risotto
>
> 1½ to 2 tablespoons canola oil
>
> Gluten-free marinara sauce or other pasta sauce, heated (optional)

Preheat oven to 450F (230C).

Place the bread crumbs in a small shallow bowl. Fill a small bowl with cold water. With slightly wet fingers and palms, form the risotto into 8 firm round balls, using 2 tablespoons risotto for each. Gently roll each ball in the bread crumbs until thoroughly coated; place on an ungreased baking sheet and repeat with remaining risotto.

Brush all sides of each risotto ball evenly with the oil, turning carefully so as not to break apart. Bake on the center oven rack 8 to 10 minutes without turning, or until golden brown. Serve at once, accompanied by marinara sauce, if desired.

PER SERVING (per rice ball without sauce): Calories 98; Protein 1g; Total Fat 5g; Sat Fat 0g; Cholesterol 0mg; Carbohydrate 11g; Dietary Fiber 0g; Sodium 101mg

Cook's Tip

To make gluten-free Italian-seasoned dry bread crumbs out of prepared gluten-free unseasoned dry bread crumbs: For every 1 cup of plain gluten-free dry bread crumbs, add ½ teaspoon salt, ½ teaspoon dried parsley flakes, ½ teaspoon ground black pepper, ½ teaspoon garlic powder, ¼ teaspoon onion powder, ¼ teaspoon dried oregano, and ¼ teaspoon dried basil. Place in a self-sealing bag, seal, and shake until thoroughly blended. Store for several weeks at room temperature. If gluten-free vegan Italian-seasoned dry bread crumbs are required, make sure the prepared gluten-free unseasoned dry variety is egg-free and dairy-free.

Variation

To make Baked Risotto Balls with Mozzarella, cut a 1-ounce piece of fresh mozzarella cheese into 6 equal cubes. Form the risotto into 6 round balls (use about 2½ tablespoons risotto per ball), molding the risotto around a cube of mozzarella. Prepare and bake as otherwise directed in the above recipe. If rice balls split apart during baking, let cool a few minutes on the baking sheet before gently reshaping with a spoon. Sprinkle with a little freshly grated Parmesan cheese, if desired, and return to the hot oven for 1 minute, or until grated cheese is melted. Serve at once, accompanied by marinara sauce, if using.

Slow-Roasted Herbed Tomatoes

(VEGAN/LOW-CARB)

Slow-roasting concentrates the inherent sweetness of plum tomatoes. Enjoy as part of an antipasti platter, alone as a healthy snack, in salads and sandwiches, or tossed with gluten-free pasta or rice.

MAKES 8 SERVINGS

> 2 pounds large plum tomatoes (about 8 to 10), quartered lengthwise
> 2 tablespoons extra-virgin olive oil
> ½ tablespoon sugar
> ½ teaspoon coarse salt
> ½ teaspoon Italian seasoning
> Freshly ground black pepper, to taste

Preheat oven to 175F (80C).

In a large bowl, gently toss the tomatoes with all the remaining ingredients until thoroughly coated. Arrange tomatoes, cut sides up, on a large baking sheet. Roast 6 hours (do not turn or stir), or until reduced and wrinkled. Serve at room temperature. Refrigerate tomatoes in a resealable plastic bag up to 1 week, or freeze up to 2 months.

PER SERVING (per 4 pieces, or ⅛ of recipe): Calories 55; Protein 1g; Total Fat 4g; Sat Fat 1g; Cholesterol 0mg; Carbohydrate 6g; Dietary Fiber 1g; Sodium 127mg

Sun-Dried Tomato and Green Onion Dip

(LACTO-OVO/LOW-CARB)

This recipe makes a great party dip—celery, bell peppers, broccoli, and baby carrots make great dippers. For an egg-free appetizer, use vegan mayonnaise.

MAKES ABOUT 2 CUPS

> 8 ounces gluten-free light cream cheese, softened
> ½ cup gluten-free light mayonnaise
> ½ cup gluten-free light sour cream
> 4 scallions, green parts only, chopped
> ⅓ cup drained and chopped marinated sun-dried tomato pieces
> ½ teaspoon salt
> Freshly ground black pepper, to taste
> Assorted fresh raw vegetables, to serve

Combine all ingredients, except the assorted raw vegetables, in a food processor fitted with the knife blade; process until smooth. Refrigerate, covered, a minimum of 2 hours or up to 2 days. Serve chilled or return to room temperature, accompanied with the assorted raw vegetables.

PER SERVING (per ¼ cup dip only, or ⅛ of recipe): Calories 118; Protein 4g; Total Fat 9g; Sat Fat 4g; Cholesterol 22mg; Carbohydrate 7g; Dietary Fiber 0g; Sodium 385mg

Lemon-Pesto Dip with Assorted Raw Vegetables

(LACTO-OVO/LOW-CARB)

This makes an excellent dip for fresh broccoli and cauli-flower. For a vegan variation, prepare with a vegan may-onnaise, nondairy sour cream or plain soy yogurt, and Rustic Pesto Sauce, page 92.

MAKES 1½ CUPS

¾ cup gluten-free light mayonnaise
½ cup gluten-free light sour cream
¼ cup gluten-free prepared pesto sauce
1 to 2 teaspoons fresh lemon juice
Salt and freshly ground black pepper, to taste
Assorted fresh raw vegetables, to serve

In a small bowl, mix together all ingredients except the vegetables until thoroughly blended. Cover and chill a minimum of 1 hour, or up to 2 days. Serve chilled, with assorted raw vegetables for dipping.

PER SERVING (per ¼ cup dip only): Calories 127; Protein 2g; Total Fat 11g; Sat Fat 2g; Cholesterol 15mg; Carbohydrate 6g; Dietary Fiber 0g; Sodium 223mg

Zucchini Carpaccio

(VEGAN/LOW-CARB)

Carpaccio (car-PAH-chee-oh) is a popular Italian appetizer consisting of thinly sliced raw meat, fish, or vegetables drizzled with olive oil and lemon juice or vinegar. The mar-inated zucchini slices can be rolled and secured with wooden picks before serving, if desired.

MAKES 6 SERVINGS

¼ cup extra-virgin olive oil
2 tablespoons balsamic vinegar
1 teaspoon coarse salt
3 medium zucchini (about 6 ounces each), trimmed, cut lengthwise into ⅛-inch thick slices
Freshly ground black pepper (optional)

In an 11 × 7-inch baking dish, combine the oil, vinegar, and salt; add the zucchini, tossing to thoroughly coat. Let stand about 20 minutes at room temperature, turning the zucchini in the marinade a few times. Cover and marinate in the refrigerator 1 hour, or overnight. Season with freshly ground black pepper, if desired. Serve chilled or return to room temperature.

PER SERVING: Calories 92; Protein 1g; Total Fat 9g; Sat Fat 1g; Cholesterol 0mg; Carbohydrate 3g; Dietary Fiber 1g; Sodium 316mg

TWO

Soups

While the Italians may not have invented soup—that distinction has yet to be decided—they may well have perfected it. In winter, what could be more comforting than a steaming bowl of St. Scholastica Winter White Bean and Arborio Rice Soup with Rosemary, or more filling than a hearty bowl of Tuscan-Style Minestrone with Fennel and Herbed Polenta Dumplings? To herald spring, what could be more renewing than a warm bowl of Italian Spring Soup, simmered with asparagus and tender young greens, and enriched with an optional egg? In summer, what could be more refreshing than a chilled bowl of Raw Tomato and Basil Soup, a no-cook blender recipe embodying the full flavors of the season? Come autumn, what could be more inviting than a light yet creamy bowl of Roasted Butternut Squash and Garlic Soup with Sage to commence a Thanksgiving feast? Whatever the occasion, there's a slurp-worthy bowl of gluten-free goodness among the following recipes for everyone gathered at the table.

Light Soups

Italian Vegetable Broth with Roasted Garlic (vegan/low-carb)

Asparagus Soup with Basil and Tarragon (vegan/low-carb)

Black-Eyed Pea Soup (vegan)

Roasted Cauliflower Soup with Rosemary (vegan/low-carb)

Butter Bean Soup with Rosemary (vegan)

Roasted Butternut Squash and Garlic Soup with Sage (vegan)

Creamy Carrot-Zucchini Soup (vegan/low-carb)

Escarole Soup (vegan/low-carb)

Herbed Potato Soup with Roasted Garlic (vegan)

Italian Spring Soup (vegan)

Chilled Raw Tomato and Basil Soup (vegan/low-carb)

Roasted Tomato Soup with Basil (vegan)

Creamy Yellow Squash Soup (vegan/low-carb)

Zucchini-Rice Soup (vegan/low-carb)

Heartier Soups and Stews

Broccoli and Mascarpone Soup (egg-free/low-carb)

Quick Cannellini and Italian-Cut Green Bean Stew (vegan)

Cauliflower and Spaghetti Soup (vegan)

Italian Lentil Soup (vegan)

Autumn Minestrone Soup (vegan)

Minestrone Soup with Potatoes and Pesto (egg-free)

Minestrone Soup with Roman Beans and Brown Rice (vegan)

Ricotta Cheese Gnocchi in Vegetable Broth (lacto-ovo/low-carb)

Italian Split Pea Soup (vegan)

Tuscan-Style Minestrone Soup with Fennel and Herbed Polenta Dumplings (egg-free)

Sweet Potato Minestrone Soup (vegan)

St. Scholastica Winter White Bean and Arborio Rice Soup with Rosemary (vegan)

Winter Vegetable Stew (vegan)

Italian Vegetable Broth with Roasted Garlic

(VEGAN/LOW-CARB)

Use this flavorful vegetable broth in any of the book's recipes calling for low-sodium vegetable broth.

MAKES 3½ TO 4 QUARTS; 14 TO 16 CUPS

1 medium garlic head, left whole

2 tablespoons extra-virgin olive oil

1 large onion (about 8 ounces), coarsely chopped

8 ounces celery (about 6 small stalks), coarsely chopped

8 ounces carrots (about 4 small), coarsely chopped

1 medium leek (about 5 ounces), trimmed, halved lengthwise, coarsely chopped

4 quarts (16 cups) water

1½ pounds very ripe tomatoes (about 4 medium)

1 pound russet potatoes (about 2 large), peeled, coarsely chopped

6 ounces cremini mushrooms, quartered

1 medium turnip (about 4 ounces), peeled and quartered

12 sprigs flat-leaf parsley

10 sprigs fresh thyme or 1 tablespoon dried thyme

4 bay leaves

1 tablespoon whole black peppercorns

1 tablespoon sugar, or to taste

¼ teaspoon whole allspice

Salt, to taste (optional)

Freshly ground black pepper (optional)

Preheat the oven to 400F (205C). Wrap the garlic head in aluminum foil and set aside.

In an 8-quart stockpot, heat the oil over medium-low heat. Add the onion, celery, carrots, and leek and cook, covered, stirring occasionally, until softened, 15 to 20 minutes. Uncover and raise heat to medium-high; cook, stirring, until lightly browned, 3 to 5 minutes. Add a few cups of the water, scraping the bottom of the pot to release any browned bits. Add the remaining ingredients and bring to a boil over high heat. Reduce the heat, cover, and simmer, partially covered, for 2 hours. Turn off the heat and let stand, covered, 1 hour.

Meanwhile, roast the garlic head about 50 minutes, or until soft. Remove the foil and set the garlic aside to cool slightly. Cut the roasted garlic head crosswise in half and squeeze the softened cloves into a small bowl; mash well and set aside.

Strain the broth through a fine-meshed sieve into another pot, pressing down hard on the vegetables with the back of a wooden spoon to extract their liquids. Discard remaining solids.

Clean the original pot. Line the sieve with cheesecloth and strain the broth into the cleaned pot. Add the mashed garlic and cook over low heat, whisking often, until thoroughly blended, about 3 minutes; season with additional salt and pepper, if necessary. Remove from heat and let cool to room temperature. Completely cooled broth can be tightly covered and stored in the refrigerator for up to 5 days, or frozen up to 4 months. For smaller quantities, freeze the broth in ice cube trays then pop the frozen cubes into freezer bags. Each cube is equal to about 2 tablespoons of broth.

PER SERVING (about 1 cup, or ¹⁄₁₄ of recipe, without salt): Calories 50; Protein 1g; Total Fat 2g; Sat Fat 0g; Cholesterol 0mg; Carbohydrate 8g; Dietary Fiber 0g; Sodium 13mg

Asparagus Soup with Basil and Tarragon

(VEGAN/LOW-CARB)

This luxurious springtime soup can be enjoyed anytime of the year using frozen asparagus. A dollop of dairy or non-dairy sour cream, though optional, provides additional richness.

MAKES 4 SERVINGS

> 2 tablespoons canola oil
> 1 large onion (about 8 ounces), chopped
> 1 medium carrot (about 4 ounces), chopped
> 2 large cloves garlic, finely chopped
> 2 cups low-sodium vegetable broth
> 1½ cups water
> 1¼ pounds fresh asparagus, trimmed, cut into 1-inch pieces, tips reserved, or 1 (12-ounce) package frozen asparagus spears, thawed, cut into 1-inch pieces, tips reserved
> ½ cup chopped fresh basil
> 1 to 2 teaspoons chopped fresh tarragon or ¼ to ½ teaspoon dried tarragon
> ½ teaspoon salt, or to taste
> Freshly ground black pepper, to taste
> Gluten-free sour cream or non-dairy sour cream (optional)

In a medium stockpot, heat the oil over medium heat. Add the onion and carrot and cook, stirring, until softened, about 3 to 4 minutes. Add the garlic and cook, stirring constantly, 1 minute. Add the broth, water, asparagus pieces, basil, tarragon, salt, and pepper; bring to a boil over high heat. Reduce the heat to between low and medium-low, cover, and simmer 20 minutes, stirring occasionally, or until vegetables are tender. Let cool slightly.

In a blender or food processor fitted with the knife blade, working in batches, as necessary, blend or process the asparagus mixture until smooth and pureed. Return to the pot and add the reserved asparagus tips; bring to a gentle simmer over medium-high heat, stirring occasionally. Reduce the heat to low and cook, covered, stirring once, until tips are crisp-tender, about 3 minutes. Serve warm, garnished with a dollop of sour cream, if desired.

PER SERVING: Calories 135; Protein 8g; Total Fat 7g; Sat Fat 1g; Cholesterol 0mg; Carbohydrate 12g; Dietary Fiber 5g; Sodium 537mg

Black-Eyed Pea Soup

(VEGAN)

Black-eyed peas, though not typically associated with Italian cuisine, are popular additions to soups and stews. Though optional, liquid smoke lends this tasty soup a smoky appeal.

MAKES 5 TO 6 SERVINGS

> 2 tablespoons extra-virgin olive oil
> 1 small onion (about 4 ounces), finely chopped
> 2 stalks celery, finely chopped
> 2 large cloves garlic, finely chopped
> 2 (15-ounce) cans black-eyed peas, rinsed and drained
> 4 cups low-sodium vegetable broth
> 1 (14.5-ounce) can stewed tomatoes, broken into small pieces, liquids included
> 1 tablespoon double-strength tomato paste
> ½ teaspoon dried oregano
> ¼ teaspoon dried thyme leaves

¼ teaspoon dried rosemary leaves

¼ teaspoon salt, or to taste

Pinch crushed red pepper flakes, or to taste (optional)

Freshly ground black pepper, to taste

¼ teaspoon liquid smoke (optional)

In a medium stockpot, heat the oil over medium heat. Add the onion and celery and cook, stirring, until softened, about 3 minutes. Add the garlic and cook, stirring constantly, 1 minute. Add the remaining ingredients and bring to a boil over high heat. Reduce the heat to between medium-low and medium and simmer, uncovered, 20 minutes, stirring occasionally. Serve warm.

PER SERVING: Calories 242; Protein 18g; Total Fat 6g; Sat Fat 1g; Cholesterol 0mg; Carbohydrate 31g; Dietary Fiber 11g; Sodium 766mg

Roasted Cauliflower Soup with Rosemary

(VEGAN/LOW-CARB)

Roasting intensifies the delicious flavors of this creamy plant-based soup.

MAKES 5 TO 6 SERVINGS

1 extra-large cauliflower (about 3½ pounds), separated into bite-size florets

¼ cup plus ½ tablespoon extra-virgin olive oil

1 tablespoon dried whole rosemary leaves

½ teaspoon coarse salt

Freshly ground black pepper, to taste

½ cup chopped onion

3 large cloves garlic, finely chopped

4 cups low-sodium vegetable broth

Table salt, to taste

1 tablespoon fresh whole rosemary leaves (optional)

Preheat oven to 425F (220C).

In a large bowl, toss together the cauliflower, ¼ cup of oil, dried rosemary, coarse salt, and pepper until thoroughly combined. Arrange in a single layer on a large ungreased baking sheet with sides. Bake 30 minutes, turning cauliflower once halfway through cooking, or until lightly browned and tender. Remove from oven and set aside to cool a few minutes.

Meanwhile, in a medium stockpot, heat the remaining ½ tablespoon of oil over medium heat. Add the onion and cook, stirring, until lightly browned, about 4 to 5 minutes. Add the garlic and cook, stirring constantly, 30 seconds. Add the broth, table salt, and pepper; bring to a boil over high heat. Add the roasted cauliflower (use a spatula to remove all ingredients from the baking sheet) and return to a boil. Reduce the heat to low and simmer, uncovered, stirring occasionally, 3 minutes. Remove from heat and let soup mixture cool slightly.

Transfer about two-thirds of the soup mixture to a blender or food processor fitted with the knife blade; blend or process until smooth and pureed. Return the pureed soup mixture to the pot and stir in the fresh rosemary, if using. Cook over low heat until heated through. Serve hot.

PER SERVING: Calories 224; Protein 15g; Total Fat 13g; Sat Fat 2g; Cholesterol 0mg; Carbohydrate 18g; Dietary Fiber 10g; Sodium 684mg

Butter Bean Soup with Rosemary

(VEGAN)

This rib-sticking, meal-in-a-bowl soup is a wintertime family favorite. It can be prepared with large lima beans, as well.

MAKES 6 SERVINGS

2 tablespoons extra-virgin olive oil

1 small onion (about 4 ounces), chopped

2 stalks celery, chopped

4 ounces carrots (about 2 small), chopped

2 large cloves garlic, finely chopped

3 tablespoons all-purpose gluten-free flour

4 cups low-sodium vegetable broth

2 (15-ounce) cans butter beans, rinsed and drained

1 (14.5-ounce) can stewed tomatoes, broken into small pieces, liquids included

¼ cup chopped fresh flat-leaf parsley

1 teaspoon dried whole rosemary

¼ teaspoon salt, or to taste

Freshly ground black pepper, to taste

In a medium stockpot, heat the oil over medium heat. Add the onion, celery, and carrot and cook, stirring, until softened, about 3 minutes. Add the garlic and cook, stirring constantly, 1 minute. Add the flour and cook, stirring constantly, 1 minute. Gradually add the broth, stirring constantly. Add the remaining ingredients and bring to a boil over high heat, stirring often. Reduce the heat to medium-low and simmer, uncovered, 10 to 12 minutes, or until slightly thickened, stirring often. Serve warm.

PER SERVING: Calories 233; Protein 16g; Total Fat 5g; Sat Fat 1g; Cholesterol 0mg; Carbohydrate 33g; Dietary Fiber 11g; Sodium 630mg

Roasted Butternut Squash and Garlic Soup with Sage

(VEGAN)

Create a warm and welcome respite from fall's and winter's chill with this pretty pureed squash soup, ideal as a Thanksgiving opener for 6 people.

MAKES 4 TO 6 SERVINGS

1¼ pounds peeled and cubed butternut squash (about 3 cups)

1 medium onion (about 6 ounces), cut into 8 wedges

1 whole head garlic, cloves separated and peeled

½ teaspoon dried rubbed sage

½ teaspoon salt

Freshly ground black pepper, to taste

3 tablespoons extra-virgin olive oil

4 cups low-sodium vegetable broth

½ to 1 cup water

¼ cup chopped fresh flat-leaf parsley

Preheat oven to 375F (190C).

In a large bowl, toss the squash, onion, garlic, sage, salt, and pepper with the oil. Place in a single layer on a large ungreased rimmed baking sheet. Roast until tender and browned, about 40 minutes, stirring and turning the squash mixture a few times.

Transfer squash mixture to a food processor fitted with the knife blade, or to a blender; add about 2 cups of broth. Process or blend until smooth and pureed. Transfer to a medium stockpot and add the remaining 2 cups broth and ½ cup water; bring to a boil over medium-high heat, stirring occasionally. Reduce heat to low and add the parsley; cook, stirring, 2 minutes, thinning with additional water, if desired. Serve warm.

PER SERVING: Calories 224; Protein 13g; Total Fat 10g; Sat Fat 1g; Cholesterol 0mg; Carbohydrate 23g; Dietary Fiber 6g; Sodium 794mg

Creamy Carrot-Zucchini Soup

(VEGAN/LOW-CARB)

Not one drop of cream is used in this decidedly creamy and downright delicious plant-based soup. For additional color, use equal parts green and yellow zucchini.

MAKES 4 SERVINGS

1 large onion (about 8 ounces), halved
    crosswise
8 ounces carrots (about 2 medium),
    cut into 1-inch pieces
½ celery stalk, thinly sliced
¼ teaspoon garlic salt
2 cups low-sodium vegetable broth,
    plus additional, as necessary
2 tablespoons extra-virgin olive oil
1 pound zucchini, chopped
6 ounces plum tomatoes, chopped
½ to 1 teaspoon dried rosemary leaves

Chop one of the onion halves and set aside. Cut the other half into eight wedges and place in a medium saucepan, along with the carrot, celery, garlic salt, and broth; bring to a boil over high heat. Reduce the heat and simmer, covered, 20 minutes, or until vegetables are tender, stirring occasionally. Transfer to a food processor fitted with the knife blade, or a blender; process or blend until smooth and pureed. Set aside.

Meanwhile, in a medium stockpot, heat the oil over medium heat. Add the zucchini and chopped onion and cook, stirring occasionally, until soft-ened, about 5 minutes. Add the tomatoes and rosemary and cook, stirring occasionally, 5 minutes. Stir in the pureed carrot mixture and reduce the heat to low; cook, covered, stirring occasionally, 5 minutes. Serve warm.

PER SERVING: Calories 154; Protein 8g; Total Fat 7g; Sat Fat 1g; Cholesterol 0mg; Carbohydrate 16g; Dietary Fiber 6g; Sodium 418mg

Escarole Soup

(VEGAN/LOW-CARB)

If time permits, prepare this near-instant soup with Italian Vegetable Broth with Roasted Garlic, page 35, for a special first course.

MAKES 4 SERVINGS

2 tablespoons extra-virgin olive oil
2 large cloves garlic, finely chopped
4 cups low-sodium vegetable broth
¼ teaspoon sugar, or to taste
Salt and freshly ground black pepper, to taste
1 medium bunch escarole (about 1 pound),
    trimmed and coarsely chopped
Freshly grated gluten-free Parmesan cheese,
    to serve (optional)

In a medium stockpot, heat the oil over medium heat. Add the garlic and cook, stirring, until fragrant, about 30 seconds. Add the broth, sugar, salt, and pepper; bring to a boil over high heat. Add the escarole, stirring until wilted. Remove from heat and serve warm, with the Parmesan passed separately, if using.

PER SERVING: Calories 136; Protein 13g; Total Fat 7g; Sat Fat 1g; Cholesterol 0mg; Carbohydrate 7g; Dietary Fiber 6g; Sodium 543mg

Herbed Potato Soup with Roasted Garlic

(VEGAN)

Roasting garlic brings out its inherent sweetness and adds richness to this humble potato soup.

MAKES 4 TO 6 SERVINGS

1 whole bulb garlic, any papery outer skin removed

About ¼ cup vegetable broth or water

2 tablespoons extra-virgin olive oil

1 large onion (about 8 ounces), chopped

1¼ pounds russet potatoes (about 2 large), peeled and cut into ½-inch cubes

4 cups low-sodium vegetable broth

2 cups water

½ teaspoon dried rosemary leaves

½ teaspoon dried thyme leaves

¼ teaspoon ground sage

1 bay leaf

Salt and freshly ground black pepper

Chopped fresh flat-leaf parsley, for garnish (optional)

Preheat oven to 450F (230C).

Slice off the top of the garlic bulb to expose the tips of the cloves. Place the bulb in an ovenproof 6-ounce ramekin or similar dish and cover with the broth. Roast for about 30 minutes, basting once or twice, or until the cloves are soft and browned. Remove the garlic from the broth and let cool slightly. Discard broth.

When garlic is cool enough to handle (but still warm), squeeze out the cloves from the skin into a small bowl. Mash well with a fork and set aside.

In a medium stockpot, heat the oil over medium heat. Add the onion and cook, stirring, until softened, about 3 minutes. Add the potatoes and cook, stirring, 3 minutes. Add the reserved mashed garlic and cook, stirring, 30 seconds. Add remaining ingredients except the optional parsley; bring to a boil over high heat. Reduce heat to between low and medium-low, cover, and simmer, stirring occasionally, until potatoes are tender, 20 to 25 minutes. Remove and discard the bay leaf.

Working in batches, if necessary, transfer the soup mixture to a food processor fitted with the knife blade, or to a blender. Process or blend until smooth and pureed. Return to the pot and reheat over low heat as necessary. Serve warm, garnished with the parsley, if using.

PER SERVING: Calories 235; Protein 15g; Total Fat 7g; Sat Fat 1g; Cholesterol 0mg; Carbohydrate 30g; Dietary Fiber 3g; Sodium 560mg

Italian Spring Soup

(VEGAN)

This renewing soup makes a light and lovely first course to herald spring. With the addition of the eggs, it becomes a nourishing supper.

MAKES 6 SERVINGS

2 tablespoons extra-virgin olive oil

2 small leeks (about 4 ounces each), white parts only, halved lengthwise, thinly sliced crosswise, or the white parts of 2 bunches of scallions, thinly sliced crosswise

4 ounces baby arugula and/or baby kale leaves, torn

4 ounces baby spinach leaves, torn

6 cups low-sodium vegetable broth

2 cups water

½ teaspoon salt, or to taste

Freshly ground black pepper, to taste

¾ pound pencil-thin asparagus, trimmed and cut into 1-inch lengths

1 cup fresh or frozen young peas

1½ to 2 cups cooked white or brown rice (use 1½ cups, if using eggs and bread crumbs)

1 tablespoon chopped fresh flat-leaf parsley

1 tablespoon chopped fresh chives or the green parts of scallions

4 eggs (optional)

2 tablespoons gluten-free Italian-seasoned bread crumbs (optional)

In a large stockpot, heat the oil over medium heat. Add the leeks and cook, stirring, until softened, about 3 minutes. Add the arugula and spinach and cook, tossing and stirring, until just wilted, about 2 minutes. Add the broth, water, salt, and pepper; bring to a boil over high heat. Add the asparagus and peas; when liquids return to a boil, reduce the heat to medium-high and simmer briskly 2 to 3 minutes, stirring occasionally, or until asparagus is just crisp-tender. Reduce heat to low and add the rice, parsley, and chives; cook, stirring, until rice is heated through, about 2 minutes. Serve at once.

If using the optional eggs and bread crumbs: In a small bowl, whisk together the eggs and bread crumbs. Return the soup to a boil over high heat; quickly remove from heat and immediately add the egg mixture in a slow, thin, steady stream, whisking constantly for about 1 minute (eggs will form thread-like strands). Serve at once.

PER SERVING (without the eggs and bread crumbs): Calories 196; Protein 16g; Total Fat 5g; Sat Fat 1g; Cholesterol 0mg; Carbohydrate 24g; Dietary Fiber 6g; Sodium 722mg

Chilled Raw Tomato and Basil Soup

(VEGAN/LOW-CARB)

Redolent of garden-fresh tomatoes, basil, and garlic, this no-cook summertime soup embodies the full flavors of summer.

MAKES 4 SERVINGS

2½ pounds vine-ripened tomatoes, cut into chunks

¼ cup water

½ cup chopped fresh basil leaves

2 tablespoons extra-virgin olive oil

½ tablespoon balsamic vinegar

2 large cloves garlic, finely chopped

½ teaspoon sugar, preferably raw

½ teaspoon coarse salt, or to taste

Freshly ground black pepper, to taste

Tabasco sauce, to taste (optional)

In a food processor fitted with the knife blade, or in a blender, process or blend the tomatoes and water until smooth and pureed. Force through a fine sieve into a large bowl; add the basil, oil, vinegar, garlic, sugar, salt, and pepper, stirring well to thoroughly blend. Refrigerate, covered, a minimum of 3 hours or up to 1 day. Stir well before serving chilled, with Tabasco sauce, if using, passed separately.

PER SERVING: Calories 120; Protein 2g; Total Fat 8g; Sat Fat 1g; Cholesterol 0mg; Carbohydrate 13g; Dietary Fiber 3g; Sodium 259mg

Roasted Tomato Soup with Basil

(VEGAN)

I love the versatility of this scrumptious soup recipe. For a thick and "creamy" vegan soup to serve 3 people, use the least amount of broth and skip the tomato paste and cream. For an elegant first course to serve 4, use the maximum amount of broth and include the tomato paste and cream, nonfat half-and-half, or soy creamer.

MAKES 3 TO 4 SERVINGS

6 medium tomatoes (about 6 ounces each), quartered

1 small onion (about 4 ounces), cut into eighths

2 tablespoons extra-virgin olive oil

2 large cloves garlic, peeled and halved lengthwise

1 teaspoon dried thyme leaves

½ teaspoon coarse salt

Freshly ground black pepper, to taste

1 cup loosely packed fresh basil leaves, ½ cup left whole, ½ cup torn

½ to 2 cups low-sodium vegetable broth

1 tablespoon tomato paste (optional)

¼ to ½ cup heavy cream, nonfat half-and-half, or soy creamer (optional)

½ to 1 teaspoon sugar

Preheat oven to 400F (205C).

In a large bowl, toss the tomatoes, onion, oil, garlic, thyme, salt, and pepper until thoroughly coated. Transfer to a baking sheet with sides and spread in a single layer. Roast 25 to 30 minutes, or until tender and lightly browned, turning tomato mixture halfway through cooking. Remove from oven and let cool about 10 minutes.

Transfer tomato mixture and whole basil leaves to a food processor fitted with the knife blade, or to a blender; process or blend until smooth and pureed. ·

Transfer tomato-basil mixture to a medium stockpot and add ½ to 2 cups broth, depending on desired consistency, and tomato paste, if using. Bring to a simmer over medium-high heat, stirring. Reduce heat to low and add the desired amount of cream, if using, torn basil, and sugar; cook, stirring, 2 minutes. Serve warm.

PER SERVING: Calories 188; Protein 6g; Total Fat 11g; Sat Fat 1g; Cholesterol 0mg; Carbohydrate 22g; Dietary Fiber 5g; Sodium 431mg

Creamy Yellow Squash Soup

(VEGAN/LOW-CARB)

This creamy plant-based soup is ideal to prepare in late summer with the last of the season's squash harvest. Green zucchini can replace all or part of the yellow variety, if desired.

MAKES 4 SERVINGS

2 tablespoons extra-virgin olive oil

2 scallions, thinly sliced, white and green parts separated

1 large clove garlic, finely chopped

1 pound yellow summer squash, coarsely chopped

4 cups low-sodium vegetable broth

1 tablespoon chopped fresh oregano or ½ teaspoon dried oregano

Salt and freshly ground black pepper, to taste
Freshly shredded gluten-free Parmesan
cheese, to serve (optional)

In a medium stockpot, heat the oil over medium heat. Add the white parts of the scallions and cook, stirring, until softened, about 2 minutes. Add the garlic and cook, stirring constantly, 30 seconds. Add the squash and cook, stirring, until softened, about 5 minutes. Add the broth, oregano, salt, and pepper; bring to a boil over high heat. Reduce the heat to between low and medium-low and simmer, covered, about 30 minutes, or until squash is very tender, stirring occasionally.

Working in batches, as necessary, transfer the soup mixture to a food processor fitted with the knife blade, or to a blender; process or blend until smooth but still slightly chunky. Return to the pot and stir in the reserved scallion greens; reheat over low heat as necessary, stirring occasionally. Serve warm, with the Parmesan cheese passed separately, if using.

PER SERVING: Calories 137; Protein 13g; Total Fat 7g; Sat Fat 1g; Cholesterol 0mg; Carbohydrate 8g; Dietary Fiber 6g; Sodium 522mg

Zucchini-Rice Soup

(VEGAN/LOW-CARB)

This beloved Italian classic can be enriched with Rustic Pesto Sauce, page 92, if desired, and served with a tossed green salad and Herbed Italian Bread Sticks, page 86, for a simple, satisfying supper.

MAKES 4 SERVINGS

1 tablespoon extra-virgin olive oil
½ cup chopped onion
¼ cup chopped celery
2 cloves garlic, finely chopped
4 cups low-sodium vegetable broth
1 cup water
½ teaspoon dried thyme leaves
½ teaspoon salt, or to taste
Freshly ground black pepper, to taste
¼ cup uncooked long-grain or Arborio
white rice
2 medium zucchini (about 1 pound),
quartered lengthwise, thinly sliced
crosswise
2 tablespoons chopped fresh flat-leaf parsley

In a medium stockpot, heat the oil over medium heat. Add the onion and celery and cook, stirring, until softened, about 3 minutes. Add the garlic and cook, stirring constantly, 30 seconds. Add the broth, water, thyme, salt, and pepper; bring to a boil over high heat. Add the rice, reduce heat to medium-high, and boil gently until rice is barely tender, about 8 minutes. Add the zucchini and return to a boil over high heat. Reduce the heat and simmer gently, uncovered, stirring occasionally, until the zucchini is tender and the rice is cooked al dente, 5 to 10 minutes. Stir in the parsley and serve warm.

PER SERVING: Calories 150; Protein 14g; Total Fat 4g; Sat Fat 1g; Cholesterol 0mg; Carbohydrate 17g; Dietary Fiber 5g; Sodium 798mg

Broccoli and Mascarpone Soup

(EGG-FREE/LOW-CARB)

This rich and creamy soup is a meal in itself with Gluten-Free Italian Bread, page 86, and a tossed green salad. For a lighter dish, use all Neufchâtel cream cheese.

MAKES 4 SERVINGS

> 1½ tablespoons extra-virgin olive oil
> ½ cup chopped red onion
> ¾ pound broccoli florets, cut into 1-inch pieces
> 2 cups low-sodium vegetable broth
> 1 cup water
> Salt and freshly ground black pepper, to taste
> ½ cup (4 ounces) mascarpone cheese, cut into chunks
> ¼ cup (2 ounces) gluten-free Neufchâtel cream cheese, cut into chunks
> 4 teaspoons chopped fresh chives

In a medium stockpot, heat the oil over medium heat. Add the onion and cook, stirring, until softened, about 3 minutes. Add the broccoli and cook, stirring, 1 minute. Add the broth, water, salt, and pepper; bring to a boil over high heat. Reduce heat to medium-low and simmer, partially covered, until broccoli is tender, about 10 minutes. Remove from heat and let cool slightly.

Working in batches, as necessary, transfer soup to a food processor fitted with the knife blade or to a blender; process or blend until smooth and pureed. Return to pot and add the mascarpone and cream cheese; cook, whisking often, over medium-low heat until cheese is thoroughly blended. Serve warm, garnished with the chives. Completely cooled soup can be stored, covered, in the refrigerator up to 2 days before reheating gently and serving.

PER SERVING: Calories 267; Protein 11g; Total Fat 22g; Sat Fat 3g; Cholesterol 50mg; Carbohydrate 9g; Dietary Fiber 5g; Sodium 347mg

Quick Cannellini and Italian-Cut Green Bean Stew

(VEGAN)

Frozen Italian-cut green beans, canned tomatoes, and canned cannellini beans make quick work of this simple stew, delicious over rice or polenta, or on its own, with Herbed Italian Bread Sticks, page 86, to sop up the tasty sauce. Regular green beans can replace the Italian-cut, if desired.

MAKES 4 TO 6 SERVINGS

> 2 tablespoons olive oil
> 1 large onion (about 8 ounces), chopped
> 2 stalks celery, chopped
> 1 small carrot (about 2 ounces), chopped
> 2 cloves garlic, finely chopped
> 2 (14.5-ounce) cans diced tomatoes, preferably with garlic and onions, juices included
> 1 (14.5-ounce) can no-salt added diced tomatoes, juices included
> 3 cups low-sodium vegetable broth
> 1 (16-ounce) package frozen Italian-cut green beans, partially thawed
> 1 teaspoon dried oregano
> 1 teaspoon sugar, or to taste
> ½ teaspoon dried thyme leaves

½ teaspoon dried rosemary leaves

½ bay leaf

Salt and freshly ground black pepper, to taste

1 (15-ounce) can cannellini beans or other white beans, rinsed and drained

¼ cup chopped fresh basil

2 tablespoons tomato paste

1 to 2 tablespoons dry white wine (optional)

In a medium stockpot, heat the oil over medium heat. Add the onion, celery, and carrot and cook, stirring, until softened, about 5 minutes. Add the garlic and cook, stirring constantly, 30 seconds. Add the canned tomatoes and their juices, broth, green beans, oregano, sugar, thyme, rosemary, bay leaf, salt, and pepper; bring to a boil over high heat. Reduce the heat to medium and simmer briskly, uncovered, until green beans are almost tender, 10 to 15 minutes, stirring often. Add the cannellini beans, basil, tomato paste, and wine, if using; cook, stirring, until green beans are very tender, 10 to 15 minutes. Serve warm.

PER SERVING: Calories 335; Protein 21g; Total Fat 8g; Sat Fat 1g; Cholesterol 0mg; Carbohydrate 50g; Dietary Fiber 17g; Sodium 833mg

Cauliflower and Spaghetti Soup

(VEGAN)

This tasty pasta soup, or minestra, *is ideal to make with all those accumulated broken pieces of gluten-free spaghetti (or other similar thin pasta) lurking at the bottom of the package. Broccoli can replace all or part of the cauliflower, if desired. Note that the pasta will take a bit longer to cook in the broth.*

MAKES 4 TO 6 SERVINGS

5 cups low-sodium vegetable broth

4 cups water

Salt and freshly ground black pepper, to taste

1 large head cauliflower (about 2½ pounds), cut into bite-size florets

4 ounces gluten-free brown rice spaghetti, or other gluten-free thin pasta, broken into approximate 1½-inch lengths

½ cup grape or cherry tomatoes, halved (optional)

¼ to ½ cup chopped fresh flat-leaf parsley and/or basil

1½ tablespoons extra-virgin olive oil

1½ tablespoons garlic-flavored olive oil (or additional plain extra-virgin olive oil)

Freshly grated gluten-free Parmesan cheese, to serve (optional)

In a large stockpot, bring the broth, water, salt, and pepper to a boil over high heat. Add the cauliflower and return to a boil. Reduce heat to low and simmer, covered, about 5 minutes, or until cauliflower is barely tender, stirring a few times. Return mixture to a boil and add the pasta. When mixture returns to a boil, reduce heat to between medium and medium-low, and simmer, uncovered, until pasta is cooked al dente, about 10 to 15 minutes, stirring occasionally. Stir in the tomatoes, if using, parsley, and oils. Serve hot, with the Parmesan passed separately, if using.

PER SERVING: Calories 330; Protein 23g; Total Fat 11g; Sat Fat 2g; Cholesterol 0mg; Carbohydrate 39g; Dietary Fiber 12g; Sodium 736mg

Italian Lentil Soup

(VEGAN)

Warm up on a chilly night with this protein-rich, fiber-filled favorite. Cooked rice or gluten-free pasta can be added toward the end of simmering for an even heartier soup—in that instance, use additional broth or water.

MAKES 6 SERVINGS

¼ cup extra-virgin olive oil

1 medium onion (about 6 ounces), chopped

2 small carrots (about 2 ounces each), chopped

2 stalks celery, chopped

2 large cloves garlic, finely chopped

4 to 5 cups low-sodium vegetable broth

4 to 5 cups water

2 cups lentils, rinsed and picked over

1 (14.5-ounce) can crushed tomatoes or tomato puree

1 teaspoon dried oregano

½ teaspoon salt, or to taste

Freshly ground black pepper, to taste

1 large bay leaf

2 ounces baby spinach, torn

2 tablespoons cider vinegar

¼ teaspoon sugar, or to taste (optional)

In a large stockpot, heat the oil over medium heat. Add the onion, carrot, and celery and cook, stirring, until softened, about 5 minutes. Add the garlic and cook, stirring constantly, 1 minute. Add broth, water, lentils, tomatoes, oregano, salt, pepper, and bay leaf; bring to a boil over high heat. Reduce heat to medium-low and simmer, covered, stirring occasionally, about 45 minutes, or until lentils are tender, adding additional broth or water if a thinner consistency is desired. Add the spinach, vinegar, and sugar, if using; cook, stirring, until spinach is wilted. Remove and discard the bay leaf and serve warm.

PER SERVING: Calories 368; Protein 27g; Total Fat 10g; Sat Fat 1g; Cholesterol 0mg; Carbohydrate 47g; Dietary Fiber 24g; Sodium 701mg

Autumn Minestrone Soup

(VEGAN)

Butternut squash, a perfect counterpoint to the rutabaga's inherent bitterness, lends this delicious soup a hint of sweetness.

MAKES 6 SERVINGS

2 tablespoons extra-virgin olive oil

1 medium onion (about 6 ounces), chopped

1 medium carrot (about 4 ounces), chopped

1 stalk celery, chopped

2 cloves garlic, finely chopped

1¼ pounds peeled and cubed butternut squash (3 cups)

1 small rutabaga (about 8 ounces), or 2 medium turnips (about 4 ounces each), peeled and chopped

4 cups low-sodium vegetable broth

2 cups water

1 (15-ounce) can diced tomatoes, drained

1 (15-ounce) can cannellini or other white beans, rinsed and drained

2 ounces stemmed kale or spinach leaves, coarsely chopped, or 2 ounces baby spinach leaves, torn

2 tablespoons chopped fresh flat-leaf parsley

½ teaspoon dried thyme leaves

½ teaspoon dried rosemary

⅛ teaspoon ground sage

1 bay leaf

½ teaspoon salt, or to taste

Freshly ground black pepper, to taste

In a medium stockpot, heat the oil over medium heat. Add the onion, carrot, and celery and cook, stirring, until softened, about 4 to 5 minutes. Add the garlic and cook, stirring constantly, 30 seconds. Add the squash and rutabaga and cook, stirring often, until just softened, about 5 minutes. Add the broth, water, tomatoes, beans, kale, parsley, thyme, rosemary, sage, bay leaf, salt, and pepper; bring to a boil over high heat. Reduce heat to between medium and medium-low and simmer, uncovered, 20 to 25 minutes, or until vegetables are tender, stirring occasionally. Remove bay leaf and serve warm.

PER SERVING: Calories 225; Protein 15g; Total Fat 5g; Sat Fat 1g; Cholesterol 0mg; Carbohydrate 34g; Dietary Fiber 9g; Sodium 705mg

Minestrone Soup with Potatoes and Pesto

(EGG-FREE)

The flavor of this superb soup improves with age. For a vegan dish, prepare with Rustic Pesto Sauce, page 92.

MAKES 6 SERVINGS

3 tablespoons extra-virgin olive oil

1 medium onion (about 6 ounces), chopped

3 large cloves garlic, finely chopped

1 pound boiling potatoes, preferably red-skinned, cut into ½-inch cubes

4 ounces carrots (about 2 small), chopped

2 stalks celery, chopped

4 cups low-sodium vegetable broth

3 cups water

1 (14.5-ounce) can diced tomatoes, liquids included

¾ pound yellow squash (about 2 medium), halved lengthwise, thinly sliced crosswise

4 ounces baby spinach leaves

1½ to 2 tablespoons tomato paste

½ teaspoon salt, or to taste

1½ cups frozen peas, thawed

3 to 4 tablespoons gluten-free prepared pesto, Classic Basil Pesto Sauce, page 97, or Rustic Pesto Sauce, page 92

Freshly ground black pepper, to taste

In a large stockpot, heat the oil over medium heat. Add the onion and garlic and cook, stirring often, 3 minutes. Add the potatoes, carrots, and celery; cook, stirring often, 5 minutes. Add the broth, water, tomatoes and their liquids, squash, spinach, tomato paste, and salt; bring to a boil over high heat. Reduce the heat to medium-low and simmer, partially covered, about 20 to 25 minutes, or until vegetables are tender, stirring occasionally. Add the peas, pesto, and pepper and cook, uncovered, 5 minutes, stirring occasionally. Serve hot.

PER SERVING: Calories 260; Protein 14g; Total Fat 11g; Sat Fat 2g; Cholesterol 2mg; Carbohydrate 29g; Dietary Fiber 9g; Sodium 842mg

Minestrone Soup with Roman Beans and Brown Rice

(VEGAN)

While you can use other beans in place of the Roman variety, also known as cranberry beans or borlotti beans, some culinary experts would argue that genuine minestrone is made only with Roman beans. White rice can replace the brown variety, if desired; in this instance, reduce the final simmering time by about half.

MAKES 6 TO 8 SERVINGS

2 tablespoons extra-virgin olive oil

1 medium onion (about 6 ounces), finely chopped

2 small thin carrots (about 2 ounces each), peeled and thinly sliced crosswise

2 stalks celery, halved lengthwise, thinly sliced crosswise

2 large cloves garlic, finely chopped

5 cups low-sodium vegetable broth

3 cups water

½ cup dry red wine

1 (28-ounce) can whole tomatoes, crushed, juices included

1 medium zucchini (about 8 ounces), quartered lengthwise, thinly sliced crosswise

1 teaspoon dried oregano

Salt and freshly ground black pepper, to taste

½ cup brown rice

1 (15-ounce) can Roman beans or kidney beans, rinsed and drained

2 cups shredded cabbage

½ cup chopped fresh basil

1 tablespoon double-strength tomato paste

1 teaspoon sugar, or to taste

In a large stockpot, heat the oil over medium heat. Add the onion, carrot, and celery and cook, stirring often, until softened, about 4 to 5 minutes. Add the garlic and cook, stirring constantly, 1 minute. Add the broth, water, wine, tomatoes and their liquids, zucchini, oregano, salt, and pepper; bring to a boil over high heat. Reduce heat to medium-low and simmer, partially covered, 30 minutes, stirring occasionally. Add the rice and return to a boil over high heat; stir in the remaining ingredients. When mixture returns to a boil, reduce the heat to between medium and medium-low and simmer, partially covered, 35 to 45 minutes, or until rice is cooked al dente, stirring occasionally. Serve warm.

PER SERVING: Calories 277; Protein 17g; Total Fat 6g; Sat Fat 1g; Cholesterol 0mg; Carbohydrate 39g; Dietary Fiber 9g; Sodium 783mg

Ricotta Cheese Gnocchi in Vegetable Broth

(LACTO-OVO/LOW-CARB)

In this delectable variation of a medieval recipe for gnocchi, ricotta cheese replaces the modern New World ingredients of potatoes or polenta. Though I prefer to serve the dumplings in a simple vegetable broth, they are ideal in a hearty stew—in either instance, serve immediately for best results. For a more contemporary rendition, see Ricotta Cheese Gnocchi with Spinach–Sunflower Seed Pesto, page 120.

MAKES 6 SERVINGS

6 cups reduced-sodium vegetable broth, or Italian Vegetable Broth with Roasted Garlic, page 35

2 cups water

3 to 4 stalks celery, thinly sliced

2 small carrots (about 2 ounces each),
    thinly sliced

¼ cup chopped fresh flat-leaf parsley

Salt and freshly ground black pepper,
    to taste

½ small bay leaf

1 recipe cooked Ricotta Cheese Gnocchi,
    page 121

In a medium stockpot, bring the broth, water, celery, carrots, parsley, salt, pepper, and bay leaf to a boil over high heat. Reduce heat to medium and simmer briskly, partially covered, until carrots are tender, about 15 minutes. Reduce heat to low and add the cooked gnocchi; stir gently until heated through.

Remove and discard the bay leaf. Using a slotted spoon, place about 8 gnocchi in each of 6 large soup bowls; cover with equal amounts of hot broth and vegetables. Serve at once.

PER SERVING: Calories 241; Protein 22g; Total Fat 9g; Sat Fat 5g; Cholesterol 63mg; Carbohydrate 18g; Dietary Fiber 5g; Sodium 833mg

Italian Split Pea Soup

(VEGAN)

This rustic, rib-sticking split pea soup will perfume your kitchen for hours with the fragrance of thyme, rosemary, and bay. Though optional, I wouldn't dream of passing on the final addition of Marsala for a taste of heaven. Additional carrots may replace the parsnips, if desired.

MAKES 4 TO 6 SERVINGS

1 tablespoon extra-virgin olive oil

¼ cup finely chopped red onion

¼ cup chopped carrot

¼ cup chopped celery

¼ cup chopped parsnips

2 large cloves garlic, finely chopped

4 cups low-sodium vegetable broth

1 cup water, plus additional, as necessary

½ pound dried split peas, rinsed and picked
    over

½ teaspoon dried thyme leaves

¼ teaspoon dried rosemary leaves

¼ teaspoon salt, or to taste

Freshly ground black pepper, to taste

1 large bay leaf

1 tablespoon Marsala or dry sherry (optional)

In a medium stockpot, heat the oil over medium heat. Add the onion, carrot, celery, and parsnips and cook, stirring, until softened, 4 to 5 minutes. Add the garlic and cook, stirring constantly, 30 seconds. Add the broth, water, split peas, thyme, rosemary, salt, pepper, and bay leaf; bring to a boil over high heat. Reduce the heat to between low and medium-low; simmer, covered, until split peas are tender, about 1½ hours, stirring every 10 minutes or so, and adding additional water, if necessary. Stir in the Marsala, if using, and serve hot.

PER SERVING: Calories 291; Protein 26g; Total Fat 4g; Sat Fat 1g; Cholesterol 0mg; Carbohydrate 40g; Dietary Fiber 19g; Sodium 676mg

Tuscan-Style Minestrone Soup with Fennel and Herbed Polenta Dumplings

(EGG-FREE)

This is my newfound favorite main-dish minestrone to make for company. The subtle licorice scents of fennel lend intrigue, while the tiny polenta dumplings add delight. For a vegan dish, omit the dumplings and add ½ teaspoon of Italian seasoning along with the bay leaf.

MAKES 6 SERVINGS

2 tablespoons extra-virgin olive oil

1 medium fennel bulb (about 12 ounces), trimmed, cored, and chopped

1 medium onion (about 6 ounces), chopped

1 small carrot (about 2 ounces), chopped

3 large cloves garlic, finely chopped

6 cups low-sodium vegetable broth

8 ounces plum tomatoes, seeded and coarsely chopped

4 ounces fresh green beans, trimmed and cut into 1-inch lengths

2 cups shredded green cabbage

1 bay leaf

Salt and freshly ground black pepper, to taste

1 (15-ounce) can cannellini or other white beans, rinsed and drained

2 ounces coarsely chopped fresh spinach leaves

2 tablespoons tomato paste

½ recipe Herbed Polenta Dumplings, page 136

In a medium stockpot, heat the oil over medium-low heat. Add the fennel, onion, and carrot and cook, stirring occasionally, until softened but not browned, about 10 minutes. Add the garlic and raise heat to medium; cook, stirring, 1 minute. Add the broth, tomatoes, green beans, cabbage, bay leaf, salt, and pepper; bring to a boil over high heat, stirring a few times. Reduce the heat to between low and medium-low, cover, and simmer for 20 minutes, stirring occasionally, or until vegetables are tender. Add the cannellini beans, spinach, and tomato paste, stirring well to combine. Add the dumplings, gently stirring at the top to immerse in the broth. Cover and cook 5 minutes, gently stirring the dumplings in the broth a few times, or until dumplings are heated through. Remove and discard the bay leaf, if desired. Serve warm.

PER SERVING: Calories 309; Protein 23g; Total Fat 9g; Sat Fat 2g; Cholesterol 8mg; Carbohydrate 38g; Dietary Fiber 14g; Sodium 890mg

Variation

To make Tuscan-Style Minestrone with Fennel and Ricotta Cheese Gnocchi, replace the Herbed Polenta Dumplings with ½ recipe of cooked Ricotta Cheese Gnocchi, page 121.

Sweet Potato Minestrone Soup

(VEGAN)

This hearty, heart-healthy soup makes a superb supper on a cold winter's day. For extra protein, stir in a can of rinsed and drained kidney or cannellini beans.

MAKES 4 TO 6 SERVINGS

1½ tablespoons extra-virgin olive oil

1 large onion (about 8 ounces), chopped

2 stalks celery, chopped

3 large cloves garlic, finely chopped

4 cups low-sodium vegetable broth

1 cup water

1 (14.5-ounce) can diced tomatoes, liquids
    included

1 (8-ounce) can no-salt added tomato sauce

1 pound sweet potatoes (about 2 large),
    peeled and cut into ½-inch cubes

6 ounces fresh green beans, trimmed, cut into
    1-inch lengths

4 ounces carrots (about 2 small), thinly sliced

2 tablespoons chopped fresh flat-leaf parsley

1½ to 2 tablespoons chopped fresh sage
    leaves

¼ teaspoon dried rosemary leaves

¼ teaspoon dried thyme leaves

½ teaspoon sugar

Salt and freshly ground black pepper, to taste

In a medium stockpot, heat the oil over medium heat. Add the onion and celery and cook, stirring, until softened, 3 to 4 minutes. Add the garlic and cook, stirring constantly, 1 minute. Add the broth, water, tomatoes and their liquids, tomato sauce, potatoes, green beans, carrots, parsley, sage, rosemary, thyme, sugar, salt, and pepper; bring to a boil over high heat. Reduce the heat to medium-low and simmer, stirring occasionally, until vegetables are tender, about 30 minutes. Serve warm.

PER SERVING: Calories 313; Protein 17g; Total Fat 6g; Sat Fat 1g; Cholesterol 0mg; Carbohydrate 51g; Dietary Fiber 12g; Sodium 800mg

St. Scholastica Winter White Bean and Arborio Rice Soup with Rosemary

(VEGAN)

The feast of St. Scholastica, twin sister of St. Benedict, is celebrated on February 10, the anniversary of her death. It's been said that three days earlier, pleading with her reluctant twin to extend his annual visit, she had asked for God's help—within minutes, a violent storm erupted, leaving Benedict no choice but to break his own Rule and spend a night away from the monastery. Upon his return to Monte Cassino, Benedict had a vision of his sister's soul leaving her body in the form of a pure white dove, ascending to heaven—ah, to be a saint! But not to worry—this simple, soul-satisfying soup, full of the goodness of hearty white kidney beans, creamy white Arborio rice, and purifying rosemary, is for saints as well as sinners. It's also one I like to picture Scholastica—the patron saint of storms—serenely stirring over a fire, subliminally persuading her beloved brother to stay for supper, storm or no storm.

SERVES 5 TO 6

2 tablespoons extra-virgin olive oil

¾ cup white Arborio rice

3 large cloves garlic, finely chopped

1 teaspoon dried rosemary leaves

6 cups low-sodium vegetable broth

2 cups coleslaw mix

1 bay leaf

¼ teaspoon salt, or to taste

Freshly ground black pepper, to taste

1 (15-ounce) can cannellini or other
    white beans, rinsed and drained

In a medium stockpot, heat the oil over medium heat. Add the rice and cook, stirring often, until lightly toasted, 3 to 5 minutes. Add the garlic and rosemary and cook, stirring constantly, 1 minute, or until fragrant. Add the broth, coleslaw mix, bay leaf, salt, and pepper; bring to a boil over high heat. Reduce the heat to medium-low and simmer, partially covered, 10 minutes, stirring occasionally. Add the beans and bring to a brisk simmer over medium-high heat. Reduce the heat to medium-low and simmer, partially covered, until rice is cooked al dente, about 5 minutes, stirring occasionally. Remove the bay leaf and serve warm.

PER SERVING: Calories 293; Protein 21g; Total Fat 6g; Sat Fat 1g; Cholesterol 0mg; Carbohydrate 40g; Dietary Fiber 7g; Sodium 741mg

Winter Vegetable Stew

(VEGAN)

Serve this soul-warming stew with Herbed Italian Bread Sticks, page 86, and a tossed spinach salad for a satisfying supper. For a heartier dish, add 1 (15-ounce) can of rinsed and drained cannellini or red kidney beans the last 15 minutes or so of cooking.

MAKES 4 TO 6 SERVINGS

2 tablespoons extra-virgin olive oil

1 medium leek (about 6 ounces), mostly white part, halved lengthwise, thinly sliced crosswise, or the mostly white parts of scallions to measure 1 cup sliced

2 large cloves garlic, finely chopped

1 (28-ounce) can whole tomatoes, coarsely chopped, juices included

½ cup water

1 tablespoon finely chopped fresh flat-leaf parsley or basil, or 1 teaspoon dried

1 teaspoon sugar

½ teaspoon salt, or to taste

½ teaspoon dried oregano

¼ teaspoon dried thyme

1 small or ½ large bay leaf

Freshly ground black pepper, to taste

1 medium head green cabbage (about 2½ pounds), bruised outer leaves discarded, quartered, cored, and cut crosswise into ½-inch-thick slices

1½ pounds boiling potatoes, peeled and cut into bite-size pieces

1 medium fennel bulb (about 12 ounces), trimmed, cored, and cut lengthwise into eighths

2 medium carrots (about 4 ounces each), sliced into ½-inch rounds

1 tablespoon tomato paste (optional)

In a large stockpot, heat the oil over medium heat. Add the leek and cook, stirring, until softened, about 3 minutes. Add the garlic and cook, stirring constantly, 30 seconds. Add the tomatoes and their juices, water, parsley, sugar, salt, oregano, thyme, bay leaf, and pepper; bring to a brisk simmer over medium-high heat, stirring often. Add the cabbage, potatoes, fennel, and carrots; cook, stirring, until cabbage begins to wilt. Reduce the heat to between medium-low and medium, cover, and simmer gently, stirring occasionally, until the vegetables are tender, about 45 minutes, stirring in the tomato paste, if using, the last 15 minutes or so of

cooking. Remove and discard the bay leaf and
serve warm.

PER SERVING: Calories 327; Protein 10g; Total Fat 8g;
Sat Fat 1g; Cholesterol 0mg; Carbohydrate 60g; Dietary
Fiber 14g; Sodium 705mg

THREE

Salads

The greatest Italian salads start with the freshest ingredients; fortunately, most are naturally gluten-free. Lettuces such as romaine, iceberg, Bibb, and Boston; greens such as arugula, escarole, spinach, and radicchio; tomatoes such as plum, cherry, beefsteak, and heirloom; and vegetables such as bell peppers, mushrooms, red onion, and cucumbers are mixed and matched and dressed with a light vinaigrette to accompany any given meal as a side dish or first course. Cheeses, eggs, beans, potatoes, olives, nuts, dried fruits, and an assortment of marinated or pickled vegetables are frequently added to create a second course or luncheon meal, while grains such as rice and millet often form the base of a casual cold-salad supper. In this chapter you will find salads for all occasions and all seasons—served with a piece of good gluten-free Italian bread and a glass of heart-healthy red wine, they epitomize the Mediterranean diet at its finest.

First-Course and Side Salads

Arugula and Orange Salad (vegan/low-carb)

Raw Beet and Fennel Salad with Goat Cheese and Walnuts (egg-free/low-carb)

Broccoli and Cauliflower Salad with Gorgonzola Dressing (lacto-ovo/low-carb)

Broccoli, Mushroom, and Tomato Salad with Tarragon Vinaigrette (vegan/low-carb)

Cannellini Bean Salad (vegan)

Easy Italian-Style Cucumber Salad (vegan)

Green Bean Salad with Tomato-Basil Dressing (vegan/low-carb)

Mesclun Salad with Goat Cheese, Pine Nuts, and Raisins (egg-free/low-carb)

Warm Portobello Mushroom and Spinach Salad with Roasted Red Pepper–Ricotta Pesto (egg-free/low-carb)

Beefsteak Tomato and Ricotta Salata Salad (egg-free/low-carb)

Roasted Onion Salad (vegan/low-carb)

St. Benedict 7-Vegetable Summer Salad (vegan/low-carb)

Tomato, Basil, and Olive Salad with Potato Croutons (vegan/low-carb)

Italian Potato Salad with Garlic and Parsley (vegan/low-carb)

Warm Potato and Bell Pepper Salad (vegan/low-carb)

Radicchio and Green Apple Salad (vegan/low-carb)

Spinach and Mushroom Salad with Basil Vinaigrette (vegan/low-carb)

Main-Dish Salads

Sicilian Bread Salad (lacto-ovo)

Italian Brown Rice Salad with Cannellini Beans and Basil (vegan)

Cauliflower, Chickpea, and Egg Salad with Capers and Olives (dairy-free/low-carb)

Italian Lentil Salad with Artichokes and Goat Cheese (egg-free/low-carb)

Italian Millet Salad (vegan)

Polenta Caprese Salad with Olives (egg-free)

Grilled Romaine Salad with Parmesan–Bread Crumb Crust (egg-free/low-carb)

Basil Omelet and Green Bean Salad (dairy-free/low-carb)

Our Lady of Loreto Rosary Salad with Job's Tears, Roasted Red Peppers, and Black Olives (vegan)

Watermelon and Ricotta Salata Salad with Pine Nuts and Basil (egg-free/low-carb)

Rice Fusilli Primavera Salad with Grilled Vegetables and Raw Tomato Sauce (vegan)

FIRST-COURSE AND SIDE SALADS

Arugula and Orange Salad

(VEGAN/LOW-CARB)

Versions of this simple yet delicious salad abound in Italy—feel free to add some thinly sliced red onion and/or black olives, if desired.

MAKES 4 SERVINGS

3 tablespoons extra-virgin olive oil

1 tablespoon orange juice

1 tablespoon balsamic vinegar

Salt and freshly ground black pepper, to taste

6 cups arugula

2 large navel oranges, peeled (all white pith removed), cut into segments

In a large salad bowl, whisk together the oil, juice, vinegar, salt, and pepper. Add the arugula and oranges; toss well to combine. Serve at once.

PER SERVING: Calories 132; Protein 2g; Total Fat 10g; Sat Fat 1g; Cholesterol 0mg; Carbohydrate 10g; Dietary Fiber 1g; Sodium 9mg

Raw Beet and Fennel Salad with Goat Cheese and Walnuts

(EGG-FREE/LOW-CARB)

Julienne strips of raw beets and fennel, tossed in citrus vinaigrette, along with mixed greens, toasted walnuts, and goat cheese, make for a sophisticated—and delicious— first-course salad.

MAKES 6 SERVINGS

⅓ cup fresh orange juice

⅓ cup fresh lemon juice

3 tablespoons extra-virgin olive oil

Salt and freshly ground black pepper, to taste

2 medium beets (about 2 ounces each), peeled, cut into ⅛-inch-thick slices, and julienned

1 medium fennel bulb (about 12 ounces), trimmed, cored, cut into ⅛-inch-thick slices, and julienned

6 cups mixed salad greens

4 ounces (½ cup) gluten-free crumbled goat cheese

2 tablespoons finely chopped fresh chives or the green parts of scallions

3 tablespoons toasted chopped walnuts

In a large bowl, whisk together the orange juice, lemon juice, oil, salt, and pepper until thoroughly blended. Let stand a few minutes to allow the flavors to blend; whisk again. Add the beets and fennel strips, tossing well to combine. Let stand 10 minutes at room temperature to allow the flavors to blend; toss again.

To serve, divide the greens equally among each of 6 salad plates. Using a slotted spoon, top with equal amounts of the beet mixture. Sprinkle each salad with 4 teaspoons of cheese, 1 teaspoon of chives, and ½ tablespoon of walnuts. Drizzle evenly with the remaining dressing in the bowl. Serve at once.

PER SERVING: Calories 212; Protein 9g; Total Fat 16g; Sat Fat 6g; Cholesterol 20mg; Carbohydrate 11g; Dietary Fiber 3g; Sodium 120mg

Broccoli and Cauliflower Salad with Gorgonzola Dressing

(LACTO-OVO/LOW-CARB)

This tangy salad is always a hit at a picnic or potluck. It can be prepared exclusively with broccoli or cauliflower, or any combination of the two—for a gorgeous presentation, use equal parts green broccoli, purple cauliflower, and yellow cauliflower. For an egg-free version, use all vegan mayonnaise.

MAKES 6 SERVINGS

- ½ cup gluten-free reduced-fat mayonnaise
- ¼ cup gluten-free full-fat mayonnaise
- ½ cup gluten-free crumbled Gorgonzola cheese (4 ounces)
- 1 teaspoon cider vinegar
- Salt and freshly ground black pepper, to taste
- ¾ pound fresh broccoli, trimmed, cut into florets, and coarsely chopped
- ¾ pound fresh cauliflower, trimmed, cut into florets, and coarsely chopped

In a large bowl, using a fork, mash together both mayonnaises, cheese, vinegar, salt, and pepper until thoroughly blended and any large crumbles of cheese are broken down. Add the broccoli and cauliflower, tossing well to combine. Serve at room temperature. Alternatively, cover and refrigerate up to 24 hours and serve chilled, or return to room temperature.

PER SERVING: Calories 182; Protein 5g; Total Fat 15g; Sat Fat 4g; Cholesterol 19mg; Carbohydrate 9g; Dietary Fiber 3g; Sodium 341mg

Broccoli, Mushroom, and Tomato Salad with Tarragon Vinaigrette

(VEGAN/LOW-CARB)

This makes a nice late-summer salad, when tomatoes are still in season and the first of the cool-weather broccoli and mushroom crops are appearing in the markets. Cauliflower can replace all or part of the broccoli, if desired.

MAKES 4 SERVINGS

- 1 pound fresh broccoli crowns, trimmed and cut into bite-size florets
- ¼ cup extra-virgin olive oil
- 2 tablespoons tarragon vinegar
- ½ tablespoon water
- ¼ teaspoon dried thyme
- ¼ teaspoon lemon pepper seasoning
- ¼ teaspoon sugar
- ½ teaspoon salt, or to taste
- Freshly ground black pepper, to taste
- 3 small plum tomatoes (about 2 ounces each), quartered
- ½ cup sliced fresh white button mushrooms
- 2 scallions, white and green parts, thinly sliced

Bring a medium stockpot filled with water to a boil. Cook the broccoli 1 to 2 minutes, or until barely tender. Drain in a colander and rinse under cold-running water until cooled; drain again.

In a medium bowl, whisk together the oil, vinegar, water, thyme, lemon pepper, sugar, salt, and black pepper until thoroughly blended. Let stand about 5 minutes at room temperature to let the flavors blend; whisk again. Add the drained broccoli and remaining ingredients, and toss gently to combine. Refrigerate, covered, a minimum of 3 hours or overnight and serve chilled, or return to room temperature.

PER SERVING: Calories 168; Protein 4g; Total Fat 14g; Sat Fat 2g; Cholesterol 0mg; Carbohydrate 10g; Dietary Fiber 4g; Sodium 313mg

Cannellini Bean Salad

(VEGAN)

Here is a great dish to bring to a picnic or potluck as it holds up well at room temperature.

MAKES 6 SERVINGS

- 2 (15-ounce) cans cannellini or other white beans, rinsed and drained
- 1 (7-ounce) jar roasted red bell peppers, drained and cut into thin strips
- 1 small red onion (about 4 ounces), sliced into thin half-rounds, soaked in cold water to cover 15 minutes, drained
- ¼ cup chopped fresh basil
- 2 tablespoons extra-virgin olive oil
- 2 tablespoons balsamic vinegar
- 1 tablespoon cider vinegar or lemon juice
- ¼ teaspoon salt, or to taste
- Freshly ground black pepper, to taste

In a medium bowl, toss all ingredients until thoroughly combined. Let stand 15 minutes at room temperature to allow the flavors to blend; toss again and serve at room temperature. Alternatively, cover and refrigerate 3 hours or up to 2 days and serve chilled, or return to room temperature.

PER SERVING: Calories 182; Protein 9g; Total Fat 5g; Sat Fat 1g; Cholesterol 0mg; Carbohydrate 27g; Dietary Fiber 6g; Sodium 96mg

Easy Italian-Style Cucumber Salad

(VEGAN/LOW-CARB)

If you're in need of a quick and easy side salad to bring to a picnic or potluck, look no further—just be ready to pass out the recipe.

MAKES 6 SERVINGS

- 2 medium cucumbers (about 8 ounces each), peeled, halved lengthwise, seeded, and thinly sliced crosswise
- 1 cup grape or cherry tomatoes, halved
- ½ small red onion (about 2 ounces), sliced into thin half-rounds, soaked in cold water to cover 15 minutes, and drained
- ½ cup chopped green bell pepper
- ⅓ to ½ cup gluten-free, dairy-free light Italian dressing
- 1 tablespoon extra-virgin olive oil
- Salt and freshly ground black pepper, to taste

In a large bowl, toss together all ingredients until well combined. Let stand 15 minutes at room temperature to allow the flavors to blend. Toss again and serve at room temperature. Alternatively, cover and refrigerate up to 2 days and serve chilled, or return to room temperature.

PER SERVING: Calories 57; Protein 1g; Total Fat 4g; Sat Fat 1g; Cholesterol 0mg; Carbohydrate 6g; Dietary Fiber 1g; Sodium 110mg

Green Bean Salad with Tomato-Basil Dressing

(VEGAN/LOW-CARB)

This delicious green and red salad is attractive on a winter holiday buffet or summer picnic table. The versatile tomato-basil dressing can be tossed with lightly cooked asparagus and zucchini, or spooned over grilled eggplant and Portobello mushrooms, as well.

MAKES 6 SERVINGS

1½ pounds fresh green beans, trimmed

2 medium plum tomatoes (about 6 ounces total), seeded and finely chopped

2 scallions, white and green parts, thinly sliced

2 tablespoons finely chopped fresh basil

3 tablespoons extra-virgin olive oil

1½ tablespoons red wine vinegar

2 cloves garlic, finely chopped

½ teaspoon sugar

½ teaspoon coarse salt, or to taste

Freshly ground black pepper, to taste

Bring a large stockpot of salted water to a boil. Cook the green beans until crisp-tender, about 5 minutes. Meanwhile, prepare an ice-water bath. Drain the cooked green beans and immediately refresh in the ice-water bath for 5 minutes. Drain well in a colander.

In a large bowl, toss the remaining ingredients until thoroughly combined. Let stand about 10 minutes to allow the flavors to blend; toss again. Add the drained green beans and toss well to combine. Serve at room temperature. Salad can be refrigerated, covered, up to 1 day before serving chilled or returning to room temperature.

PER SERVING: Calories 106; Protein 3g; Total Fat 7g; Sat Fat 1g; Cholesterol 0mg; Carbohydrate 11g; Dietary Fiber 4g; Sodium 167mg

Mesclun Salad with Goat Cheese, Pine Nuts, and Raisins

(EGG-FREE/LOW-CARB)

Celebrate spring with this lovely first-course salad, which can be prepared with any mix of young salad greens, or baby spinach.

MAKES 4 SERVINGS

4 tablespoons extra-virgin olive oil

2 tablespoons white wine vinegar

1 tablespoon finely chopped fresh flat-leaf parsley

1 tablespoon finely chopped fresh chives or the green parts of scallions

½ teaspoon sugar

¼ teaspoon salt

Freshly ground black pepper, to taste

8 cups Mesclun or other mixed young salad greens

2 ounces (¼ cup) gluten-free crumbled goat cheese

2 tablespoons raisins, soaked in warm water to cover 10 minutes, drained

2 tablespoons toasted pine nuts

In a large bowl, whisk together the oil, vinegar, parsley, chives, sugar, salt, and pepper until thoroughly blended. Let stand at room temperature a few minutes to allow the sugar to dissolve; whisk again. Add the Mesclun and toss gently to combine. Add half the goat cheese and toss again. Divide the Mesclun mixture evenly among each of 4 salad plates or bowls. Top each with ½ tablespoon of the raisins, ½ tablespoon of the pine nuts, and ½ tablespoon of the remaining cheese. Serve at once.

PER SERVING: Calories 246; Protein 8g; Total Fat 21g; Sat Fat 6g; Cholesterol 15mg; Carbohydrate 9g; Dietary Fiber 2g; Sodium 212mg

Warm Portobello Mushroom and Spinach Salad with Roasted Red Pepper–Ricotta Pesto

(EGG-FREE/LOW-CARB)

Grace your table with this gorgeous first-course or luncheon salad. Served between gluten-free bread, it also makes a yummy—albeit a bit messy—sandwich.

MAKES 4 SERVINGS

1 (6-ounce) bag baby spinach
4 large Portobello mushroom caps (about 2 ounces each)
2 teaspoons extra-virgin olive oil
Salt and freshly ground black pepper, to taste
Roasted Red Pepper–Ricotta Pesto, page 156

Divide the spinach evenly among each of 4 salad plates; set aside.

Heat a nonstick grill pan over medium-high heat. Brush each mushroom on rounded side and rim with ½ teaspoon of the oil; season lightly with salt and pepper. Place the mushrooms, gill sides down, in pan and grill for 3 minutes. Turn, gill sides up, and grill until nicely browned, 3 to 4 minutes, rotating each mushroom a half-turn after 2 minutes. While the mushrooms are finishing cooking, fill each cap with 2 tablespoons of the pesto. Transfer each mushroom, gill side up, to the center

of each prepared salad plate. Serve at once, with the remaining pesto (about 4 tablespoons) passed separately.

PER SERVING: Calories 142; Protein 5g; Total Fat 11g; Sat Fat 2g; Cholesterol 5mg; Carbohydrate 9g; Dietary Fiber 3g; Sodium 323mg

Beefsteak Tomato and Ricotta Salata Salad

(EGG-FREE/LOW-CARB)

While Jersey beefsteak tomatoes are incomparably delicious, any good-quality ripe tomato can be substituted. If ricotta salata is not available, use crumbled feta or goat cheese.

MAKES 4 SERVINGS

4 large ripe beefsteak or other round tomatoes (about 8 ounces each), cut into ½-inch-thick rounds
Salt, preferably the coarse variety, and freshly ground black pepper, to taste
2 ounces gluten-free ricotta salata, coarsely grated or crumbled (about ¼ cup)
2 tablespoons extra-virgin olive oil
2 to 3 tablespoons shredded fresh basil leaves

Arrange the tomato slices on a serving platter in attractive concentric circles. Season with salt and pepper. Sprinkle evenly with the ricotta salata, then drizzle evenly with the oil. Garnish with the basil and serve at room temperature.

PER SERVING: Calories 141; Protein 4g; Total Fat 11g; Sat Fat 3g; Cholesterol 13mg; Carbohydrate 10g; Dietary Fiber 2g; Sodium 177mg

Roasted Onion Salad

(VEGAN/LOW-CARB)

Harkening back to medieval times, when onions were cooked in the embers then dressed with oil, vinegar, and spices, this recipe easily adapts to the backyard grill. Serve as a side dish or as a topping for grilled eggplant, Portobello mushrooms, tofu, and veggie burgers.

MAKES 6 SERVINGS

6 medium-size red onions, peeled,
  left whole
3 tablespoons extra-virgin olive oil,
  divided
¼ cup chopped fresh flat-leaf parsley
2 tablespoons red wine vinegar
1 tablespoon chopped fresh oregano or
  ½ teaspoon dried
1 teaspoon sugar
½ teaspoon salt, or to taste
Freshly ground black pepper, to taste
Salt and pepper to taste

Prepare a medium-hot charcoal or gas grill, or preheat the oven to 450F (230C). Position the grill rack 4 to 6 inches from the heat source, or place oven rack in the center.

Rub each onion with ½ teaspoon of oil (1 tablespoon total) and wrap individually in heavy-duty aluminum foil. Roast in covered grill or in the oven about 1 hour, or until tender. Let cool about 15 minutes before carefully unwrapping; cut into thin slices and place in a large bowl. Add the remaining ingredients, tossing well to combine. Serve slightly warm or at room temperature. Completely cooled mixture can be refrigerated, covered, up to 5 days before returning to room temperature and serving.

PER SERVING: Calories 129; Protein 2g; Total Fat 7g; Sat Fat 1g; Cholesterol 0mg; Carbohydrate 16g; Dietary Fiber 3g; Sodium 184mg

St. Benedict 7-Vegetable Summer Salad

(VEGAN/LOW-CARB)

I created this simple yet colorful summer salad in celebration of St. Benedict's Feast Day, on July 11. The seven vegetables represent the seven sacraments, tangible signs of God's abundant grace to His people on Earth, which strengthened and nourished Benedict's deep and abiding faith throughout his lifetime. Feel free to vary the vegetables, so long as the total number remains seven—always seven.

MAKES 4 TO 6 SERVINGS

1 cup trimmed and cut fresh green beans,
  about 2½ to 3 inches in length
1 cup sliced yellow summer squash rounds,
  about 3/8-inch thick
1 cup sliced zucchini rounds, about 3/8-inch
  thick
1 cup sliced red onion half-rounds, about
  ¼-inch thick
2 small plum tomatoes (about 2 ounces each),
  chopped
1 cup sliced cucumber rounds (preferably
  from a pickling cucumber), about 3/8-inch
  thick
1 cup shredded carrots
6 tablespoons gluten-free, reduced-fat,
  dairy-free Italian salad dressing
1 tablespoon extra-virgin olive oil
1 tablespoon balsamic vinegar

1 tablespoon finely chopped fresh chives or
the green parts of scallions
1 tablespoon finely chopped fresh basil
Salt and freshly ground black pepper, to taste

In a large steaming basket set over about 2 inches of water, place the green beans, squash, zucchini, and onion; bring to a boil over high heat. Reduce heat to medium, cover, and steam 4 to 5 minutes, or until vegetables are just crisp-tender. Drain in a colander, then rinse under cold-running water until cooled. Drain again, then pat dry with paper towels.

Transfer steamed vegetables to a large bowl and add the remaining ingredients; toss gently to combine. Cover and refrigerate a minimum of 3 hours, or up to 24 hours, and serve chilled, or return to room temperature.

PER SERVING: Calories 110; Protein 3g; Total Fat 6g; Sat Fat 1g; Cholesterol 0mg; Carbohydrate 14g; Dietary Fiber 4g; Sodium 194mg

Tomato, Basil, and Olive Salad with Potato Croutons

(VEGAN/LOW-CARB)

This sensational summer salad can be assembled a day in advance, before tossing with the potato croutons and serving.

MAKES 6 SERVINGS

4 tablespoons extra-virgin olive oil
1½ tablespoons red wine vinegar
6 medium vine-ripened tomatoes (about 6
ounces each), cut into 1-inch pieces

½ cup chopped red onion
¼ cup finely chopped fresh basil leaves
2 tablespoons finely chopped kalamata olives
Salt, preferably the coarse variety, and
freshly ground black pepper, to taste
Potato Croutons, page 68

In a large bowl, whisk together the oil and vinegar. Add the tomatoes, onion, basil, olives, salt, and pepper; toss well to thoroughly combine. Let stand about 15 minutes to let the flavors blend; toss again. Just before serving, add the potato croutons, tossing well to thoroughly combine. Serve at once.

PER SERVING: Calories 194; Protein 2g; Total Fat 15g; Sat Fat 2g; Cholesterol 0mg; Carbohydrate 14g; Dietary Fiber 3g; Sodium 180mg

Variations

To make Tomato, Basil, and Olive Salad with Italian Bread Croutons, replace the Potato Croutons with 4 ounces of cubed Italian Bread, page 86, prepared and baked according to the recipe for Sicilian Bread Salad, page 68.

To make Tomato and Basil Salad with Rosemary and Olive Croutons, omit the olives from the recipe and replace the potato croutons with 4 ounces of cubed Olive Bread with Rosemary, page 85, prepared and baked according to the recipe for Sicilian Bread Salad, page 68.

Italian Potato Salad with Garlic and Parsley

(VEGAN/LOW-CARB)

Simple and delicious, this potato salad is a welcome change from traditional mayonnaise-based versions. Chopped celery and/or red onion can be added, if desired.

MAKES 6 SERVINGS

> 1½ pounds small red-skinned potatoes, scrubbed and halved or quartered, depending on size
> ¼ cup extra-virgin olive oil
> 2 tablespoons white wine vinegar
> 3 large cloves garlic, finely chopped
> ½ teaspoon salt, or to taste
> Freshly ground black pepper, to taste
> ¼ cup finely chopped fresh flat-leaf parsley

In a medium stockpot, bring the potatoes and enough salted water to cover to a boil over high heat. Reduce the heat slightly and boil until potatoes are tender through the center but not mushy, 15 to 20 minutes. Drain and set aside to cool 10 to 15 minutes.

In a large bowl, whisk together the oil, vinegar, garlic, salt, and pepper. Stir in the parsley and let stand a few minutes at room temperature to allow the flavors to blend; stir again. When the potatoes are cool enough to handle but still quite warm, cut into smaller pieces. Add potatoes to the bowl, tossing gently to combine. Let cool to room temperature, about 15 minutes, before tossing gently again and serving. Alternatively, cover and refrigerate up to 24 hours before returning to room temperature and serving.

PER SERVING: Calories 151; Protein 2g; Total Fat 9g; Sat Fat 1g; Cholesterol 0mg; Carbohydrate 16g; Dietary Fiber 2g; Sodium 184mg

Warm Potato and Bell Pepper Salad

(VEGAN/LOW-CARB)

No one will ever know that bottled Italian dressing is the secret behind the success of this sublime potato and bell pepper salad.

MAKES 6 SERVINGS

> 1¼ pounds small Yukon Gold or red-skinned potatoes, scrubbed and halved or quartered, depending on size
> 1 tablespoon canola oil
> 1 medium green bell pepper (about 6 ounces), cored, seeded, and thinly sliced
> 1 medium red bell pepper (about 6 ounces), cored, seeded, and thinly sliced
> 1 small red onion (about 4 ounces), thinly sliced into half-rounds
> ¼ teaspoon crushed red pepper flakes, or to taste (optional)
> ⅓ to ½ cup gluten-free reduced-fat Italian dressing, at room temperature
> 1 tablespoon extra-virgin olive oil
> Garlic salt, to taste
> Freshly ground black pepper, to taste

In a medium stockpot, bring the potatoes and enough salted water to cover to a boil over high heat. Reduce the heat slightly and boil until potatoes are tender through the center but not mushy, 15 to 20 minutes. Drain and set aside to cool 10 to 15 minutes.

Meanwhile, in a large nonstick skillet, heat the canola oil over medium-high heat. Add the bell peppers, onion, and red pepper flakes, if using; cook, stirring, until vegetables are softened and beginning to brown, 4 to 5 minutes. Remove skillet from heat and set briefly aside.

Cut the warm potatoes into smaller pieces, as

necessary. Add to the skillet along with the dressing, olive oil, garlic salt, and black pepper; toss gently to combine. Serve warm or at room temperature. Completely cooled salad can be refrigerated, covered, up to 2 days before serving chilled, or returning to room temperature.

PER SERVING: Calories 132; Protein 2g; Total Fat 6g; Sat Fat 1g; Cholesterol 0mg; Carbohydrate 18g; Dietary Fiber 3g; Sodium 111mg

Radicchio and Green Apple Salad

(VEGAN/LOW-CARB)

This attractive red and green salad is a perfect first course for a winter holiday gathering.

MAKES 4 SERVINGS

2 tablespoons extra-virgin olive oil
½ tablespoon balsamic vinegar
½ tablespoon cider vinegar
½ teaspoon sugar
Salt and freshly ground black pepper, to taste
2 medium heads radicchio (about 6 ounces each), cored, rinsed, and drained, cut lengthwise into ½-inch-thick slices
1 large apple (about 8 ounces), preferably the Granny Smith variety, cored and cut into thin matchstick pieces
2 tablespoons coarsely chopped toasted walnuts

In a salad bowl, whisk together the oil, balsamic vinegar, cider vinegar, sugar, salt, and pepper. Let stand a few minutes to allow the sugar to dissolve; whisk again. Add the radicchio and apple; toss well to combine. Sprinkle with the walnuts and serve at once.

PER SERVING: Calories 129; Protein 2g; Total Fat 9g; Sat Fat 1g; Cholesterol 0mg; Carbohydrate 11g; Dietary Fiber 1g; Sodium 18mg

Spinach and Mushroom Salad with Basil Vinaigrette

(VEGAN/LOW-CARB)

If serving as a first course, garnish this classic salad with cherry or grape tomatoes for a welcoming touch.

MAKES 4 SERVINGS

4½ tablespoons extra-virgin olive oil
1½ tablespoons cider vinegar
2 tablespoons finely chopped fresh basil
1 clove garlic, finely chopped
¼ teaspoon dried thyme leaves
¼ teaspoon sugar
¼ teaspoon salt
Freshly ground black pepper, to taste
8 cups baby spinach leaves
2 cups sliced fresh cultivated white mushrooms

In a large bowl, whisk together all ingredients except the spinach and mushrooms until thoroughly combined. Let stand at room temperature a few minutes (or up to 1 hour) to allow the flavors to blend; whisk again. Just before serving, add the spinach and mushrooms and toss to thoroughly coat. Serve at once.

PER SERVING: Calories 159; Protein 2g; Total Fat 16g; Sat Fat 2g; Cholesterol 0mg; Carbohydrate 5g; Dietary Fiber 2g; Sodium 46mg

Potato Croutons

(VEGAN/LOW-CARB)

These tasty croutons are a bit like a thick potato chip—like the latter, they can be enjoyed alone.

MAKES 6 SERVINGS

2 tablespoons extra-virgin olive oil
½ tablespoon balsamic vinegar
¼ teaspoon dried oregano
¼ teaspoon dried thyme leaves
¼ teaspoon garlic salt
Freshly ground black pepper, to taste
Cayenne red pepper, to taste (optional)
1 (8-ounce) russet potato, unpeeled,
    scrubbed, sliced into ¼-inch-thick
    rounds and halved

PREHEAT OVEN TO 400F (205C).

In a medium bowl, whisk together the oil, vinegar, oregano, thyme, garlic salt, black pepper, and red pepper, if using. Let stand a few minutes to allow the flavors to blend; whisk again. Add the potatoes and toss thoroughly to coat. Transfer the potatoes in a single layer to an ungreased baking sheet. Bake 15 minutes; turn and bake an additional 7 to 12 minutes, or until crisp and edges are browned. Transfer to a wire cooling rack to cool completely before using as directed in the recipe. For best results, use on the day made.

PER SERVING: Calories 63; Protein 1g; Total Fat 5g; Sat Fat 1g; Cholesterol 0mg; Carbohydrate 5g; Dietary Fiber 1g; Sodium 87mg

MAIN-DISH SALADS

Sicilian Bread Salad

(LACTO-OVO)

This hearty bread salad embodies all the essential flavors of Sicily—tomatoes, bell peppers, chickpeas, pesto, and olives—always olives. If you don't have garlic-flavored olive oil, use plain oil and replace the coarse salt with garlic salt.

MAKES 4 SERVINGS

4 ounces (about ⅓ recipe) Olive Bread with
    Rosemary, page 85, Gluten-Free Italian
    Bread, page 86, or other gluten-free
    Italian-style bread, cut into ¾-inch cubes
1½ tablespoons garlic-flavored olive oil
¼ teaspoon coarse salt
3 tablespoons Classic Basil Pesto Sauce,
    page 97, Rustic Pesto Sauce, page 92,
    or gluten-free prepared pesto sauce
1½ tablespoons balsamic vinegar
1 tablespoon water
1 to 2 tablespoons chopped fresh rosemary
    (1 tablespoon, if using Olive Bread with
    Rosemary), or 1 to 2 teaspoons dried
    rosemary
Salt and freshly ground black pepper, to taste
1 cup canned chickpeas, rinsed and drained
1 cup cherry or grape tomatoes, halved
½ small red onion (about 2 ounces), sliced
    into thin half-rounds, soaked in cold water
    to cover 15 minutes and drained well
½ cup chopped green and/or red bell
    pepper
6 to 12 kalamata olives, pitted and halved
    (6 if using Olive Bread with Rosemary)
6 green olives, pitted and halved

4 cups romaine lettuce, spinach, or other lettuce leaves, torn into bite-size pieces

Preheat oven to 350 F (175C). In a medium bowl, toss the bread cubes with the oil to evenly coat. Sprinkle with coarse salt, and toss again. Arrange the bread in a single layer on an ungreased baking sheet. Bake until lightly brown, 10 to 12 minutes, turning once. Remove from oven and let cool completely. (At this point, bread cubes can be stored in an airtight container at room temperature up to 2 days before continuing with the recipe.)

In a large bowl, whisk together the pesto, vinegar, water, rosemary, salt, and black pepper. Add the chickpeas, tomatoes, onion, bell pepper, and olives; toss until thoroughly coated. Let stand 30 minutes at room temperature; alternatively, cover and refrigerate up to 24 hours. Toss again and add the cooled bread; toss gently to combine. Let stand 20 to 30 minutes at room temperature to allow bread to soften; toss gently again. To serve, divide the romaine evenly among 4 salad bowls or plates. Spoon equal portions of the bread mixture over the romaine and serve at once.

PER SERVING: Calories 316; Protein 10g; Total Fat 17g; Sat Fat 3g; Cholesterol 3mg; Carbohydrate 34g; Dietary Fiber 3g; Sodium 522mg

Italian Brown Rice Salad with Cannellini Beans and Basil

(VEGAN)

This outstanding rice salad is an excellent choice for a picnic or buffet—if prepared and refrigerated a day ahead, the flavor improves as it returns to room temperature.

MAKES 6 MAIN-COURSE OR 8 SIDE-DISH SERVINGS

3 tablespoons extra-virgin olive oil

3 tablespoons balsamic vinegar

2 cloves garlic, finely chopped

½ teaspoon salt

Freshly ground black pepper, to taste

4 scallions, white and green parts, thinly sliced

1 cup cherry or grape tomatoes, halved or quartered, depending on size

1 cup chopped fresh basil

8 pitted kalamata or other high-quality black olives, chopped

1 cup uncooked brown rice, cooked according to package directions, slightly warm (about 3½ to 4 cups)

1 (15-ounce) can cannellini or other white beans, rinsed and drained

In a large mixing bowl, whisk together the oil, vinegar, garlic, salt, and pepper until thoroughly blended. Let stand 5 minutes to allow the salt to dissolve; whisk again. Add the scallions, tomatoes, basil, and olives, stirring to thoroughly combine. Let stand a few minutes to allow the flavors to blend.

Add rice and beans to the bowl, tossing to thoroughly combine. Let stand 20 minutes at room temperature to allow the flavors to blend, stirring a few times. Serve at room temperature. Alternatively, cover and refrigerate up to 24 hours and serve chilled, or return to room temperature.

PER SERVING: Calories 270; Protein 7g; Total Fat 10g; Sat Fat 2g; Cholesterol 0mg; Carbohydrate 40g; Dietary Fiber 3g; Sodium 267mg

Cauliflower, Chickpea, and Egg Salad with Capers and Olives

(DAIRY-FREE/LOW-CARB)

For a simple yet superb late summer's supper, serve this delicious cold salad with Chilled Raw Tomato and Basil Soup (page 41), using the first of the incoming season's cauliflower and the last of the outgoing season's tomatoes.

MAKES 5 TO 6 SERVINGS

4½ tablespoons extra-virgin olive oil, divided

3 tablespoons white wine vinegar

½ teaspoon salt, plus additional, to taste

Freshly ground black pepper, to taste

1 large head of cauliflower (2 to 2½ pounds), cut into 1-inch florets

2 to 3 tablespoons drained capers

2 to 3 tablespoons chopped kalamata or other good-quality black olives

3 to 4 hard-cooked eggs, at room temperature, peeled, cut lengthwise into eighths and halved crosswise (See Cook's Tip, Italian Egg Salad in Lettuce Cups recipe, page 20)

1 cup rinsed and drained canned chickpeas

In a large bowl, whisk together 4 tablespoons of oil, vinegar, salt, and pepper. Let stand at room temperature a few minutes to let the flavors blend; whisk again.

Bring a large stockpot filled with salted water to a boil. Cook the cauliflower for about 3 minutes, or until crisp-tender. Drain in a colander. While still hot, add to the bowl, along with the capers and olives; toss well to combine. Let cool to room temperature, tossing a few times. Add the eggs, chickpeas, and remaining ½ tablespoon oil; toss well to thoroughly combine. Season with addi-

tional salt and pepper, as necessary. Serve at room temperature, or cover and refrigerate up to 2 days, and serve chilled, or return to room temperature.

PER SERVING: Calories 271; Protein 10g; Total Fat 18g; Sat Fat 3g; Cholesterol 129mg; Carbohydrate 20g; Dietary Fiber 5g; Sodium 432mg

Italian Lentil Salad with Artichokes and Goat Cheese

(EGG-FREE/LOW-CARB)

Trader Joe's convenient pouches of gluten-free steamed lentils make quick work of this protein-packed and delicious salad.

MAKES 6 SERVINGS

1 (17-ounce) package gluten-free steamed lentils or about 2 cups gluten-free canned lentils, rinsed and drained

1 (6-ounce) jar marinated quartered artichoke hearts, drained

½ small red onion (about 2 ounces), cut into very thin half-rounds, soaked in cold water to cover 15 minutes and drained well

¼ cup extra-virgin olive oil

¼ cup chopped fresh basil

2 tablespoons chopped fresh flat-leaf parsley

1 tablespoon balsamic vinegar

2 large cloves garlic, finely chopped

Salt and freshly ground black pepper, to taste

4 ounces gluten-free crumbled goat cheese (about ½ cup), divided

6 cups baby spinach or arugula

Cherry or grape tomatoes, halved, for garnish (optional)

In a large bowl, mix together all ingredients except the goat cheese, spinach, and tomatoes, if using. Add all but 3 tablespoons of the goat cheese, tossing gently to combine. Line 6 salad plates with the spinach; top with equal amounts of the lentil mixture. Sprinkle each serving with ½ tablespoon of the remaining cheese and serve at once, garnished with the tomatoes, if using.

PER SERVING: Calories 273; Protein 14g; Total Fat 16g; Sat Fat 6g; Cholesterol 20mg; Carbohydrate 20g; Dietary Fiber 6g; Sodium 130mg

Italian Millet Salad

(VEGAN)

Millet, commonly used as bird food in the United States, is a staple grain in many Italian households. This delicious tabbouleh-like salad is even better the next day. Slivered almonds or chopped walnuts can replace the pine nuts, if desired.

MAKES 6 SERVINGS

- ¼ cup pine nuts
- 1 cup millet
- 2 cups low-sodium vegetable broth
- ½ cup water
- ¼ cup currants or raisins
- ½ teaspoon salt, or to taste, divided
- Freshly ground black pepper, to taste
- ¼ cup extra-virgin olive oil
- Juice of 1 medium lemon (about 3 tablespoons), or more, to taste
- 3 large cloves garlic, finely chopped
- 4 scallions, white and green parts, thinly sliced
- 1 cup grape or cherry tomatoes, halved
- ½ cup finely chopped fresh flat-leaf parsley
- ½ cup drained marinated quartered artichoke hearts, chopped
- ¼ cup chopped kalamata olives

Heat a medium deep-sided skillet over medium heat; add the nuts and cook, stirring, until lightly toasted, 3 to 5 minutes. Immediately remove nuts from skillet and transfer to a holding plate. Add the millet to the hot skillet and toast, stirring frequently, until lightly browned and fragrant, about 5 minutes. Stir in the broth, water, currants, ¼ teaspoon salt, and pepper and bring to a brisk simmer over high heat. Reduce the heat to between low and medium-low, cover, and cook until millet is tender and most of the liquid has been absorbed, about 20 minutes. Remove skillet from heat and let stand, covered, 5 minutes. Spread millet mixture in a single layer on a baking sheet and let cool about 5 minutes.

Meanwhile, in a large bowl, whisk together the oil, lemon juice, garlic, remaining ¼ teaspoon salt, and pepper. Add the millet mixture, reserved nuts, and all remaining ingredients; toss well to thoroughly combine. Let stand 20 minutes at room temperature to allow the flavors to blend; toss again and serve at room temperature. Alternatively, cover and refrigerate up to 2 days and serve chilled, or return to room temperature.

PER SERVING: Calories 324; Protein 11g; Total Fat 17g; Sat Fat 2g; Cholesterol 0mg; Carbohydrate 37g; Dietary Fiber 6g; Sodium 531mg

Polenta Caprese Salad with Olives

(EGG-FREE)

This downright delicious salad makes an ideal casual supper or special luncheon in the summertime. Unlike typical bread salads, it's also a great potluck, picnic, or buffet choice as it holds up well at room temperature.

MAKES 6 SERVINGS

1 cup low-sodium vegetable broth

1 cup water

¾ cup quick-cooking or regular polenta (coarse-ground yellow cornmeal)

6 tablespoons extra-virgin olive oil, divided

¼ teaspoon dried thyme leaves

¼ teaspoon dried rosemary leaves

¼ teaspoon garlic salt

Freshly ground black pepper, to taste

2½ tablespoons balsamic vinegar

2 to 3 large cloves garlic, finely chopped

Salt and freshly ground black pepper, to taste

24 cherry or grape tomatoes, halved

12 pitted kalamata olives, or other good-quality black olives, halved

12 pitted small green olives, halved, or 6 jumbo green olives, quartered

12 bite-size fresh mozzarella cheese balls (about 4 ounces), halved

2 to 3 scallions, white and green parts, thinly sliced

½ cup chopped fresh basil

Fresh whole basil leaves, for garnish (optional)

Lightly grease an 8-inch-square glass baking dish; set aside.

If using quick-cooking polenta: In a large saucepan or medium stockpot, bring the broth, water, polenta, 1 teaspoon of oil, thyme, rosemary, garlic salt, and pepper to a boil over high heat. Immediately reduce the heat to medium and cook, stirring often with a long-handled spoon (polenta will sputter), 5 minutes. Immediately spoon polenta into the prepared baking dish, pressing down with the back of a large spoon or spatula (dampen slightly, if necessary) to form a smooth surface. Let stand about 15 minutes to become firm. (At this point, polenta can be held up to 1 hour at room temperature before continuing with the recipe. Alternatively, cover and refrigerate up to 24 hours before returning to room temperature and proceeding.)

If using regular polenta: In a large saucepan or medium stockpot, bring the broth, water, 1 teaspoon of oil, thyme, rosemary, garlic salt, and pepper to a boil over high heat. Slowly add the polenta, stirring constantly with a long-handled spoon. Reduce the heat to low and cook, covered, stirring occasionally, until the polenta is tender, about 15 minutes. Immediately spoon polenta into the prepared baking dish, pressing down with the back of a large spoon or spatula (dampen slightly, if necessary) to form a smooth surface. Let stand about 15 minutes to become firm. (At this point, polenta can be held up to 1 hour at room temperature before continuing with the recipe. Alternatively, cover and refrigerate up to 24 hours before returning to room temperature and proceeding.)

Preheat oven to broil and position rack 4 to 6 inches from heating element. Lightly oil a baking sheet and set aside.

Cut the polenta into fourths and transfer to the prepared baking sheet. Brush the top of the polenta evenly with 1 teaspoon oil. Broil until lightly browned, 3 to 5 minutes. Turn the polenta over and brush evenly with 1 teaspoon of remaining oil.

Broil until lightly browned, 3 to 4 minutes. Set aside to cool a few minutes.

In a large bowl, whisk together remaining 5 tablespoons oil, vinegar, garlic, salt, and pepper. Add the tomatoes, both olives, cheese, scallions, and chopped basil, tossing well to combine. Let stand a few minutes to allow flavors to blend; toss again. Cut each polenta quarter into 16 (1-inch) squares; add to the bowl, tossing gently to combine. Let stand about 10 minutes to allow the flavors to blend; toss gently again and serve at room temperature, garnished with the whole basil leaves, if using.

PER SERVING: Calories 310; Protein 9g; Total Fat 22g; Sat Fat 5g; Cholesterol 17mg; Carbohydrate 22g; Dietary Fiber 4g; Sodium 454mg

Grilled Romaine Salad with Parmesan–Bread Crumb Crust

(EGG-FREE/LOW-CARB)

For a delicious contradiction, I like to serve this slightly warm, slightly crunchy salad with Chilled Raw Tomato and Basil Soup, page 41.

MAKES 4 SERVINGS

- ½ cup gluten-free freshly grated Parmesan cheese
- ¼ cup gluten-free, egg-free, dairy-free Italian-seasoned bread crumbs
- ⅓ cup prepared gluten-free nonfat Italian dressing
- 3 tablespoons extra-virgin olive oil, divided
- 2 tablespoons balsamic vinegar
- 1 to 2 large cloves garlic, finely chopped
- 2 large hearts of romaine (6 to 8 ounces each), tough outer leaves removed, cut lengthwise in half
- Salt, preferably the coarse variety, and freshly ground pepper, to taste

Preheat the oven to broil. Position oven rack 6 to 8 inches from heat source. Lightly oil a baking sheet with sides and set aside.

In a small bowl, combine the Parmesan and bread crumbs; set aside. In another small bowl, whisk together the dressing, 1 tablespoon oil, vinegar, and garlic; set aside.

Place a stovetop grilling pan with grids over medium-high heat. Brush romaine hearts on all sides evenly with 1 tablespoon oil; season with salt and pepper. Place the romaine hearts, leaf side down, on the grill and cook for 2 minutes, or until grill marks appear. Turn each romaine heart over and grill the cut sides 1 minute. Transfer each romaine heart, cut side up, to the prepared baking sheet. Sprinkle evenly with the Parmesan–bread crumb mixture, then drizzle evenly with the remaining 1 tablespoon oil. Broil 6 to 8 inches from the heat source until the cheese begins to melt and the bread crumbs are lightly toasted, about 3 minutes.

To serve, transfer romaine hearts to each of 4 salad plates, cut-sides up. Whisk the reserved dressing mixture; drizzle equal amounts (about 2 tablespoons) evenly over each romaine heart. Serve at once.

PER SERVING: Calories 198; Protein 8g; Total Fat 14g; Sat Fat 4g; Cholesterol 10mg; Carbohydrate 11g; Dietary Fiber 2g; Sodium 720mg

Basil Omelet and Green Bean Salad

(DAIRY-FREE/LOW-CARB)

While I prefer the combination of green beans and potatoes, you can make this tasty egg salad using just about any leftover vegetable of your choice.

MAKES 3 MAIN-DISH OR 4 TO 6 FIRST-COURSE SERVINGS

3 eggs

1 tablespoon finely chopped fresh basil

Salt and freshly ground black pepper, to taste

1 tablespoon extra-virgin olive oil

½ recipe leftover Green Bean Salad with Tomato-Basil Vinaigrette, page 62, green beans cut crosswise in half

½ recipe Potato Croutons, page 68 (optional)

In a small bowl, whisk together the eggs, basil, salt, and pepper; set aside

Heat an omelet pan or 8-inch nonstick skillet over medium-high heat until a drop of water sizzles on its surface. Add the oil and swirl to coat the pan. Quickly add the egg mixture. Swirl pan with 1 hand while stirring eggs in a circular motion with a fork (tines should be parallel to but not touching bottom of pan). When the eggs begin to set, quickly push cooked egg toward center of the pan, allowing uncooked egg to run underneath. Lift pan from heat and turn off heat. Return pan to the same burner, cover, and let stand for 2 to 3 minutes, or until eggs are completely set. Slide omelet onto a plate and let cool. Cut into ¾-inch-thick strips; set aside.

In a medium bowl, toss together the green bean salad and egg strips. Divide evenly among 4 plates or bowls and serve at room temperature, garnished with the potato croutons, if using.

PER SERVING: Calories 221; Protein 9g; Total Fat 17g; Sat Fat 3g; Cholesterol 213mg; Carbohydrate 11g; Dietary Fiber 4g; Sodium 230mg

Our Lady of Loreto Rosary Salad with Job's Tears, Roasted Red Peppers, and Black Olives

(VEGAN)

Job's tears, the hulled and cooked pale grains of which resemble pearl barley, gets its name from the shape of the unhulled grain, which suggests a blackish-colored teardrop. Throughout the world, rosary beads and other prayer beads, as well as jewelry, are made from unhulled Job's tears. In the Adriatic city of Loreto, a vast basilica enshrines one of the most revered of all Marian shrines—the Holy House of Jesus, Mary, and Joseph, a humble cottage whose interior measures a mere thirty-one feet by thirteen. Above an altar stands a replica of a wooden statue of the Madonna and Child destroyed in a fire—like the original, darkened by soot from the oil lamps burning in unceasing prayer over the centuries, it is a striking ebony, similar in color to unhulled Job's tears. Like the hulled tears accomplish in this satisfying salad, its promise of mercy and love fills the hungry with good things.

MAKES 4 SERVINGS

1 (8-ounce) red bell pepper, cored, seeded, and ribbed, and cut into eighths

1 cup hulled Job's tears, rinsed and picked over (remove any dark grains), drained well

3 tablespoons extra-virgin olive oil

2 tablespoons red wine vinegar

1 tablespoon fresh lemon juice

½ teaspoon salt, or to taste

¼ teaspoon sugar

Freshly ground black pepper, to taste

3 large plum tomatoes, about 3 ounces each, chopped

4 scallions, white and green parts, thinly sliced

1 cup fresh or frozen peas, cooked and drained (optional)

¼ cup crumbled gluten-free feta cheese (optional)

¼ cup chopped fresh flat-leaf parsley

¼ cup chopped fresh basil

¼ cup chopped kalamata or other good-quality black olives

Preheat the oven to broil. Position the oven rack 4 inches from heat source. Lightly oil a baking sheet.

Place bell pepper pieces, skin sides up, on the prepared baking sheet; flatten pieces with your hand. Broil until skins are partially charred and puffy, about 5 minutes, turning the baking sheet to promote even cooking. Transfer peppers to a paper bag and twist to seal. Alternatively, place in a self-sealing plastic bag and seal. Let rest 15 to 20 minutes.

Meanwhile, bring a medium stockpot filled with salted water to a boil over high heat. Add Job's tears, reduce heat to medium-high, and simmer briskly, stirring occasionally, until tender, about 30 minutes. Drain and let cool slightly, about 5 minutes.

In a large bowl, whisk together the oil, vinegar, lemon juice, salt, sugar, and black pepper. Let stand a few minutes to allow the flavors to blend. Remove the bell pepper pieces from the bag; peel and discard skins. Coarsely chop the bell pepper and transfer to the bowl. Add the Job's tears and remaining ingredients; toss well to combine. Let cool to room temperature, tossing a few times before

serving. Alternatively, completely cooled salad can be refrigerated, covered, up to 2 days before serving chilled or returning to room temperature.

PER SERVING: Calories 344; Protein 7g; Total Fat 15g; Sat Fat 2g; Cholesterol 0mg; Carbohydrate 49g; Dietary Fiber 10g; Sodium 518mg

Watermelon and Ricotta Salata Salad with Pine Nuts and Basil

(EGG-FREE/LOW-CARB)

Ricotta salata is salted dry ricotta cheese; it is available in specialty stores, Italian markets, and some well-stocked supermarkets. Crumbled gluten-free feta or goat cheese can be substituted, if necessary.

MAKES 6 SERVINGS

2 tablespoons extra-virgin olive oil

2 tablespoons fresh lemon juice (about ½ large lemon)

2 tablespoons finely chopped fresh basil

Salt and freshly ground black pepper, to taste

6 cups cubed seedless watermelon (from about a 4-pound whole watermelon)

½ pound gluten-free ricotta salata, cut into ¼-inch cubes

¼ cup toasted pine nuts

In a large bowl, whisk together the oil, lemon juice, basil, salt, and pepper. Add the watermelon and ricotta salata; toss gently to thoroughly combine. Serve at once, sprinkled with the pine nuts.

PER SERVING: Calories 227; Protein 8g; Total Fat 17g; Sat Fat 7g; Cholesterol 34mg; Carbohydrate 15g; Dietary Fiber 1g; Sodium 426mg

Rice Fusilli Primavera Salad with Grilled Vegetables and Raw Tomato Sauce

(VEGAN)

Perfect for a party, this delicious grilled vegetable pasta salad dressed in a raw tomato sauce gives new life to the tired deli counter variety. While the recipe easily doubles to feed a crowd, you will need your biggest pasta bowl for the final tossing. Tiny Italian or Japanese eggplant can be found in the produce section of well-stocked supermarket throughout the year.

MAKES 5 TO 6 MAIN-DISH OR 8 TO 10 SIDE-DISH SERVINGS

3 tablespoons extra-virgin olive oil, divided

½ tablespoon Italian seasoning

½ teaspoon coarse salt, divided

Freshly ground black pepper, to taste

Cayenne red pepper, to taste

2 (4-ounce) Italian or Japanese eggplants, trimmed and cut lengthwise into ½-inch-thick slices

1 (4-ounce) zucchini, trimmed and cut lengthwise into ½-inch-thick slices

1 (4-ounce) yellow summer squash, trimmed and cut lengthwise into ½-inch-thick slices

½ medium red bell pepper (about 3 ounces), cut lengthwise into eighths

½ medium red onion (about 3 ounces), cut into ½-inch-thick rounds

2 tablespoons balsamic vinegar, divided

Dried oregano, to taste

Table salt, to taste

1 tablespoon fresh lemon juice

2 large cloves garlic, finely chopped

¼ teaspoon sugar

1½ pounds ripe plum tomatoes, quartered

2 scallions, white and green parts, thinly sliced

¼ cup chopped fresh basil

¼ cup chopped fresh flat-leaf parsley

2 tablespoons chopped kalamata or other good-quality black olives

2 tablespoons chopped green olives

1 tablespoon drained capers

8 ounces brown rice fusilli pasta or similar gluten-free pasta

Gluten-free crumbled goat cheese or feta cheese, to serve (optional)

In a large bowl, whisk together 1½ tablespoons oil, Italian seasoning, ¼ teaspoon coarse salt, black pepper, and cayenne, if using. Add the eggplant, zucchini, summer squash, bell pepper, and onion, tossing to thoroughly coat; set aside.

Prepare a medium-hot charcoal or gas grill, or preheat a broiler. Position the grill rack or oven rack 4 to 6 inches from the heat source. If grilling, lightly oil a vegetable grid and set aside. If broiling, lightly oil a large baking sheet and set aside. Or place a stovetop grilling pan with grids over medium-high heat. Working in batches, as necessary, grill or broil the vegetables until lightly browned and tender, about 3 to 4 inches per side for the bell pepper, about 2 to 3 minutes per side for the eggplant, zucchini, squash, and onion. Place the vegetables on a large baking sheet as they finish cooking.

When all the vegetables have finished cooking, cut the eggplant crosswise into 1-inch-wide strips. Drizzle the vegetables with ½ tablespoon of the vinegar and ½ tablespoon oil. Sprinkle lightly with oregano, table salt, and black pepper; toss gently with a large spatula. Set aside to cool on the baking sheet.

Meanwhile, in the same large bowl used for vegetables, whisk together the remaining 1½ tablespoons vinegar and remaining 1 tablespoon oil with the lemon juice, garlic, sugar, remaining ¼ teaspoon coarse salt, and black pepper. Let stand a few minutes to allow the sugar and salt to dissolve; whisk again. In a food processor fitted with the knife blade, or a blender, process or blend the tomatoes until smooth and pureed. Add the tomatoes to the bowl, along with the scallions, basil, parsley, olives, and capers; stir well to combine. Add the grilled vegetables and toss well to combine. (At this point, mixture can be refrigerated, covered, overnight before proceeding with the recipe.)

In a large stockpot filled with boiling salted water, cook the fusilli according to package directions until al dente. Drain in a colander. While still hot, add to the grilled vegetable–tomato sauce mixture, tossing well to thoroughly combine. Let cool to room temperature before tossing again and serving, sprinkled with the goat cheese, if using. Alternatively, cover and refrigerate up to 1 day and serve chilled, or return to room temperature.

PER SERVING: Calories 323; Protein 9g; Total Fat 11g; Sat Fat 1g; Cholesterol 0mg; Carbohydrate 49g; Dietary Fiber 5g; Sodium 347mg

FOUR

Breads, Pizzas, Sandwiches, and Other Lighter Fare

Everyone on planet Earth loves pizza—if they could possibly sample a piece, everyone in the universe would, too. Few can resist a crispy panini sandwich, prepared with crusty Italian bread, packed with succulent grilled vegetables, and often bursting with melted cheese. What's not to like about chewy Italian bread sticks dipped in marinara or, better still, a little "evoo"? Yet, with the meager selection of both fresh and frozen gluten-free pizza crusts and Italian breads in most supermarkets (alas, even in some health food stores), adherents of a gluten-free diet are often resigned to putting these forbidden foods out of their minds. Happily, the following collection of homemade breads, pizzas, paninis, and other lighter fare will not only allow you to contemplate these culinary delights once again, but to actually sink your teeth into them. What are you waiting for? Preheat the oven and get started!

Breads

Gluten-Free Brown Ciabatta Bread (vegan/low-carb)

Focaccia Bread with Rosemary and Coarse Salt (dairy-free)

Olive Bread with Rosemary (dairy-free/low-carb)

Gluten-Free Italian Bread (dairy-free)

Herbed Italian Bread Sticks (vegan)

Sun-Dried Tomato and Pesto Quick Bread (lacto-ovo/low-carb)

Pizzas

Three-Cheese Artichoke and Sun-Dried Tomato Pizza with Spaghetti-Olive Crust (lacto-ovo)

Pizza Margherita with Prebaked Pizza Crust (lacto-ovo)

Cheese Pizza with Rice Crust (lacto-ovo)

Eggplant Pizza with Zucchini Crust (lacto-ovo/low-carb)

Roasted Vegetable Pizza with Brown Rice Flour Crust (vegan)

Classic Pizza alla Marinara with White Rice Flour Crust (vegan)

Spinach and Goat Cheese Pesto Pizza with Cornmeal Crust (lacto-ovo)

Polenta Pizza with Grape Tomatoes and Rustic Pesto Sauce (vegan)

Polenta Skillet Pizza Pie with Broccoli and Gorgonzola (egg-free/low-carb)

Roasted Red Pepper, Caper, and Basil Pizza with Cauliflower Crust (lacto-ovo/low-carb)

Sandwiches and Other Lighter Fare

English Muffin Pizzas (lacto-ovo)

Panini with Grilled Eggplant and Sun-Dried Tomato-Basil Pesto (vegan)

Grilled Portobello Mushroom Pizza Burgers (egg-free)

Italian Veggie Patties (dairy-free)

Tomato-Basil Grilled Cheese Sandwiches (egg-free)

Spinach Roll-Ups with Italian Egg Salad (dairy-free/low-carb)

Gluten-Free Brown Ciabatta Bread

(VEGAN/LOW-CARB)

Best toasted, this rustic vegan bread is perfect for making panini sandwiches, bruschetta, and garlic bread, to name a few. A teaspoon or so of dried herbs—such as rosemary, thyme, and/or oregano—can be added when mixing the dry ingredients, if desired.

MAKES 1 LOAF

Cornmeal, for dusting
1 tablespoon plus 2 teaspoons extra-virgin
    olive oil, divided
1 cup warm water (105F to 115F;
    40C to 45C)
1 (¼-ounce) packet active dry yeast
    (about 1 tablespoon)
2 teaspoons sugar
½ cup brown rice flour
½ cup garbanzo bean (chickpea) flour
½ cup amaranth flour
½ cup tapioca flour
2 teaspoons xanthan gum
½ teaspoon salt

Preheat oven to 400F (205C). Generously grease a baking sheet and dust with cornmeal; set aside. Grease a large mixing bowl with 2 teaspoons of the oil and set aside.

In a small bowl, combine the warm water and yeast, stirring to dissolve; add the sugar, stirring to dissolve. Set aside about 10 minutes to allow the mixture to foam. Meanwhile, in a clean large mix-

ing bowl, whisk together the flours, xanthan gum, and salt until thoroughly blended. Using a wooden spoon, make a well in the center by stirring the flour mixture to the edges of the bowl. When yeast mixture is foamy, add the remaining 1 tablespoon oil, stirring to blend; pour the yeast mixture into the center of the well. With the spoon, slowly mix the wet ingredients with the dry. Using your hands, finish mixing until a dough is formed (mixture will be sticky; do not over-mix).

With wet fingers, form the dough into a ball and transfer to the oiled bowl, turning to coat on all sides. Cover the bowl with a damp kitchen towel and set in a draft-free warm place (about 70F/20C) to rise until doubled in bulk, about 1 hour.

Transfer the risen dough to the prepared baking sheet and shape into a rectangle about 8 inches in length. With the tip of a sharp knife, make a few evenly spaced shallow slashes across the top or sides of the dough. Bake for 30 to 35 minutes, or until bread is golden brown and sounds hollow when lightly tapped. If bread is browning too quickly after about 25 minutes, cover loosely with foil or transfer to lower rack until done. Transfer bread to a cooling rack and cool for a minimum of 20 minutes before slicing. Store completely cooled bread in an airtight container at room temperature up to 24 hours, or freeze for up to 2 months.

PER SERVING (¹⁄₁₆ *of recipe):* Calories 81; Protein 1g; Total Fat 2g; Sat Fat 0g; Cholesterol 0mg; Carbohydrate 15g; Dietary Fiber 1g; Sodium 68mg

Focaccia Bread with Rosemary and Coarse Salt

(DAIRY-FREE)

I like to serve this Italian flatbread with a saucer of extra-virgin olive oil mixed with some freshly ground black pepper—and a pinch of red pepper flakes—for dipping. It's also a great companion to many meals, namely soups. The coarse salt can be omitted, and dried thyme leaves can replace the rosemary, if desired.

MAKES 1 (11 × 7-INCH) LOAF

Cornmeal, for dusting

1 cup warm water (105F to 115F; 40C to 45C)

2 teaspoons sugar

1 (¼-ounce) package gluten-free rapid-rise (quick-acting) dry yeast (about 1 tablespoon)

1 cup white rice flour

½ cup tapioca flour

½ tablespoon xanthan gum

½ teaspoon table salt

1 egg

3½ tablespoons extra-virgin olive oil, divided

1 tablespoon dried rosemary leaves

½ teaspoon coarse salt, or to taste

Lightly grease an 11 × 7-inch baking dish and dust with cornmeal; set aside.

In a small bowl, combine the warm water, sugar, and yeast, stirring to dissolve. Set aside about 10 minutes to allow the mixture to foam. Meanwhile, in a large mixing bowl, whisk together the rice flour, tapioca flour, xanthan gum, and table salt until thoroughly blended.

When yeast mixture is foamy, add to the flour mixture, stirring to combine. Add the egg and 2 tablespoons of oil; beat on high speed 2 minutes. Using a spoon, transfer to the prepared baking dish. With a damp spatula or your fingers, smooth the top of the dough. Cover with a damp kitchen towel and set aside in a draft-free warm area (about 70F/20C) until doubled in bulk, 30 minutes to 1 hour.

Preheat oven to 400F (205C). With two wet fingertips, make several indentations across the top of the dough at regular intervals. Brush the dough evenly with the remaining 1½ tablespoons of oil, then sprinkle evenly with the rosemary and coarse salt. Bake 20 to 25 minutes, or until lightly browned and cooked through the center. Let cool in the baking dish 10 minutes before cutting into wedges and serving warm or at room temperature. Store completely cooled focaccia in an airtight container at room temperature for up to 24 hours, or freeze for up to 2 months.

PER SERVING (⅛ of recipe): Calories 176; Protein 3g; Total Fat 7g; Sat Fat 1g; Cholesterol 27mg; Carbohydrate 26g; Dietary Fiber 1g; Sodium 260mg

Variations

To make Flat Bread Salad Pizza, top completely cooled focaccia loaf with about 4 cups of mixed greens that have been tossed with prepared gluten-free Italian dressing or balsamic vinaigrette. Garnish with olives, capers, artichokes, tomatoes, onion, etc., and/or gluten-free cheese (such as mozzarella, Parmesan, feta, goat, Gorgonzola), if desired; cut into wedges and serve at once.

To make Flat Bread Salad Bruschetta, cut completely cooled focaccia loaf into 8 wedges. Grill or toast each wedge; while still warm, rub on one side with the cut side of a halved garlic clove. When completely cooled, top the garlic-rubbed side with equal portions of the dressed mixed greens, as per above. Garnish with the suggested toppings, as per above, and serve at once.

Olive Bread with Rosemary

(DAIRY-FREE/LOW-CARB)

This fragrant bread is my favorite—serve it with just about any Italian- or Mediterranean-style entrée, soup, or salad. As an appetizer, it's fabulous for dipping in olive oil, while center-cut slices make great sandwich or panini bread. Dried thyme can replace the rosemary, if desired.

MAKES 1 LOAF

Cornmeal, for dusting

1 tablespoon plus 2 teaspoons extra-virgin olive oil, divided

⅔ cup lukewarm water (105F to 115F; 40C to 45C)

½ tablespoon sugar

½ tablespoon gluten-free rapid-rise yeast

¾ cup tapioca flour

½ cup brown rice flour

6 tablespoons sorghum flour

½ tablespoon xanthan gum

½ teaspoon salt

1 large egg, at room temperature

¼ cup pitted kalamata or other good-quality black olives, finely chopped

1 tablespoon fresh rosemary leaves, finely chopped, or 1 teaspoon dried

Lightly grease a baking sheet and dust with cornmeal; set aside. Grease a large mixing bowl with 1 teaspoon of the oil; set aside.

In a small bowl, combine the warm water, sugar, and yeast, stirring to dissolve. Set aside about 10 minutes to allow the mixture to foam. Meanwhile, in a large mixing bowl, whisk together the flours, xanthan gum, and salt until thoroughly blended.

When yeast mixture is foamy, add to the flour mixture, stirring to combine. Add the egg and remaining 4 teaspoons of oil; beat on low speed 2 minutes. Using a spoon, mix in the olives and rosemary; transfer dough to the prepared large mixing bowl. Cover with a damp kitchen towel and let rise in a draft-free warm area (about 70F/20C) until doubled in bulk, about 1 hour.

Preheat oven to 400F (205C).

Transfer dough to the prepared baking sheet and shape into a rounded loaf about 6 inches long. Smooth the dough with a damp spatula. With the tip of a sharp knife, make a few evenly spaced shallow slashes across the top. Bake on the center rack about 35 to 45 minutes, or until loaf is lightly browned and sounds hollow when lightly tapped. (If bread is browning too quickly after 30 minutes, cover loosely with foil.) Transfer loaf to a rack and cool a minimum of 15 minutes before slicing and serving warm, or at room temperature. Completely cooled bread can be stored in an airtight container at room temperature up to 24 hours, or frozen for up to 2 months.

PER SERVING (¹⁄₁₂ *of recipe*): Calories 97; Protein 2g; Total Fat 3g; Sat Fat 0g; Cholesterol 18mg; Carbohydrate 17g; Dietary Fiber 1g; Sodium 97mg

Gluten-Free Italian Bread

(DAIRY-FREE)

This easy recipe produces gluten-free Italian bread with a crusty exterior and soft interior similar to the wheat-based traditional variety. Though this bread is best eaten the day it is baked, day-old bread can be used successfully to make toasted garlic bread, bruschetta, or grilled panini sandwiches. Freeze the second loaf for up to 2 months.

MAKES 2 LOAVES

Cornmeal, for dusting

1½ cups warm water (105F to 115F;
    40C to 45C)

2 tablespoons sugar

1 (¼-ounce) package gluten-free
    rapid-rise (quick-acting) dry yeast
    (about 1 tablespoon)

2 cups white rice flour

1 cup tapioca flour

1 tablespoon xanthan gum

½ tablespoon salt

3 egg whites

2 tablespoons extra-virgin olive oil

1 teaspoon plain white vinegar

Lightly grease 2 standard-size baking sheets and dust with cornmeal; set aside.

In a small bowl, combine the warm water, sugar, and yeast, stirring to dissolve. Set aside about 10 minutes to allow the mixture to foam. Meanwhile, in a large mixing bowl, whisk together the rice flour, tapioca flour, xanthan gum, and salt until thoroughly blended.

When yeast mixture is foamy, add to the flour mixture, stirring to combine. Add the egg whites, oil, and vinegar; beat on high speed 3 minutes. Using a spoon, transfer equal amounts of the dough onto the prepared baking sheets, shaping into 2 loaves about 8 inches in length. Smooth top of dough with a damp spatula or your fingers, if desired. Cover with a damp kitchen towel and set aside in a draft-free warm area (about 70F/20C) until doubled in bulk, 30 minutes to 1 hour.

Meanwhile, preheat oven to 350F (175C). With the tip of a sharp knife, make about 6 evenly spaced shallow, diagonal slashes across the top of each loaf. Bake 45 minutes to 1 hour, or until loaves are nicely browned and crusty and cooked through the center. (If loaves are browning too quickly, cover loosely with foil after about 40 minutes.) Place on a wire rack to cool about 15 minutes before serving warm or at room temperature. For optimal freshness, store completely cooled loaves in an airtight container at room temperature for up to 24 hours, or freeze for up to 2 months.

PER SERVING (¹⁄₁₆ *of recipe*): Calories 131; Protein 2g; Total Fat 2g; Sat Fat 0g; Cholesterol 0mg; Carbohydrate 26g; Dietary Fiber 1g; Sodium 211mg

Herbed Italian Bread Sticks

(VEGAN)

Serve these scrumptious bread sticks as accompaniments to soups, salads, and gluten-free pasta dishes, or serve with heated marinara or pizza sauce as a snack. Split lengthwise, they make ideal mini sub rolls.

MAKES 4 WHOLE BREAD STICKS OR 8 HALF-PIECES

⅔ cup brown rice flour

½ cup tapioca starch flour

1 (¼-ounce) package gluten-free active dry
    yeast (about 1 tablespoon)

1 teaspoon xanthan gum

1 teaspoon Italian seasoning

½ teaspoon sugar

½ teaspoon salt

⅔ cup water

1 tablespoon extra-virgin olive oil, divided

1 teaspoon cider vinegar

Dried oregano, to taste

Garlic salt, to taste

Preheat oven to 425F (220C). Lightly grease a baking sheet and set aside.

In a large mixing bowl, whisk together the rice flour, tapioca flour, yeast, xanthan gum, Italian seasoning, sugar, and salt until thoroughly combined. Slowly add the water, stirring to combine. Add ½ tablespoon oil and vinegar and beat on medium speed 2 minutes. Cover bowl with a damp kitchen towel and let stand at room temperature 10 minutes.

Using a spoon, transfer 4 equal portions of dough onto the prepared baking sheet. With damp fingers and a damp spatula, shape into 4 cylinders about 6 inches long. Smooth the dough with the damp spatula. Brush evenly with the remaining ½ tablespoon of oil. Sprinkle lightly with the oregano and garlic salt. Bake about 12 minutes, or until golden. Cut crosswise in half, if desired, and serve warm, within 1 hour of baking for best results. Completely cooled bread sticks can be stored at room temperature in an airtight container up to 1 day before being reheated in a warm oven. Alternatively, they can be frozen for up to 2 months.

PER SERVING (per whole bread stick, or ¼ of recipe): Calories 201; Protein 3g; Total Fat 4g; Sat Fat 1g; Cholesterol 0mg; Carbohydrate 37g; Dietary Fiber 2g; Sodium 272mg

Sun-Dried Tomato and Pesto Quick Bread

(LACTO-OVO/LOW-CARB)

Ready in under an hour from start to finish, this savory yeast-free bread requires no rising time—no one will ever guess it's gluten-free unless you tell them.

MAKES 1 (9 × 5-INCH) LOAF

2 cups tapioca starch flour

1½ teaspoons xanthan gum

1 teaspoon gluten-free baking powder

½ teaspoon baking soda

2 teaspoons Italian seasoning

½ teaspoon salt

1 cup (4 ounces) gluten-free freshly shredded Parmesan cheese

⅓ cup skim milk

2 eggs

2 tablespoons gluten-free prepared pesto sauce

1 tablespoon water

½ tablespoon extra-virgin olive oil

¼ cup drained and finely chopped marinated sun-dried tomato strips, 1 tablespoon marinade reserved

Preheat oven to 400F (205C). Lightly oil a nonstick 9 × 5-inch loaf pan; set aside.

In a large bowl, whisk together the flour, xanthan gum, baking powder, baking soda, Italian seasoning, and salt until thoroughly combined. Add the cheese, mixing well to evenly distribute. In a small bowl, whisk together the milk, eggs, pesto, water, and oil until thoroughly blended; stir in the tomatoes. Add the wet mixture to the dry ingredients, stirring well to thoroughly combine. Transfer to prepared loaf pan. Bake in the center of the oven for 15 to 18 minutes, or until loaf is lightly browned and sounds hollow when lightly tapped.

Remove the loaf from the pan and transfer to a wire rack. With the tip of a thin, sharp knife, poke about 8 to 12 evenly spaced ½-inch-deep slits across the top; brush evenly with the reserved sun-dried tomato marinade. Let cool to room temperature before serving. For optimal freshness, store completely cooled bread in an airtight container for up to 24 hours, or freeze for up to 2 months.

PER SERVING (¹⁄₁₆ of recipe): Calories 112; Protein 4g; Total Fat 4g; Sat Fat 2g; Cholesterol 31mg; Carbohydrate 16g; Dietary Fiber 0g; Sodium 251mg

PIZZAS

Three-Cheese Artichoke and Sun-Dried Tomato Pizza with Spaghetti-Olive Crust

(LACTO-OVO)

I use Trader Joe's organic brown rice spaghetti and marinated julienne-sliced sun-dried tomatoes for this filling gluten-free pizza dish—mangia!

MAKES 8 SERVINGS

1 pound gluten-free spaghetti
2 cups prepared gluten-free marinara sauce, divided
2 cups gluten-free reduced-fat shredded mozzarella cheese, divided
3 eggs, beaten
6 to 8 kalamata olives, finely chopped
½ teaspoon garlic salt, plus additional, to taste

4 ounces marinated artichoke hearts, drained (about ½ cup packed), thinly sliced lengthwise
⅓ cup packed and drained marinated julienne-sliced sun-dried tomatoes
⅓ cup fresh basil leaves, torn
½ cup gluten-free shredded provolone cheese
½ cup gluten-free shredded Parmesan cheese
Italian seasoning or dried oregano, to taste
1 tablespoon extra-virgin olive oil

Preheat oven to 350F (175C). Lightly oil a large baking sheet with sides and set aside.

Bring a large stockpot of salted water to a boil. Cook the pasta according to package directions until just al dente; drain. Rinse under cold-running water until cool; drain again. Return to the pot and add 1 cup marinara sauce, 1 cup mozzarella cheese, eggs, olives, and garlic salt; mix until spaghetti is thoroughly coated. Spread the spaghetti mixture evenly in the prepared baking sheet. Bake on the center oven rack until mixture is set and lightly browned, about 15 to 18 minutes.

Remove baking sheet from oven and spread the spaghetti crust evenly with remaining 1 cup marinara sauce. Arrange the artichokes and sun-dried tomato slices evenly over top, followed by the torn basil leaves. Sprinkle evenly with the remaining 1 cup mozzarella cheese, followed with the provolone and Parmesan cheeses. Sprinkle lightly with Italian seasoning and additional garlic salt, if desired; drizzle evenly with the oil. Bake on the center rack about 12 to 15 minutes, or until cheese is melted and pizza is heated through. Cut into wedges and serve at once.

PER SERVING: Calories 443; Protein 23g; Total Fat 16g; Sat Fat 7g; Cholesterol 105mg; Carbohydrate 53g; Dietary Fiber 3g; Sodium 926mg

Zucchini Crust

(LACTO-OVO/LOW-CARB)

This low-carb crust can be used as the foundation for all your favorite pizza toppings. Cut into small squares, it can also double as the base for all your favorite bruschetta and crostini toppings.

MAKES 1 STANDARD-SIZE RECTANGULAR PIZZA CRUST

2 to 2½ cups grated raw zucchini
   (about ¾ pound)
Salt
2 eggs
1 cup shredded gluten-free part-skim
   mozzarella cheese
Freshly ground black pepper, to taste

Preheat the oven to 375F (190C). Lightly grease a standard-size nonstick baking sheet with sides.

Place the zucchini in a colander set in the sink and sprinkle liberally with salt; let sit for 15 minutes. Rinse under cold-running water and drain well. Transfer to several layers of paper towels and squeeze to dry thoroughly. Transfer to a large bowl and add the eggs, mozzarella, and pepper; toss well to thoroughly combine. Transfer to the prepared baking sheet, pressing mixture evenly into the sheet with your fingers. Bake in the center of the oven until light brown and crisp, 12 to 15 minutes (do not overbake). Use as directed in the recipe.

PER SERVING (per ⅙ of recipe): Calories 86; Protein 8g; Total Fat 5g; Sat Fat 3g; Cholesterol 81mg; Carbohydrate 2g; Dietary Fiber 1g; Sodium 122mg

Pizza Margherita with Prebaked Pizza Crust

(LACTO-OVO)

Both frozen and unfrozen prebaked gluten-free pizza crusts are available at Whole Foods Markets and specialty stores, as well as some well-stocked supermarkets. For best results, follow the manufacturer's suggested thawing and baking instructions. Most brands, though cholesterol-free, contain egg whites; for an egg-free alternative, check the individual labels accordingly.

MAKES 6 SERVINGS

1 (12-ounce) or 2 (6-ounce) frozen or
   unfrozen prebaked gluten-free pizza
   crust(s), thawed according to package
   directions
½ to ¾ cup prepared gluten-free pizza sauce
5 to 6 ounces fresh mozzarella cheese, thinly
   sliced
1 tablespoon extra-virgin olive oil
⅓ to ½ cup torn fresh basil leaves

Preheat oven according to manufacturer's suggested temperature (typically around 375F/190C).

Place pizza crust(s) on an ungreased standard or large baking sheet, as necessary; spread evenly with the pizza sauce. Arrange the cheese evenly over the top; drizzle evenly with the oil. Bake as directed, or until cheese is melted and crust is browned (typically about 15 minutes). Remove from oven and sprinkle with basil. Cut into wedges and serve at once.

PER SERVING (per ⅙ of recipe): Calories 275; Protein 11g; Total Fat 11g; Sat Fat 5g; Cholesterol 21mg; Carbohydrate 33g; Dietary Fiber 0g; Sodium 642mg

Cheese Pizza with Rice Crust

(LACTO-OVO)

This basic pizza happens to be my favorite—feel free to top with the veggies of your choice.

MAKES 6 SERVINGS

3 cups freshly cooked long-grain white or
    brown rice, slightly warm or at room
    temperature

2 eggs, beaten

3 cups gluten-free reduced-fat shredded
    mozzarella cheese, divided

Garlic salt, to taste (optional)

1 (15-ounce) can tomato sauce

2 cloves garlic, finely chopped

1 teaspoon dried oregano, plus additional,
    to taste

¼ teaspoon sugar

¼ teaspoon salt, or to taste

Freshly ground black pepper, to taste

1 tablespoon extra-virgin olive oil, divided

Crushed red pepper flakes, to serve (optional)

Preheat oven to 450F (230C). Lightly oil a standard-size baking sheet with sides and set aside.

In a medium bowl, mix together the rice, eggs, 1 cup of the cheese, and garlic salt, if using. Spread evenly in the prepared baking sheet, smoothing the top with the back of a spoon. Bake on the center oven rack 15 minutes, or until lightly browned. Remove from oven, and reduce oven temperature to 350F (175C). Let rice crust cool about 10 minutes, or up to 1 hour.

In a small saucepan, combine the tomato sauce, garlic, oregano, sugar, salt, and pepper; bring to a simmer over medium-high heat, stirring occasionally. Reduce the heat to medium-low and simmer, uncovered, 15 minutes, stirring occasionally. Remove from the heat and stir in ½ tablespoon of the oil; set aside. (At this point, tomato sauce can be held at room temperature up to 1 hour, or cooled to room temperature and refrigerated, covered, up to 5 days before proceeding.)

Spread the tomato sauce evenly over top of the rice crust. Sprinkle evenly with the remaining 2 cups of cheese, then sprinkle lightly with additional oregano, to taste. Drizzle evenly with the remaining ½ tablespoon oil. Bake on the center oven rack 12 to 15 minutes, or until heated through and cheese is melted. Cut into wedges and serve warm, with the crushed red pepper flakes passed separately, if desired.

PER SERVING: Calories 347; Protein 21g; Total Fat 14g; Sat Fat 7g; Cholesterol 101mg; Carbohydrate 34g; Dietary Fiber 1g; Sodium 840mg

Eggplant Pizza with Zucchini Crust

(LACTO-OVO/LOW-CARB)

This is the ideal pizza to make at the height of summer, when both eggplant and zucchini are bountiful.

MAKES 6 SERVINGS

1 small eggplant (about ½ pound), unpeeled,
    cut into ⅛-inch-thick slices

Table salt

¾ cup gluten-free pizza sauce

Zucchini Crust, page 89

1 tablespoon extra-virgin olive oil

Dried oregano, to taste

Salt and freshly ground black pepper, to taste

1 cup gluten-free shredded part-skim
   mozzarella cheese

½ cup gluten-free freshly grated Parmesan
   cheese

Preheat oven to 400F (205C). Lightly oil a baking
sheet and set aside. Place the eggplant in a colander
in the sink and sprinkle liberally with table salt; let
sit for 30 minutes. Rinse thoroughly under cold-
running water and pat dry with paper towels.

Arrange the eggplant slices in a single layer on the
prepared baking sheet. Bake 6 to 8 minutes, or until
tender and lightly browned, turning halfway through
cooking. Remove from the oven and let cool.

Reduce the oven temperature to 375F (190C).
Spread the pizza sauce over top of the baked zucchini crust. Arrange the eggplant slices evenly over
the sauce, overlapping if necessary. Brush the eggplant evenly with the oil, then sprinkle lightly with
oregano, salt, and pepper. Sprinkle evenly with the
mozzarella, then the Parmesan cheese. Bake for 10
minutes, or until cheese is melted (do not overbake). Cut into wedges and serve warm.

PER SERVING: Calories 226; Protein 17g; Total Fat 14g;
Sat Fat 7g; Cholesterol 98mg; Carbohydrate 8g; Dietary
Fiber 2g; Sodium 576mg

Brown Rice Flour Pizza Crust

(VEGAN)

*The texture of this crust is remarkably similar to a stan-
dard deep-dish wheat-based pizza crust—the brown rice
flour provides denseness while the tapioca starch provides
lightness.*

MAKES 1 (STANDARD-SIZE) RECTANGULAR PIZZA CRUST

Cornmeal, for dusting (optional)

1⅓ cups brown rice flour

1 cup tapioca starch

2 (¼-ounce) package gluten-free active dry
   yeast (about 2 tablespoons)

2 teaspoons xanthan gum

1 teaspoon sugar

1 teaspoon garlic salt

1⅓ cups water

2 tablespoons extra-virgin olive oil, divided

2 teaspoons cider vinegar

Preheat oven to 425F (220C). Lightly grease a standard-size baking sheet with a rim. Dust with cornmeal, if using, and set aside.

In a large mixing bowl, whisk together the rice
flour, tapioca starch, yeast, xanthan gum, sugar, and
garlic salt until thoroughly combined. Slowly add
the water, stirring to combine. Add 1 tablespoon of
oil and all of the vinegar; beat on medium speed 2
minutes. Cover bowl with a damp kitchen towel
and let stand at room temperature 10 minutes.

Using a spoon, transfer dough to the prepared
baking sheet; smooth top of dough with a damp
spatula. Using a pastry brush, brush evenly with
the remaining 1 tablespoon oil. Bake 10 minutes, or
until lightly browned. (If top has puffed up in
places, puncture with the tines of a fork and gently
press down to deflate.) Remove and use as directed
in recipe (preferably within 1 hour).

PER SERVING (⅛ of recipe): Calories 197; Protein 3g;
Total Fat 4g; Sat Fat 1g; Cholesterol 0mg; Carbohydrate
37g; Dietary Fiber 2g; Sodium 261mg

Roasted Vegetable Pizza with Brown Rice Flour Crust

(VEGAN)

Even cheese lovers will never miss the cheese in this yummy plant-based pizza. Feel free to vary the roasted vegetable toppings—eggplant and asparagus are other good choices.

MAKES 8 SERVINGS

1 medium red bell pepper (about 6 ounces), cut into 1-inch pieces

1 medium onion (about 6 ounces), cut into thin wedges

1 medium zucchini (about 6 ounces), sliced into ¼-inch-thick rounds

6 ounces sliced cremini and/or cultivated white mushrooms

3½ tablespoons extra-virgin olive oil, divided

¾ teaspoon coarse salt, divided

1 (6-ounce) can tomato paste

1½ tablespoons balsamic vinegar

½ tablespoon water

2 tablespoons finely chopped fresh basil

½ tablespoon sugar

2 large cloves garlic, finely chopped

¼ teaspoon dried oregano, plus additional, to taste

¼ teaspoon dried thyme leaves

¼ teaspoon dried rosemary leaves, plus additional, to taste

Freshly ground black pepper, to taste

Garlic salt, to taste (optional)

1 Brown Rice Flour Pizza Crust, page 91

Shredded fresh basil leaves (optional)

Preheat oven to 450F (230C).

On a large ungreased baking sheet with sides, toss the bell pepper, onion, zucchini, and mushrooms with 1½ tablespoons of the oil. Sprinkle with ½ teaspoon of the coarse salt and toss again. Bake 15 minutes, or until tender, turning halfway through cooking. Remove baking sheet from oven and reduce temperature to 400F (205C). (At this point, vegetables can be held at room temperature up to 1 hour before proceeding with the recipe.)

In a small bowl, combine the tomato paste, vinegar, 1 tablespoon oil, water, chopped basil, sugar, garlic, oregano, thyme, rosemary, remaining ¼ teaspoon of coarse salt, and black pepper; stir until thoroughly blended. Spread tomato paste mixture evenly over the baked pizza crust. Arrange roasted vegetables evenly over top; drizzle evenly with remaining 1 tablespoon oil, then sprinkle lightly with oregano and/or rosemary, and garlic salt, if using. Bake in the center of the oven 12 to 15 minutes, or until vegetables are beginning to brown and crust is crisp and browned. Garnish with the shredded basil, if using, and serve at once.

PER SERVING: Calories 294; Protein 5g; Total Fat 11g; Sat Fat 2g; Cholesterol 0mg; Carbohydrate 47g; Dietary Fiber 4g; Sodium 432mg

Rustic Pesto Sauce

(VEGAN/LOW-CARB)

Made from fresh basil, garlic, and olive oil, this rustic sauce is essentially a light pesto sans the nuts and cheese. If using as a base for pizza, add 1 to 2 tablespoons of water to achieve a more spreadable consistency.

MAKES ABOUT ½ CUP

3 cups loosely packed fresh basil leaves

1 tablespoon water, plus additional, as necessary

⅓ cup extra-virgin olive oil

3 cloves garlic, finely chopped

½ teaspoon coarse salt, or to taste

Process all ingredients in a food processor fitted with the knife blade, or in a blender, until smooth, adding water by the teaspoonful to achieve desired consistency. Serve at room temperature. The sauce can be stored, covered, in the refrigerator up to 3 days.

PER SERVING (per tablespoon, or ⅛ of recipe): Calories 97; Protein 2g; Total Fat 9g; Sat Fat 1g; Cholesterol 0mg; Carbohydrate 3g; Dietary Fiber 0g; Sodium 120mg

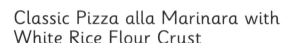

Classic Pizza alla Marinara with White Rice Flour Crust

(VEGAN)

More appetizer than meal, authentic pizza alla marinara is not only cheeseless, but delicious. Add your favorite toppings to create a filling dinner for 4 people.

MAKES 8 SERVINGS

½ recipe Easy Homemade Pizza Sauce, on the right, or 1 cup prepared gluten-free pizza sauce

1 White Rice Flour Pizza Crust, page 94

6 large cloves garlic, slivered

¾ teaspoon dried oregano, or to taste

Salt, preferably the coarse variety, and freshly ground black pepper, to taste

1 tablespoon extra-virgin olive oil

Preheat oven to 350F (175C).

Spread the pizza sauce evenly on crust, leaving a ½-inch border. Scatter the garlic slivers evenly over the sauce. Sprinkle evenly with the oregano,

salt, and pepper. Drizzle evenly with the oil. Bake 10 to 12 minutes, or until the edges are nicely browned. Cut into wedges and serve at once.

PER SERVING (with prepared pizza sauce): Calories 273; Protein 4g; Total Fat 9g; Sat Fat 1g; Cholesterol 0mg; Carbohydrate 45g; Dietary Fiber 2g; Sodium 464mg

Easy Homemade Pizza Sauce

(VEGAN/LOW-CARB)

Why bother to make your own pizza sauce? For one, it's cheaper than buying most commercially prepared brands; for another, you can control the sodium content; furthermore, it requires little effort to prepare. Best of all, it tastes better.

MAKES ABOUT 2 CUPS

1 (15-ounce) can crushed tomatoes

1½ tablespoons extra-virgin olive oil

1 teaspoon dried oregano

½ teaspoon Italian seasoning

3 large cloves garlic, finely chopped

½ teaspoon sugar

½ teaspoon salt, or to taste

Freshly ground black pepper, to taste

In a medium saucepan, combine all ingredients. Bring to a simmer over medium-high heat, stirring a few times. Remove from heat and let cool to room temperature. Use as directed in recipe. Completely cooled sauce can be refrigerated, covered, up to 5 days, or frozen up to 3 months.

PER SERVING (¼ cup, or ⅛ of recipe): Calories 48; Protein 1g; Total Fat 3g; Sat Fat 0g; Cholesterol 0mg; Carbohydrate 6g; Dietary Fiber 1g; Sodium 346mg

White Rice Flour Pizza Crust

(VEGAN)

Sweet rice flour, made from glutinous, or sticky, white rice, lends this pizza crust its chewy texture. It is available in Asian markets and specialty stores.

MAKES 1 (12- TO 14-INCH) PIZZA CRUST

Cornmeal, for dusting (optional)
1¾ cups white rice flour
¾ cup sweet rice flour
1 (¼-ounce) package gluten-free rapid-rise yeast (about 1 tablespoon)
½ tablespoon sugar
1 teaspoon table salt or garlic salt
½ teaspoon xanthan gum
1 to 1¼ cups very warm water (120F to 130F; 50C to 55C)
3 tablespoons extra-virgin olive oil

Preheat the oven to 400F (205C). Lightly grease a 12- to 14-inch nonstick pizza pan. Sprinkle with cornmeal, if using.

In a large bowl, whisk together the flours, yeast, sugar, salt, and xanthan gum. Stir in 1 cup water and the oil. Using your hands to work the dough, add enough of the remaining water to hold the mixture together. Knead the dough in the bowl for 5 minutes. Cover with a damp kitchen towel and let rest for 10 minutes.

Flatten the dough into a round disk and press into the prepared pan. Bake in the center of the oven for 10 minutes. Remove and proceed as directed in the recipe.

PER SERVING (⅛ of recipe): Calories 234; Protein 4g; Total Fat 6g; Sat Fat 1g; Cholesterol 0mg; Carbohydrate 41g; Dietary Fiber 2g; Sodium 267mg

Spinach and Goat Cheese Pesto Pizza with Cornmeal Crust

(LACTO-OVO)

The trinity of spinach, goat cheese, and pesto is divine, as one bite of this rich pizza testifies.

MAKES 8 SERVINGS

2 cups loosely packed fresh baby spinach, chopped
½ tablespoon extra-virgin olive oil
1 recipe Classic Basil Pesto Sauce, page 97, or ⅔ cup gluten-free prepared pesto sauce
1 prepared Cornmeal Pizza Crust, page 98
4 ounces gluten-free crumbled goat cheese (½ cup)
¾ cup shredded gluten-free part-skim mozzarella cheese

Preheat oven to 350F (175C).

In a small bowl, toss the spinach with the oil; set aside. Spread the pesto sauce evenly over the baked cornmeal pizza crust. Scatter the spinach evenly over the top. Sprinkle evenly with the goat cheese, followed by the mozzarella. Bake in the center of the oven for 10 to 15 minutes, or until cheese is melted and crust is lightly browned. Cut into squares and serve warm.

PER SERVING: Calories 406; Protein 19g; Total Fat 22g; Sat Fat 9g; Cholesterol 84mg; Carbohydrate 34g; Dietary Fiber 6g; Sodium 512mg

Variation

To make Spinach, Artichoke, and Goat Cheese Pesto Pizza with Cornmeal Crust, arrange 4 ounces of drained marinated sliced artichoke hearts over the spinach before topping with the cheeses; bake as directed in the recipe.

Polenta Pizza with Grape Tomatoes and Rustic Pesto Sauce

(VEGAN)

Quick-cooking polenta makes quick work of this scrumptious—and pretty—pesto pizza. Use the polenta crust as a base for many of your favorite toppings.

MAKES 6 SERVINGS

2 cups low-sodium vegetable broth

1 cup water

1 cup quick-cooking or regular polenta (coarse-ground yellow cornmeal)

4 teaspoons extra-virgin olive oil, divided

½ teaspoon garlic salt, or to taste

Freshly ground black pepper, to taste

Rustic Pesto Sauce, page 92, Classic Basil Pesto Sauce, page 97, or ½ cup prepared gluten-free pesto sauce, at room temperature, thinned with water for spreading, if necessary

1 cup grape tomatoes or small cherry tomatoes, halved

Preheat oven to broil. Lightly oil a 12-inch pizza pan or standard-size baking sheet with a rim.

If using quick-cooking polenta: In a medium stockpot, bring the broth, water, polenta, 2 teaspoons of the oil, garlic salt, and pepper to a boil over high heat. Immediately reduce the heat to medium and cook, stirring often with a long-handled spoon (polenta will sputter), 5 minutes. Immediately spoon polenta into the prepared pan, pressing down with the back of a large spoon or spatula (dampen slightly, if necessary) to form a smooth surface. Let stand about 15 minutes to become firm. (At this point, the crust can be held up to 1 hour at room temperature before continuing with the recipe.)

If using regular polenta: In a medium stockpot, bring the broth, water, 2 teaspoons of the oil, garlic salt, and pepper to a boil over high heat. Slowly add the polenta, stirring constantly with a long-handled spoon. Reduce the heat to low and cook, covered, stirring occasionally, until the polenta is tender, about 15 minutes. Immediately spoon polenta into the prepared pan, pressing down with the back of a large spoon or spatula (dampen slightly, if necessary) to form a smooth surface. Let stand about 15 minutes to become firm. (At this point, the crust can be held up to 1 hour at room temperature before continuing with the recipe.)

Brush the top of the polenta evenly with remaining 2 teaspoons of oil. Broil 4 to 6 inches from the heating element until lightly browned, 3 to 5 minutes. Remove from oven and, using a pastry brush, immediately spread with all but 1½ tablespoons of the pesto sauce. Space the tomato halves evenly over the top; using the pastry brush, dab the tomatoes with the remaining pesto. Return to the oven and broil 1 minute. Cut into wedges and serve at once. Alternatively, pizza can be held in a warm oven (about 200F/95C) on the lowest oven rack up to 1 hour before serving.

PER SERVING: Calories 269; Protein 8g; Total Fat 16g; Sat Fat 2g; Cholesterol 0mg; Carbohydrate 25g; Dietary Fiber 4g; Sodium 504mg

Polenta Skillet Pizza Pie with Broccoli and Gorgonzola

(EGG-FREE/LOW-CARB)

When pressed for time, you simply can't beat the convenience of quick-cooking polenta—if you can't locate it, I've included instructions for the regular variety as well. Gluten-free crumbled goat or feta can replace the Gorgonzola cheese, if desired.

MAKES 6 SERVINGS

2 tablespoons extra-virgin olive oil, divided

3 cups water

¾ cup instant polenta or regular polenta (coarse-ground yellow cornmeal)

½ teaspoon salt

⅔ cup prepared gluten-free pizza sauce or marinara sauce

1½ cups bite-size fresh or frozen broccoli florets

Garlic salt, to taste

Freshly ground black pepper, to taste

Dried oregano, to taste

4 ounces (½ cup) gluten-free crumbled Gorgonzola cheese

Preheat oven to 400F (205C). Brush bottom and sides of 10-inch cast-iron skillet with 1 tablespoon of the oil.

If using quick-cooking polenta: In a medium stockpot, combine water, polenta, ½ tablespoon oil, and salt; bring to a boil over high heat. Immediately reduce heat to medium and cook, stirring often with a long-handled wooden spoon (polenta will sputter), 5 minutes. Immediately transfer polenta to the prepared skillet, smoothing the top with the back of a spoon or spatula. Let stand 20 minutes (or up to 1 hour) at room temperature to firm.

If using regular polenta: In a medium stockpot, combine water, ½ tablespoon oil, and salt; bring to a boil over high heat. Slowly add the polenta, stirring constantly with a long-handled spoon. Reduce the heat to low and cook, covered, stirring occasionally, until the polenta is tender, about 15 minutes. Immediately transfer polenta to the prepared skillet, smoothing the top with the back of a spoon or spatula. Let stand 20 minutes (or up to 1 hour) at room temperature to firm.

Bake polenta 25 minutes, or until beginning to brown. Remove skillet from oven; spread polenta evenly with the sauce to form a ¼-inch border. Top with the broccoli and season with garlic salt, pepper, and oregano; drizzle evenly with remaining ½ tablespoon of oil. Bake 10 to 15 minutes, or until broccoli is lightly browned. Sprinkle evenly with the cheese and bake an additional 3 to 5 minutes, or until cheese is melted. Let stand 10 minutes at room temperature before slicing and serving.

PER SERVING: Calories 222; Protein 9g; Total Fat 13g; Sat Fat 5g; Cholesterol 20mg; Carbohydrate 20g; Dietary Fiber 3g; Sodium 421mg

Roasted Red Pepper, Caper, and Basil Pizza with Cauliflower Crust

(LACTO-OVO/LOW-CARB)

This low-carb pizza also makes a terrific party appetizer, cut into bite-size squares.

MAKES 6 SERVINGS

2 (12-ounce) bags frozen cauliflower florets,
cooked according to package directions,
drained, and cooled

1¾ cups gluten-free reduced-fat shredded
mozzarella cheese, divided

1 egg

1 teaspoon Italian seasoning, plus additional,
to taste

½ teaspoon salt, or to taste

Freshly ground black pepper, to taste

¾ cup gluten-free pizza sauce

1½ tablespoons drained capers

1 (7-ounce) jar roasted red peppers, drained
and cut into thin strips

¼ cup fresh basil leaves, torn

½ cup gluten-free freshly grated Parmesan
cheese

1 tablespoon extra-virgin olive oil

Preheat oven to 450F (230C). Lightly grease a stan-dard-size baking sheet with sides, and set aside.

In a food processor fitted with the knife blade, pulse the cauliflower until the consistency of rice. Using paper towels, squeeze out excess moisture and place in a medium bowl. Add ¾ cup cheese, egg, Italian seasoning, salt, and black pepper; stir well to thoroughly combine. Spread evenly in the prepared baking sheet, pressing down with your fingers. Bake on the center oven rack 15 to 18 minutes, or until nicely browned. Remove from oven and reduce the heat to 350F (175C).

Spread the cauliflower crust evenly with the pizza sauce. Scatter the top evenly with the capers. Arrange the roasted peppers evenly over the top, then the basil. Sprinkle evenly with the remaining 1 cup mozzarella cheese, then the Parmesan cheese. Sprinkle lightly with additional Italian seasoning, then drizzle evenly with the oil. Bake on the center oven rack 15 minutes, or until hot and cheese is melted. Let stand about 10 minutes before cutting into wedges and serving warm.

PER SERVING: Calories 211; Protein 16g; Total Fat 12g; Sat Fat 6; Cholesterol 58mg; Carbohydrate 12g; Dietary Fiber 3g; Sodium 720mg

Classic Basil Pesto Sauce

(EGG-FREE/LOW-CARB)

This classic sauce is delicious tossed with gluten-free pasta, rice, potatoes, and vegetables; stirred into soups and dips; and spread over gluten-free breads and pizzas. Chopped walnuts or slivered almonds can replace the pine nuts, if desired.

MAKES ABOUT ⅔ CUP

2½ cups loosely packed fresh basil leaves

¼ cup extra-virgin olive oil

¼ cup gluten-free freshly grated Parmesan
cheese

3 tablespoons pine nuts

3 large cloves garlic, finely chopped

½ teaspoon coarse salt, or to taste

Process all ingredients in a food processor fitted with the knife blade, or in a blender, until smooth. Serve at room temperature. Sauce can be stored, covered, in the refrigerator up to 3 days.

PER SERVING (about 1 tablespoon, or 1/10 of recipe): Calories 79; Protein 2g; Total Fat 8g; Sat Fat 1g; Cholesterol 2mg; Carbohydrate 1g; Dietary Fiber 1g; Sodium 142mg

Cornmeal Pizza Crust

(LACTO-OVO/LOW-CARB)

Dried herbs—such as oregano, rosemary, or thyme—can be added along with the garlic salt, if desired.

MAKES 1 LARGE RECTANGULAR PIZZA CRUST

2 cups coarse-ground yellow cornmeal or polenta
1 cup cold water
1 cup boiling water
2 eggs, lightly beaten
1 cup gluten-free shredded part-skim mozzarella cheese
½ teaspoon garlic salt
Freshly ground black pepper, to taste

Preheat oven to 450F (230C). Lightly oil a large nonstick baking sheet with sides.

In a large bowl, combine the cornmeal with the water. Slowly stir in the boiling water. Stir for a few minutes until the mixture cools and some of the water is absorbed by the cornmeal. Stir in the eggs, mozzarella cheese, garlic salt, and pepper. Pour the mixture onto the prepared baking sheet, spreading with a spatula and raking with a fork to evenly distribute. Bake in the center of the oven for 10 minutes, or until lightly browned. Use in the recipe as directed.

PER SERVING (⅛ of recipe): Calories 145; Protein 8g; Total Fat 6g; Sat Fat 2g; Cholesterol 70mg; Carbohydrate 17g; Dietary Fiber 0g; Sodium 311mg

---

SANDWICHES AND OTHER LIGHTER FARE

English Muffin Pizzas

(LACTO-OVO)

Trader Joe's makes a terrific gluten-free English muffin (as of this writing, dairy-free, with egg whites) that inspired this quick and easy recipe—feel free to modify the toppings.

MAKES 4 MAIN-DISH OR 8 SNACK-SIZE SERVINGS

4 gluten-free English muffins, split and lightly toasted
½ cup (about ¼ recipe) Easy Homemade Pizza Sauce, page 93, or prepared gluten-free pizza sauce
1 cup shredded gluten-free part-skim mozzarella cheese
2 teaspoons extra-virgin olive oil
Dried oregano, to taste
Garlic salt, to taste

Preheat oven to broil. Spread each muffin half with 1 tablespoon of the pizza sauce. Top each half with 2 tablespoons of the cheese. Drizzle each with ¼ teaspoon of oil, then sprinkle lightly with oregano and garlic salt. Place on an ungreased baking sheet and broil 6 to 8 inches from heating element until cheese is melted, 1 to 2 minutes. Serve at once.

PER SERVING: Calories 254; Protein 13g; Total Fat 9g; Sat Fat 4g; Cholesterol 15mg; Carbohydrate 30g; Dietary Fiber 0g; Sodium 611mg

---

Variations

To make English Muffin Pesto Pizzas, replace the pizza sauce with Classic Basil Pesto Sauce, page 97, or gluten-free prepared pesto sauce and omit the oil and oregano from the recipe. Proceed as otherwise directed in the recipe.

For a dairy-free option, replace the pizza sauce with Rustic Pesto Sauce, page 92, and omit the cheese and oregano. Top each muffin half with 2 halved grape or cherry tomatoes before drizzling with the oil and sprinkling with garlic salt, if using. Broil 1 minute, or until just heated.

Panini with Grilled Eggplant and Sun-Dried Tomato-Basil Pesto

(VEGAN)

You'll never miss the cheese in these scrumptious pressed and grilled sandwiches. If you can't locate vegan gluten-free Italian bread at the store, make the Gluten-Free Brown Ciabatta Bread, page 83, and create 8 mini paninis.

MAKES 4 LARGE SANDWICHES OR 8 MINI SANDWICHES

3 small Italian eggplants (5 to 6 ounces each), or 1 (1-pound) long Asian eggplant, unpeeled and cut into ½-inch-thick rounds

1 tablespoon plus 4 teaspoons extra-virgin olive oil, divided

Salt, preferably the coarse variety, and freshly ground black pepper, to taste

8 large slices (about 1 ounce each) gluten-free, egg-free, dairy-free Italian bread, or Gluten-Free Brown Ciabatta Bread, page 83, cut into 16 (½-inch-thick slices)

Sun-Dried Tomato-Basil Pesto, page 102, Rustic Pesto Sauce, page 92, or about ½ cup prepared gluten-free pesto sauce

Garlic salt, to taste

Brush the eggplant evenly on both sides with 1 tablespoon of the oil.

Place a stovetop grilling pan with grids over medium-high heat. Working in batches, as necessary, grill the eggplant slices until browned and tender, about 2 to 3 minutes per side. Transfer grilled eggplant to a baking sheet and season on both sides with coarse salt and pepper. When all the eggplant has been cooked, remove the grill pan from the heat; set eggplant aside to cool.

Divide the grilled eggplant evenly among 4 slices (or 8 slices) of the bread. Spoon equal portions of the pesto (about 2 tablespoons per large sandwich, 1 tablespoon per mini) evenly over top. Top each with a piece of bread. Using a pastry brush, brush the top of each sandwich evenly with 2 teaspoons of remaining oil (½ teaspoon per large sandwich, ¼ teaspoon per mini); sprinkle very lightly with garlic salt. Carefully turn the sandwiches over and brush with the remaining 2 teaspoons of oil and sprinkle lightly with garlic salt.

Wipe out the grill pan and return to the stovetop over medium heat. Working in batches, as necessary, add the sandwiches, pesto side down, and weight with a heavy skillet (preferably a 10-inch cast-iron skillet); either press down with your hands or place a filled tea kettle in the skillet. Grill 1 to 2 minutes without moving, or until grill marks appear on the undersides of the sandwiches. Carefully turn the sandwiches over and repeat with the other side. Cut sandwiches in half, if desired, and serve at once.

PER SERVING (1 large/2 mini sandwiches, or ¼ of recipe): Calories 331; Protein 9g; Total Fat 17g; Sat Fat 3g; Cholesterol 0mg; Carbohydrate 39g; Dietary Fiber 4g; Sodium 621mg

Grilled Portobello Mushroom Pizza Burgers

(EGG-FREE)

Thick and juicy grilled Portobello mushrooms are the vegetarian's answer to a gluten-free, non-processed, soy-free alternative to the hamburger.

MAKES 4 SERVINGS

- 4 large Portobello mushroom caps (about 3 ounces each)
- 2 teaspoons extra-virgin olive oil, divided
- Garlic salt and freshly ground black pepper, to taste
- 8 tablespoons prepared gluten-free pizza sauce
- 8 tablespoons gluten-free shredded part-skim mozzarella cheese
- 4 gluten-free sandwich rolls, preferably whole-grain, egg-free, and dairy-free, toasted, if desired

Heat a nonstick grill pan over medium-high heat. Brush each mushroom on rounded side and rim with ½ teaspoon of the oil; season lightly on all sides with garlic salt and pepper. Place the mushrooms, gill sides down, in pan and grill for 3 minutes. Turn, gill sides up, and grill until nicely browned, 3 to 4 minutes, rotating each mushroom a half-turn after 2 minutes. As mushrooms are cooking, fill each cap with 2 tablespoons pizza sauce, and then sprinkle with 2 tablespoons cheese. Cover the pan briefly with a lid to help melt the cheese, as necessary.

To serve, place a filled mushroom, gill side up, on the bottom half of each roll. Cover with roll tops and serve at once.

PER SERVING: Calories 215; Protein 10g; Total Fat 9g; Sat Fat 3g; Cholesterol 8mg; Carbohydrate 27g; Dietary Fiber 3g; Sodium 472mg

Variation

To make Grilled Portobello Mushroom Burgers with Pesto, for a vegan option, replace the pizza sauce with Rustic Pesto Sauce, page 92; otherwise, replace with Classic Basil Pesto Sauce, page 97, or prepared gluten-free pesto sauce. Omit the cheese, if desired; serve as otherwise directed in the recipe.

Italian Veggie Patties

(DAIRY-FREE)

These tasty patties are a welcome gluten-free answer to the various commercial brands of veggie burgers that invariably contain harmful glutens.

MAKES 6 PATTIES

- 2 tablespoons extra-virgin olive oil
- ½ cup finely chopped onion
- ½ cup finely chopped carrot
- 2 large cloves garlic, finely chopped
- 1 pound cultivated white mushrooms, finely chopped
- ½ teaspoon salt
- ½ teaspoon dried thyme leaves
- ¼ teaspoon dried oregano
- ¼ teaspoon dried rosemary leaves
- 1 (19-ounce) can chickpeas, rinsed and drained (about 1¾ cups), mashed into a coarse paste
- 1 cup finely ground fresh gluten-free bread crumbs, preferably from day-old Gluten-Free Italian Bread, page 86

¼ cup finely chopped fresh flat-leaf parsley

Freshly ground black pepper, to taste

2 eggs, lightly beaten

Gluten-free pasta sauce, heated, to serve (optional)

6 gluten-free hamburger buns (optional)

Ketchup, lettuce, tomato, raw onion, etc. (optional toppings)

In a large nonstick skillet, heat half the oil over medium heat. Add the onion and carrot and cook, stirring, 2 minutes. Add the garlic and cook, stirring constantly, 30 seconds. Add the mushrooms, salt, thyme, oregano, and rosemary; raise heat to medium-high. Cook, stirring often, until all of the liquids released by the mushrooms has evaporated, about 3 minutes. Remove from heat and stir in the mashed chickpeas, bread crumbs, parsley, and pepper. Let cool to room temperature. Add eggs to the cooled chickpea mixture, stirring thoroughly to combine. Transfer to a covered container and refrigerate a minimum of 30 minutes, or overnight.

Shape the chilled chickpea-egg mixture into 6 equal patties, about ½-inch in thickness. Place the patties on a baking sheet lined with wax paper and return to the refrigerator for 15 to 30 minutes.

Wipe out the skillet and heat the remaining 1 tablespoon of oil over medium heat. Cook the patties until nicely browned, about 3 to 4 minutes per side. Serve at once, with the heated pasta sauce, if using. Alternatively, place inside buns and serve with the optional toppings.

PER SERVING (per patty only): Calories 193; Protein 9g; Total Fat 8g; Sat Fat 1g; Cholesterol 71mg; Carbohydrate 23g; Dietary Fiber 2g; Sodium 249mg

Tomato-Basil Grilled Cheese Sandwiches

(EGG-FREE)

The common grilled cheese sandwich is raised to the sublime in this quick and easy recipe.

MAKES 4 SERVINGS

1 cup/16 tablespoons gluten-free reduced-fat shredded mozzarella cheese (4 ounces)

8 slices gluten-free bread (about 1 ounce each), preferably multi-grain

2 small plum tomatoes (about 2 ounces each), thinly sliced

Salt and freshly ground black pepper, to taste

16 medium to large fresh basil leaves, torn in half

2 tablespoons butter, softened

Garlic salt (optional)

Sprinkle 2 tablespoons of cheese on each of 4 bread slices. Top with equal amounts of tomato slices and season lightly with salt and pepper. Top with equal amounts of torn basil leaves; sprinkle each with 2 tablespoons of remaining cheese. Top each with a bread slice to form a sandwich. Spread outsides of sandwiches with equal amounts of butter; sprinkle each side lightly with garlic salt, if using.

Heat a large nonstick skillet with a lid over medium heat for 3 minutes. Add the sandwiches and cook about 3 minutes, or until underside is nicely browned. Carefully turn and press down with a spatula to flatten. Cover the skillet and cook about 2 more minutes, or until underside is nicely browned. Serve at once.

PER SERVING: Calories 276; Protein 14g; Total Fat 13g; Sat Fat 7g; Cholesterol 31mg; Carbohydrate 29g; Dietary Fiber 4g; Sodium 509mg

Sun-Dried Tomato-Basil Pesto

(VEGAN/LOW-CARB)

This tasty, tomato-intense pesto is wonderful tossed with gluten-free pasta, rice, and steamed vegetables, or spread over polenta. Thin with water, broth, or pasta-cooking liquid, as desired.

MAKES ABOUT ½ CUP

  1 cup loosely packed fresh basil leaves
  ¼ cup drained marinated sun-dried tomato
     pieces
  2 tablespoons pine nuts, chopped walnuts,
     or slivered almonds
  1 tablespoon extra-virgin olive oil
  1 tablespoon tomato paste
  1 tablespoon water, or more, as desired
  1 large clove garlic, finely chopped
  ½ teaspoon coarse salt, or to taste
  Freshly ground black pepper, to taste

In a food processor fitted with the knife blade, process all ingredients until a smooth paste is formed. Use at room temperature as directed in the recipe.

PER SERVING (per tablespoon, or ⅛ of recipe): Calories 43; Protein 1g; Total Fat 4g; Sat Fat 1g; Cholesterol 0mg; Carbohydrate 3g; Dietary Fiber 0g; Sodium 144mg

Spinach Roll-Ups with Italian Egg Salad

(DAIRY-FREE/LOW-CARB)

Serve these crunchy and creamy protein-packed spinach roll-ups with Chilled Raw Tomato and Basil Soup, page 41, for an excellent gluten-free, dairy-free summertime luncheon or light supper.

MAKES 4 ROLL-UPS

  1 recipe Italian Egg Salad (page 20)
  4 large spinach leaves
  12 cherry or grape tomatoes, halved
  ½ cup shredded carrots
  Salt and freshly ground black pepper, to taste

Place one-fourth of the egg salad in the center of each spinach leaf. Top each with 6 tomato halves, then sprinkle with 2 tablespoons of the carrots. Sprinkle with salt and pepper, to taste. Roll up and serve at once.

PER SERVING: Calories 188; Protein 7g; Total Fat 15g; Sat Fat 3g; Cholesterol 213mg; Carbohydrate 6g; Dietary Fiber 2g; Sodium 218mg

FIVE

Main Dishes

If dinner menus in U.S. homes were ever surveyed to track ethnicity, we'd probably all be Italian. Indeed, on any given evening, countless families and singles and those in between are sitting down to quick pasta suppers—or calling up for takeout pizza. Thankfully, with the advent of an expansive gluten-free market, pronto pasta dinners await those with celiac disease, gluten-intolerance, or wheat allergies when they visit their local major supermarket. Instead of the lonesome packages of mealy corn spaghetti they once had to hunt down somewhere in the remote health food section (typically about one-eighth of one side of one aisle), a prominent display of high-quality, gluten-free whole-grain brown rice, quinoa, and/or corn pastas in a variety of shapes and sizes now greets them on a well-designated health food aisle—and, sometimes, even on the conventional pasta aisle. Yet for the ambitious who would rather make their own, check out the Easy Gluten-Free Homemade Pasta (dairy-free), page 108, or the Gluten-Free, Egg-Free, Dairy-Free Homemade Pasta (vegan), page 108—not to worry, no pasta maker required. In Italy, of course, one does not live by pasta alone—particularly in northern Italian kitchens, creamy risotto and other rice dishes, hearty polenta, and healthy vegetable and legume combinations, all blessedly gluten-free, abound. If you, like me, are not Italian by birth, the following gluten-free main dishes are sure to prove your credentials as a proud adopted son or daughter of Italy, at least on some enchanted evening—or two, or three, etc.

Gluten-Free Pasta Dishes

Quinoa Linguine with Dandelion Greens and Roasted Roma Tomatoes (vegan)

Easy Gluten-Free Homemade Pasta (dairy-free)

Gluten-Free, Egg-Free, Dairy-Free Homemade Pasta (vegan)

Brown Rice Fusilli and Kidney Beans with Zucchini-Tomato Sauce (vegan)

Brown Rice Spaghetti with Checca Sauce (vegan)

One-Pot Quinoa Linguine with Cherry Tomatoes and Basil (vegan)

Brown Rice Penne with Chickpeas, Fresh Mozzarella, and Eggplant Marinara (egg-free)

Brown Rice Fusilli with Eggplant, Tomato, and Ricotta Salata (egg-free)

Brown Rice Spaghetti with Neapolitan-Style Marinara Sauce (vegan)

Brown Rice Spaghetti with Raw Tomato and Basil Sauce (vegan)

Brown Rice Fusilli with White Beans, Escarole, and Pesto (vegan)

Quinoa Linguine with Vine-Ripened Tomato Marinara Sauce (vegan)

Gnocchi Dishes

Potato Gnocchi with Roasted Red Pepper Sauce (vegan)

Pumpkin Gnocchi with Sage Brown Butter and Marinara (lacto-ovo)

Polenta Gnocchi with Blue Cheese and Tomato-Cream Sauce (egg-free)

Ricotta Cheese Gnocchi and Peas with Spinach–Sunflower Seed Pesto (lacto-ovo)

Roman-Style Polenta Gnocchi (egg-free)

Grain-Free Sweet Potato Gnocchi (dairy-free)

Risotto and Other Rice Dishes

Artichoke and Spinach Risotto (vegan)

One-Pot Risotto with Assorted Vegetables (vegan)

Microwave Cabbage Risotto with Basil (vegan)

Black and White Risotto with Tuscan Kale and Cannellini Beans (vegan)

Baked Risotto with Peas, Roasted Red Peppers, and Mushrooms (vegan)

Quick-Cooking Brown Rice Risotto with Peas and Artichokes (vegan)

Brown Arborio Rice Risotto with Fresh Pumpkin and Sage (vegan)

Red Wine Risotto with Radicchio, Peas, and Pearl Onions (vegan)

Sun-Dried Tomato and Pesto Risotto (egg-free)

Risotto Croquettes with Marinara (lacto-ovo)

Cremini Mushroom and Brown Rice Timbales (egg-free)

Baked Stuffed Tomatoes with Arborio Rice and Basil (vegan)

Polenta Dishes

Roasted Asparagus, Mushrooms, and Chickpeas over Creamy Parmesan Polenta (egg-free)

Caramelized Cabbage and Red Bean–Polenta Pie (vegan)

Roman Beans with Polenta (vegan)

Herbed Polenta Dumplings with Broccoli-Marinara Sauce (egg-free)

Polenta Gratin with Creamy Mushroom Sauce and Fontina Cheese (egg-free)

Porcini Mushroom and Tomato Ragu with White Bean Polenta (vegan)

Creamy Pumpkin Polenta (egg-free)

Sweet and Sour Root Vegetable Ragu over Herbed Polenta (vegan)

Other Entrées

Stuffed Artichokes with Kalamata Olives and Sun-Dried Tomatoes (vegan)

Cabbage Strata with Ricotta and Roman Beans (egg-free)

Cannellini Bean and Fennel Gratin (egg-free)

Buckwheat Risotto with Spinach and Goat Cheese (egg-free)

Eggplant Parmesan (lacto-ovo)

3-Cheese Eggplant Lasagna (lacto-ovo)

Eggplant Lasagna with Spinach and Sun-Dried Tomatoes (vegan)

Eggplant "Meat" Balls (lacto-ovo)

Eggplant Rolls with Spinach, Feta, and Kalamata Olives (egg-free)

Baked Stuffed Eggplant Parmesan (egg-free)

Goat Cheese and Ricotta Cheese Skillet Pie (lacto-ovo/low-carb)

Stuffed Portobello Mushrooms with Ricotta and Spinach (egg-free/low-carb)

Bell Peppers Stuffed with Quinoa and Chickpeas (vegan)

Stuffed Peppers with Sun-Dried Tomato and Pesto Risotto (vegan)

Potato and Cottage Cheese Lasagna (egg-free)

Potato Torta with Broccoli and Tomatoes (vegan)

Stuffed Baked Potatoes with Sun-Dried Tomatoes and Scallions (lacto-ovo)

Spaghetti Squash with Roasted Red Pepper–Ricotta Pesto (egg-free)

Zucchini Cakes with Pine Nuts and Basil (lacto-ovo)

Raw Zucchini Spaghetti with Sun-Dried Tomato Marinara Sauce (vegan/low-carb)

Zucchini-Rice Loaf with Chickpeas and Basil (vegan)

Stuffed Zucchini Boats with Spinach and Parmesan (egg-free/low-carb)

Zucchini-Quinoa Lasagna (egg-free)

GLUTEN-FREE PASTA DISHES

Quinoa Linguine with Dandelion Greens and Roasted Roma Tomatoes

(VEGAN)

This pasta dish is a spring tonic in Italy. Simple yet time-consuming to prepare, it can be made in stages on a relaxed weekend afternoon and served as a renewing supper that evening. Any mix of bitter greens—Belgian endive, curly endive, chicory, escarole—can replace part or all of the dandelion greens, if desired. Soaking the greens in salted water for 1 hour before cooking helps remove some of their bite.

MAKES 4 SERVINGS

- 1 pound Roma tomatoes (about 4) or large plum tomatoes, halved lengthwise and seeded
- 3 tablespoons extra-virgin olive oil, divided
- ½ teaspoon coarse salt
- Freshly ground black pepper, to taste
- ½ pound dandelion greens, soaked for 1 hour in salted water to cover, drained
- ½ cup chopped red onion
- 3 large cloves garlic, finely chopped
- Table salt, to taste
- Pinch crushed red pepper flakes, or to taste (optional)
- 8 ounces gluten-free linguine, preferably the quinoa variety
- Freshly grated gluten-free Parmesan or Romano cheese, to serve (optional)

Preheat the oven to 350F (175C).

Place the tomato halves on a rimmed baking sheet and toss with 1 tablespoon of the oil. Sprinkle evenly with coarse salt and pepper; toss again. Arrange in a single layer, cut sides up. Bake about 1¼ hours, turning halfway through cooking, or until shrunken and fragrant. Remove baking sheet from oven and let cool. Transfer tomatoes to a cutting board and coarsely chop; set aside.

Meanwhile, bring a large pot of salted water to a boil. Cook the drained dandelion greens until tender, about 5 to 7 minutes. Turn off the heat. Using a slotted spoon, remove the greens and coarsely chop; set aside. Do not drain the cooking water.

In a large nonstick skillet, heat the remaining 2 tablespoons of oil over medium heat. Add the onion and cook, stirring, until softened, about 2 to 3 minutes. Add the garlic and cook, stirring constantly, 30 seconds. Reduce the heat to low and add the chopped roasted tomatoes, table salt, black pepper, and red pepper flakes, if using. Cook, stirring occasionally, 10 minutes. Remove skillet from heat and let cool a few minutes. Transfer tomato mixture to a food processor fitted with the knife blade; process until smooth but slightly chunky. Return the pureed tomato mixture to the skillet and stir in the chopped dandelion greens; set aside.

Return the remaining cooking water to a boil over high heat; add the pasta and cook according to package directions until al dente. Drain and add to the skillet, tossing well to combine. Cook over low heat until heated through, 1 to 2 minutes. Serve warm, with the Parmesan, if using, passed separately.

PER SERVING: Calories 345; Protein 11g; Total Fat 12g; Sat Fat 2g; Cholesterol 0mg; Carbohydrate 55g; Dietary Fiber 8g; Sodium 293mg

Easy Gluten-Free Homemade Pasta

(DAIRY-FREE)

I prefer this no-fuss recipe for three simple reasons: I can get all the ingredients at my local supermarket, it requires no electrical gadgets, and it's delicious.

MAKES 4 SERVINGS (ABOUT ½ POUND UNCOOKED PASTA)

2 cups all-purpose gluten-free flour
½ tablespoon xanthan gum
1 teaspoon gluten-free baking powder
½ teaspoon salt
2 large eggs
5 to 6 tablespoons water
¼ teaspoon canola oil

In a large bowl, whisk together the flour, xanthan gum, baking powder, and salt until thoroughly blended. In a small bowl, whisk together the eggs, 5 tablespoons of water, and oil until thoroughly blended. Make a well in the center of the flour mixture and fill with the egg mixture. Using a wooden spoon, stir the wet mixture into the dry mixture; use your hands to thoroughly incorporate. If too dry, knead in an additional ½ to 1 tablespoon of water. Gather the dough into a ball and transfer to a lightly floured flat work surface; knead until the consistency of Play-Doh, about 2 minutes. Wrap in plastic wrap and let rest at room temperature 30 minutes.

If using a pasta maker, follow the manufacturer's suggestions for rolling and cutting the dough into desired shapes.

If rolling by hand, divide the dough into 4 equal balls. Working with 1 dough ball at a time (cover the others loosely with plastic wrap), using a heavy rolling pin, roll each dough ball out as thinly as possible (about ¹⁄₁₆-inch in thickness). Using a sharp knife, cut the dough into desired shapes. For spaghetti, cut into long strips about ⅛-inch thick; for linguine, about ¼-inch thick, for fettuccine, about ⅜-inch thick, etc. When finished cutting the noodles, spread out to dry for about 2 hours. (At this point, noodles can be covered and refrigerated 24 hours before cooking, or frozen up to 3 months. If frozen, thaw in the refrigerator before cooking for best results.)

Bring a large pot of salted water to a boil. Cook the pasta until al dente, about 5 to 15 minutes, depending on thickness and size. (As a general rule, when the pasta rises to the surface, take a little piece and taste it. You should be able to bite into it without it falling apart.) Drain in a colander, transfer to a bowl, and toss with pasta sauce of choice.

PER SERVING: Calories 268; Protein 10g; Total Fat 3g; Sat Fat 1g; Cholesterol 106mg; Carbohydrate 48g; Dietary Fiber 2g; Sodium 390mg

Gluten-Free, Egg-Free, Dairy-Free Homemade Pasta

(VEGAN)

This recipe works best with the use of a stand mixer; if you don't have one, use a hand-held electric mixer, setting the speeds as directed.

MAKES 4 SERVINGS (ABOUT ½ POUND UNCOOKED PASTA)

1⅓ cups sorghum flour
⅔ cup tapioca starch, plus additional 1 tablespoon, if necessary
1 teaspoon xanthan gum
½ teaspoon salt

½ cup warm water, plus additional

　　1 tablespoon cold water, if necessary

2 tablespoons extra-virgin olive oil

In the bowl of a standing mixer, whisk together the sorghum flour, tapioca starch, xanthan gum, and salt until thoroughly blended. Using the paddle attachment on its lowest setting (stir), slowly add the warm water and oil. Gradually increase the speed to medium and mix for 2 minutes. The dough should come together in a ball the consistency of Play-Doh. If too dry, add an additional 1 tablespoon of water. If too sticky, add an additional tablespoon of tapioca starch. If necessary, slowly return to medium speed and beat 1 more minute. Wrap dough in plastic wrap and let rest at room temperature 30 minutes.

If using a pasta maker, follow the manufacturer's suggestions for rolling and cutting the dough into desired shapes.

If rolling by hand, divide the dough into 4 equal balls. Working with 1 dough ball at a time (cover the others loosely with plastic wrap), using a heavy rolling pin, roll each dough ball out as thinly as possible (about ¹⁄₁₆-inch in thickness). Using a sharp knife, cut the dough into desired shapes. For spaghetti, cut into long strips about ⅛-inch thick; for linguine, about ¼-inch thick, for fettuccine, about ⅜-inch thick, etc. When finished cutting the noodles, spread out to dry for about 2 hours. (At this point, noodles can be covered and refrigerated 24 hours before cooking, or frozen up to 3 months. If frozen, thaw in the refrigerator before cooking for best results.)

Bring a large pot of salted water to a boil. Cook the pasta until al dente, about 5 to 15 minutes, depending on thickness and size. (As a general rule, when the pasta rises to the surface, take a little piece and taste it. You should be able to bite into it

without it falling apart.) Drain in a colander, transfer to a bowl, and toss with pasta sauce of choice.

PER SERVING: Calories 278; Protein 5g; Total Fat 8g; Sat Fat 1g; Cholesterol 0mg; Carbohydrate 48g; Dietary Fiber 5g; Sodium 273mg

Brown Rice Fusilli and Kidney Beans with Zucchini-Tomato Sauce

(VEGAN)

This light and rustic pasta sauce is a tasty way to use up the last of the summer's zucchini and tomatoes. For sophisticated occasions, a touch of cream is sublime. Hot cooked rice can replace the pasta, if desired.

MAKES 6 SERVINGS

　　12 ounces gluten-free brown rice fusilli or
　　　　similar pasta

　　1 (16-ounce) can kidney beans, rinsed and
　　　　drained

　　½ recipe Zucchini-Tomato Pasta Sauce (about
　　　　3 cups), page 114, heated

Bring a large stockpot of salted water to a boil. Cook the pasta according to package directions until al dente. Meanwhile, place the beans in a colander set in a sink. Slowly drain the cooked pasta over the beans; drain well. Return to the stockpot and add the Zucchini-Tomato Sauce; toss well to thoroughly combine. Serve at once.

PER SERVING: Calories 326; Protein 12g; Total Fat 6g; Sat Fat 1g; Cholesterol 0mg; Carbohydrate 56g; Dietary Fiber 4g; Sodium 267mg

Brown Rice Spaghetti with Checca Sauce

(EGG-FREE)

Checca sauce is a popular summertime sauce prepared with uncooked tomatoes, basil, and fresh mozzarella. Though traditionally served with wheat-based spaghetti or angel hair pasta, feel free to use your favorite gluten-free variety.

MAKES 4 SERVINGS

4 large plum tomatoes (about 3 ounces each), quartered

4 scallions (white and green parts), coarsely chopped

1 cup fresh basil leaves, torn

½ cup gluten-free freshly shredded Parmesan cheese

2 tablespoons extra-virgin olive oil

3 large cloves garlic, finely chopped

¼ teaspoon salt, or to taste

Freshly ground black pepper, to taste

8 ounces gluten-free brown rice spaghetti or similar pasta

4 ounces fresh mozzarella cheese, cut into ½-inch cubes, divided

In a food processor fitted with the knife blade, combine the tomatoes, scallions, basil, Parmesan cheese, oil, garlic, salt, and pepper; pulse in on/off motions until mixture is smooth but slightly chunky. Let stand 15 minutes at room temperature to allow the flavors to blend.

Meanwhile, bring a large pot of salted water to a boil. Cook the pasta according to package directions until al dente; reserve ¼ cup of the cooking water and then drain well. Return the hot pasta to the pot and add the tomato-basil mixture and half the mozzarella cheese; toss well to combine, adding the reserved cooking water if a saucier consistency is desired. Divide the pasta mixture equally among each of 4 serving plates; top with equal amounts of the remaining cheese. Serve at once.

PER SERVING: Calories 438; Protein 19g; Total Fat 18g; Sat Fat 7g; Cholesterol 33mg; Carbohydrate 51g; Dietary Fiber 3g; Sodium 436mg

One-Pot Quinoa Linguine with Cherry Tomatoes and Basil

(VEGAN)

This slightly soupy, slightly slippery one-pot pasta, known as minestra *in Italy, is as fun to make as it is to eat. Feel free to experiment with your own gluten-free pasta and veggie combinations.*

MAKES 5 TO 6 SERVINGS

2 tablespoons extra-virgin olive oil

1 large onion (about 8 ounces), cut into thin half-rounds

4 cloves garlic, slivered

¼ teaspoon crushed red pepper flakes, or to taste (optional)

4½ cups water, plus additional, as necessary

12 ounces gluten-free quinoa linguine

1½ cups cherry or grape tomatoes, halved or quartered if large

2 sprigs fresh basil, plus ½ cup torn leaves

½ teaspoon coarse salt, or to taste

Freshly ground black pepper, to taste

Freshly grated gluten-free Parmesan cheese, for serving (optional)

In a large, deep-sided skillet, heat the oil over medium heat. Add the onion and cook, stirring, until softened, about 3 minutes. Add the garlic and red pepper flakes, if using; cook, stirring, 1 minute, or until fragrant. Add the water, pasta, tomatoes, basil sprigs, salt, and pepper; bring to a boil over high heat. Boil, stirring and turning often with tongs, until pasta is cooked al dente and water has nearly evaporated, about 9 minutes. Remove skillet from heat. Remove and discard the basil sprigs; add the torn basil leaves, tossing to thoroughly combine. Serve at once, with the Parmesan passed separately, if using.

PER SERVING: Calories 323; Protein 11g; Total Fat 7g; Sat Fat 1g; Cholesterol 0mg; Carbohydrate 60g; Dietary Fiber 8g; Sodium 202mg

Neapolitan-Style Marinara Sauce

(VEGAN/LOW-CARB)

The addition of carrot and celery lends this outstanding marinara sauce its characteristic Neapolitan flavor.

MAKES ABOUT 3 CUPS

1½ tablespoons extra-virgin olive oil
1 small onion (about 4 ounces), chopped
1 small carrot (about 2 ounces), chopped
1 stalk celery, chopped
3 large cloves garlic, finely chopped
1 (28-ounce) can whole plum tomatoes, coarsely chopped, juices included, or 2 pounds fresh plum tomatoes, peeled and coarsely chopped, accumulated juices included (see Cook's Tip, page 113)

½ cup water (if using fresh tomatoes)
2 tablespoons tomato paste
2 to 4 tablespoons chopped fresh basil
2 tablespoons chopped fresh flat-leaf parsley
1 teaspoon dried oregano
½ teaspoon (if using canned tomatoes) or 1 teaspoon (if using fresh tomatoes) salt, or to taste
½ teaspoon sugar, or to taste
¼ teaspoon dried thyme
Freshly ground black pepper, to taste

In a large deep-sided nonstick skillet, heat the oil over medium heat. Add the onion, carrot, and celery and cook, stirring, until softened, about 5 minutes. Add the garlic and cook, stirring, 1 minute. Add the remaining ingredients and bring to a brisk simmer over medium-high heat. Reduce the heat to medium-low and simmer, uncovered, stirring occasionally and breaking up the tomatoes with a wooden spoon, until reduced to about 3 cups, about 20 minutes for fresh tomatoes, or 35 minutes for canned. For a smooth sauce, puree all the mixture in a blender, food processor, or food mill (*mouli*). For a slightly chunky sauce, puree half the mixture. For a chunky sauce, leave as is. Use as directed in recipe. Completely cooled sauce can be refrigerated, covered, up to 3 days; alternatively, freeze for up to 3 months.

PER SERVING (per ½ cup, or ⅙ of recipe, with canned tomatoes): Calories 78; Protein 2g; Total Fat 4g; Sat Fat 1g; Cholesterol 0mg; Carbohydrate 11g; Dietary Fiber 2g; Sodium 513mg

Brown Rice Penne with Chickpeas, Fresh Mozzarella, and Eggplant Marinara

(EGG-FREE)

Ready is under 30 minutes, this one-pot pasta dish is a rush-hour special in my house—for a vegan dish, omit the cheese and add more chickpeas.

MAKES 5 TO 6 SERVINGS

8 ounces gluten-free brown rice penne or other similar pasta

1 cup rinsed and drained canned chickpeas

1 cup prepared gluten-free marinara sauce, preferably a tomato-basil variety

1 (7.5-ounce) jar gluten-free caponata

2 teaspoons extra-virgin olive oil

4 ounces bite-size fresh mozzarella balls (about 12), well drained

2 to 3 tablespoons chopped fresh basil

Bring a medium stockpot of salted water to a boil. Cook the pasta according to package directions until al dente, adding the chickpeas the last few minutes of cooking. Drain and immediately return to the pot; add the marinara, caponata, and oil. Cook over medium-low heat, stirring, until sauce is heated through. Add the mozzarella and basil and stir gently to combine. Cover the pot, turn off the heat, and let stand 5 minutes. Uncover and toss very gently (the cheese balls should hold their shape). Serve at once.

PER SERVING: Calories 352; Protein 16g; Total Fat 12g; Sat Fat 4g; Cholesterol 20mg; Carbohydrate 51g; Dietary Fiber 5g; Sodium 416mg

Brown Rice Fusilli with Eggplant, Tomato, and Ricotta Salata

(EGG-FREE)

This summertime pasta dish can easily be made vegan with the omission of the ricotta salata—in this instance, season with additional coarse salt for a fuller flavor.

MAKES 6 SERVINGS

1 (1-pound) eggplant, peeled and cut into 1½-inch cubes

Table salt

3 tablespoons extra-virgin olive oil, divided

1 medium onion (about 6 ounces), thinly sliced into half-rounds

2 large cloves garlic, finely chopped

6 small plum tomatoes (about 12 ounces total), peeled, seeded, and cut lengthwise into eighths (see Cook's Tip, page 113)

½ cup chopped fresh basil, divided

¼ cup low-sodium vegetable broth

½ teaspoon sugar

Salt, preferably the coarse variety, and freshly ground black pepper, to taste

12 ounces brown rice fusilli pasta or other similar gluten-free pasta, cooked according to package directions until al dente and drained

3 ounces gluten-free ricotta salata, coarsely chopped

Freshly shredded gluten-free Parmesan cheese, to serve (optional)

Sprinkle the eggplant with table salt and set in a colander to drain for 30 minutes. Rinse the eggplant under cold-running water and drain well between paper towels.

In a large deep-sided nonstick skillet with a lid, heat 2 tablespoons of the oil over medium heat. Add the onion and cook, stirring, until softened, about 3 minutes. Add the garlic and cook, stirring, 1 minute. Add the eggplant, tomatoes, ¼ cup basil, broth, sugar, salt, and pepper; toss well to combine. Reduce heat to medium-low, cover, and cook until the eggplant is tender, stirring occasionally, about 12 to 15 minutes. Add the pasta, ricotta salata, remaining ¼ cup basil, and remaining 1 tablespoon oil; toss well to combine. Serve at once, with the Parmesan, if using, passed separately.

PER SERVING: Calories 351; Protein 11g; Total Fat 11g; Sat Fat 3g; Cholesterol 13mg; Carbohydrate 52g; Dietary Fiber 4g; Sodium 270mg

Vine-Ripened Tomato Marinara Sauce

(VEGAN/LOW-CARB)

As the smooth variation of this sauce freezes especially well, consider making a double-batch with the end of the season's tomatoes to enjoy throughout the winter months.

MAKES ABOUT 2½ CUPS

1 tablespoon extra-virgin olive oil

1 medium onion (about 6 ounces), chopped

3 large cloves garlic, finely chopped

½ teaspoon dried oregano

½ teaspoon dried thyme leaves

¼ to ½ cup dry red wine

2½ pounds vine-ripened tomatoes, peeled, seeded, and coarsely chopped (see Cook's Tip, on the right)

½ cup low-sodium vegetable broth, plus additional, as necessary

1 tablespoon tomato paste

1 teaspoon sugar, or to taste

1 teaspoon salt, or to taste

Freshly ground black pepper, to taste

In a medium stockpot, heat the oil over medium heat. Add the onion and cook, stirring, until golden, about 5 to 7 minutes. Add the garlic, oregano, and thyme; cook, stirring constantly, 1 minute, or until garlic is browned but not burnt. Add the wine and cook, stirring and scraping the browned bits from the bottom of the pot, 2 minutes, or until liquids have greatly reduced. Add the tomatoes (and any accumulated juices), broth, tomato paste, sugar, and salt; bring to a brisk simmer over medium-high heat, stirring a few times. Reduce the heat to medium-low and cook, partially covered, about 45 minutes, or until tomatoes have cooked down to about 2½ cups, stirring occasionally and breaking up the tomatoes with a large wooden spoon. For a smooth sauce, puree in a blender, food processor, or a food mill (*mouli*). Use as directed in the recipe. Completely cooled sauce can be refrigerated, covered, up to 3 days; alternatively, freeze for up to 3 months.

PER SERVING (per ½ cup, or ⅕ of recipe): Calories 72; Protein 2g; Total Fat 3g; Sat Fat 0g; Cholesterol 0mg; Carbohydrate 8g; Dietary Fiber 2g; Sodium 518mg

Cook's Tip

To peel tomatoes, bring a large pot of water to a boil. Drop tomatoes into boiling water 20 seconds. Drain in a colander and peel off the skins under cold-running water.

Zucchini-Tomato Pasta Sauce

(VEGAN/LOW-CARB)

Toss this flavorful sauce with your favorite gluten-free pasta, rice, and vegetables, or spoon over polenta.

MAKES ABOUT 6 CUPS

¼ cup extra-virgin olive oil

2 medium onions (about 6 ounces each), chopped

6 large cloves garlic, finely chopped

2 to 2½ pounds tomatoes (about 8 medium), chopped

1 pound zucchini, cut into ½-inch cubes

1 cup low-sodium vegetable broth

3 tablespoons tomato paste

1 teaspoon dried oregano

1 teaspoon sugar, or to taste

1 teaspoon salt, or to taste

Freshly ground black pepper, to taste

Pinch or more crushed red pepper flakes, or to taste (optional)

¼ to ½ cup heavy cream, half-and-half, or soy creamer (optional)

In a medium stockpot, heat the oil over medium heat. Add the onion and cook, stirring, until softened, about 3 to 5 minutes. Add the garlic and cook, stirring often, 1 minute. Add the remaining ingredients, except the optional cream, and bring to a simmer over medium-high heat, stirring occasionally. Reduce the heat to medium-low and simmer, uncovered, stirring occasionally, until reduced and thickened, about 1 hour, stirring in the cream, if using, the last few minutes of cooking. Serve warm.

PER SERVING (about ½ cup, or 1/12 of recipe): Calories 82; Protein 3g; Total Fat 5g; Sat Fat 1g; Cholesterol 0mg; Carbohydrate 9g; Dietary Fiber 2g; Sodium 262mg

Brown Rice Spaghetti with Neapolitan-Style Marinara Sauce

(VEGAN)

Delicious in its simplicity, spaghetti alla marinara is as popular in Italy as it is in America. This Neapolitan-style version is my favorite.

MAKES 6 SERVINGS

16 ounces gluten-free brown rice spaghetti

Neapolitan-Style Marinara Sauce, page 111, heated

Freshly shredded gluten-free Parmesan cheese, to serve (optional)

Bring a large stockpot of salted water to a boil. Cook pasta according to package directions; drain well. Return to the pot or transfer to a large bowl; add the sauce, tossing well to combine. Serve at once, with the Parmesan, if using, passed separately.

PER SERVING: Calories 341; Protein 13g; Total Fat 5g; Sat Fat 1g; Cholesterol 0mg; Carbohydrate 67g; Dietary Fiber 9g; Sodium 519mg

Brown Rice Spaghetti with Raw Tomato and Basil Sauce

(VEGAN)

The heady scents of tomato, basil, and garlic infuse this no-cook pasta sauce, which is equally tasty tossed with Arborio rice or spooned over polenta. For best results, the consistency of the sauce should resemble Mexican salsa. If you don't have coarse salt, use half the amount of table salt.

MAKES 4 MAIN SERVINGS

1 pound plum tomatoes, finely chopped

½ cup finely chopped fresh basil

3 to 4 tablespoons extra-virgin olive oil

1 tablespoon finely chopped fresh flat-leaf parsley

1½ to 2 teaspoons balsamic vinegar

3 large cloves garlic, finely chopped

¾ to 1 teaspoon coarse salt, or to taste

Freshly ground black pepper, to taste

8 ounces gluten-free brown rice spaghetti or similar gluten-free pasta

In a medium bowl, combine all ingredients except the pasta; let stand 30 minutes at room temperature, stirring 4 to 5 times to allow the flavors to blend.

Meanwhile, bring a medium stockpot of salted water to a boil. Cook the pasta according to package directions until al dente; drain well. Return the hot pasta to the pot and immediately add the tomato sauce, tossing well to combine. Let stand, covered, 5 minutes. Toss gently until most of the liquids have been absorbed by the pasta. Serve warm or at room temperature, with additional coarse salt passed separately, if desired.

PER SERVING: Calories 327; Protein 8g; Total Fat 11g; Sat Fat 2g; Cholesterol 0mg; Carbohydrate 48g; Dietary Fiber 3g; Sodium 367mg

Brown Rice Fusilli with White Beans, Escarole, and Pesto

(VEGAN)

This is a great way to sneak escarole, a bitter-tasting yet nutrient-rich green, into a well-balanced diet. Spinach, Swiss chard, or kale can replace it, if desired.

MAKES 6 SERVINGS

1 tablespoon extra-virgin olive oil

1 cup chopped red onion

1 to 2 large cloves garlic, finely chopped

½ teaspoon dried rosemary

1 medium bunch of escarole (about 1 pound), coarsely chopped, divided

¼ cup water, divided

½ teaspoon salt, or to taste

Freshly ground black pepper, to taste

1 (15-ounce) can cannellini or other white beans, rinsed and drained

½ cup Rustic Pesto Sauce, page 92, Classic Basil Pesto Sauce, page 97, or prepared gluten-free pesto sauce

12 ounces brown rice fusilli or other similar gluten-free twist pasta, cooked according to package directions until al dente, drained and ¼ cup of cooking liquid reserved

In a large deep-sided nonstick skillet, heat the oil over medium heat. Add the onion and cook, stirring, until softened, about 2 to 3 minutes. Add the garlic and rosemary and cook, stirring constantly, 30 seconds. Add half the escarole, 2 tablespoons water, and salt; cook, tossing with a wide spatula, until escarole is just wilted, about 2 minutes. Add the remaining escarole and water; cook, tossing, until escarole is just wilted, about 2 more minutes. Add the beans and cook, stirring, until beans are heated through and escarole is completely wilted, about 2 to 3 minutes. Reduce the heat to low and quickly stir in the pesto and reserved pasta cooking liquid. Add the cooked and drained pasta, tossing well to thoroughly coat. Serve at once.

PER SERVING: Calories 407; Protein 18g; Total Fat 13g; Sat Fat 3g; Cholesterol 0mg; Carbohydrate 61g; Dietary Fiber 11g; Sodium 340mg

Quinoa Linguine with Vine-Ripened Tomato Marinara Sauce

(VEGAN)

Quinoa linguine is a tasty and protein-packed alternative to rice-based gluten-free pastas. Its chewy texture lends itself well to a chunky marinara sauce.

MAKES 5 TO 6 SERVINGS

12 ounces quinoa linguine or other gluten-free pasta

Vine-Ripened Tomato Marinara Sauce, page 113, heated

½ cup chopped fresh flat-leaf parsley and/or basil

Freshly shredded gluten-free Parmesan cheese, to serve (optional)

In a large stockpot, cook the pasta in boiling salted water according to package directions; drain well. Return to the pot or transfer to a large bowl; add the sauce and parsley, tossing well to combine. Serve at once, with the Parmesan passed separately, if using.

PER SERVING: Calories 311; Protein 12g; Total Fat 4g; Sat Fat 1g; Cholesterol 0mg; Carbohydrate 60g; Dietary Fiber 8g; Sodium 527mg

GNOCCHI DISHES

Potato Gnocchi with Roasted Red Pepper Sauce

(VEGAN)

This is a terrific company dish, as the gnocchi can be made a day ahead before cooking and serving with the sauce, which can also be made well in advance. For best results, use boiling potatoes, such as Yukon Gold, in lieu of the baking variety, as the former absorb less moisture and will allow the gnocchi to retain their firmness during cooking. Beating the potatoes with an electric mixture is preferable over mashing, as the former ensures that all small lumps will be removed, resulting in smoother dough.

MAKES 4 TO 6 SERVINGS (ABOUT 6 DOZEN GNOCCHI)

1 pound boiling potatoes, preferably Yukon Gold, unpeeled and quartered

1 cup gluten-free all-purpose flour

1 teaspoon xanthan gum

2 tablespoons extra-virgin olive oil

½ teaspoon salt

Fresh ground black pepper, to taste

2 to 4 tablespoons water

Roasted Red Pepper Sauce, page 117, heated

In a large saucepan, bring the potatoes and enough salted water to cover to a boil over high heat. Reduce the heat slightly and cook until the potatoes are very tender, 15 to 20 minutes, depending on size. Drain well; when cool enough to handle, remove skins.

Meanwhile, in a small bowl, whisk together the

flour and xanthan gum until thoroughly blended; set aside.

Transfer potatoes to a large mixing bowl. Add the oil, salt, and black pepper; using an electric mixer, beat until very smooth, adding enough water as necessary (mixture will become glue-like). Immediately add half the flour mixture and beat on low speed until just incorporated. Using your fingers, knead in the remaining flour mixture until thoroughly incorporated and dough is smooth but slightly sticky. Mold dough into a ball and place on a flat work surface.

Divide the dough ball into three equal balls. Roll each dough ball into a 12-inch cylinder about ¾ inch in diameter. Cut each cylinder crosswise into ½-inch-thick pieces (for about 6 dozen pieces total). Press each piece gently against the inside curve of a fork and gently roll up, so that decorative rib marks appear on the dough. You can also flatten each piece gently with your thumb into an indented disk. Alternatively, shape each piece into an oval. (At this point, gnocchi can be refrigerated, covered, up to 24 hours before continuing with the recipe.)

Bring a large stockpot of salted water to a boil over high heat. Working in batches so as not to crowd the pot, drop the gnocchi into the boiling water. As soon as they have all risen to the surface, about 1 minute, reduce the heat to medium-high and simmer briskly for 2 minutes, or until cooked through the center. (If previously refrigerated, add another 30 seconds or so.) Using a slotted spoon, transfer the cooked gnocchi to a serving bowl; cover to keep warm. Return the water to a boil over high heat and repeat the cooking process with the remaining uncooked gnocchi.

To serve, add the Roasted Red Pepper Sauce to the gnocchi; toss very gently to combine. Serve at once.

PER SERVING: Calories 351; Protein 8g; Total Fat 14g; Sat Fat 2g; Cholesterol 0mg; Carbohydrate 49g; Dietary Fiber 6g; Sodium 377mg

Variation

To make Potato Gnocchi with Roasted Red Pepper Sauce and Peas, add 1 cup cooked fresh or frozen peas to the gnocchi along with the sauce.

Roasted Red Pepper Sauce
(VEGAN/LOW-CARB)

Use this versatile sauce on countless pasta, gnocchi, and polenta dishes, and vegetables, as well.

MAKES ABOUT 1 CUP

2 tablespoons extra-virgin olive oil
2 large cloves garlic, finely chopped
1 (12-ounce) jar roasted red bell peppers, rinsed, drained, and coarsely chopped
½ cup chopped onion
½ cup chopped carrot
¾ cup low-sodium vegetable broth, plus additional, as necessary
¼ teaspoon crushed red pepper flakes, or to taste (optional)
Salt and freshly ground black pepper, to taste
2 to 4 tablespoons chopped fresh basil or flat-leaf parsley (optional)

In a small saucepan, heat the oil over medium heat. Add the garlic and cook, stirring constantly, 30 seconds. Add the roasted pepper, onion, and carrot; cook, stirring, until liquids from peppers are greatly reduced, 5 to 7 minutes. Add the broth, red pepper flakes, if using, salt, and black pepper; bring to a simmer over medium-high heat. Reduce the heat to medium-low, cover, and simmer 20 minutes, stirring a few times. Let cool a few minutes before transferring to a food processor fitted with the knife blade, or to a blender. Process or blend until smooth and pureed. Return to the pan and stir in the basil, if using; cook over low heat, stirring, until heated through, 1 to 2 minutes, thinning with additional broth, if desired. Use as directed in recipe. Completely cooled sauce can be stored, covered, in refrigerator up to 3 days before reheating over low heat and serving.

PER SERVING (about ¼ cup, or ¼ of recipe): Calories 103; Protein 2g; Total Fat 7g; Sat Fat 1g; Cholesterol 0mg; Carbohydrate 9g; Dietary Fiber 3g; Sodium 18mg

Variation

To make Roasted Red Pepper Cream Sauce, stir in ¼ cup of nonfat half-and-half, or soy creamer, along with the basil.

Pumpkin Gnocchi with Sage Brown Butter and Marinara

(LACTO-OVO)

I prefer the powdery consistency of canned grated Parmesan-Romano cheese, versus the freshly shredded refrigerated variety, in this tasty recipe—if using the former, read the label carefully to ensure it's gluten-free. For a special party appetizer, serve this dish on a heated platter with the marinara in the center and provide wooden picks for dipping.

MAKES 6 SERVINGS (ABOUT 4 DOZEN GNOCCHI)

1 pound russet potatoes (about 2 large), peeled and cut into chunks

⅟₁₆ teaspoon ground nutmeg

Salt and freshly ground black pepper, to taste

⅓ cup pumpkin puree

¾ cup gluten-free all-purpose flour

1 large egg

2 tablespoons extra-virgin olive oil

2 tablespoons butter

6 large fresh sage leaves, chopped

⅔ cup finely grated gluten-free Parmesan-Romano cheese blend, divided, plus additional, to serve

1 (24-ounce) jar gluten-free marinara sauce, heated

Fresh whole sage leaves, for garnish (optional)

In a large saucepan, place the potatoes in enough salted water to cover by a few inches; bring to a boil over high heat. Reduce the heat to medium-high, and cook until potatoes are very tender, about 25 minutes. Drain well in a colander.

Transfer the potatoes to a large bowl and add the nutmeg, salt, and pepper; mash with a potato masher until smooth. Add the pumpkin puree; mash until thoroughly blended (no white should remain). Gradually mash in the flour, and then the egg. Stir with a spoon until smooth.

Divide dough into 4 equal parts. Shape each section of dough into a ¾-inch-thick cylinder, about 12 inches long. Cut each cylinder into 1-inch pieces; form each piece into an oval (for a total of about 4 dozen gnocchi). (At this point, gnocchi can be refrigerated, covered, separated from each other to prevent sticking together, up to 12 hours before continuing with the recipe.)

Meanwhile, bring a large pot of salted water to a boil over high heat. Working in batches so as not to crowd the pot, drop the gnocchi into the boiling water. As soon as they have all risen to the surface (1 to 2 minutes), immediately reduce the heat to medium and simmer gently for 5 minutes (if refrigerated, simmer an additional 1 minute). Transfer the gnocchi with a slotted spoon to a colander to drain. Return the water to a boil over high heat and repeat the process with the next batch.

In a 12-inch nonstick skillet, heat the oil over medium-high heat. Add the gnocchi and cook, turning frequently, until crisp and browned on all sides, about 4 to 5 minutes. Remove skillet from heat and add the butter. Return skillet to medium heat and add the chopped sage; cook, stirring often, 3 minutes. Increase heat to medium-high and cook, stirring often, 1 minute, or until gnocchi are beginning to caramelize and sage is crispy. Remove from heat and transfer gnocchi to a large bowl. Sprinkle with half the cheese, tossing gently to thoroughly coat. Repeat with remaining cheese.

To serve, spoon equal portions (about ½ cup) of the heated marinara sauce onto each of 4 deep-welled serving plates. Top with equal portions (about 8) of the gnocchi. Serve at once, garnished with a sage leaf, if desired, with additional cheese passed separately.

PER SERVING: Calories 324; Protein 11g; Total Fat 17g; Sat Fat 6g; Cholesterol 54mg; Carbohydrate 36g; Dietary Fiber 2g; Sodium 975mg

Variation

For Pumpkin Gnocchi with Pesto, omit the last 6 ingredients (oil through whole sage leaves). Prepare and boil the gnocchi as directed in the stockpot, omitting the pan-frying step. Toss the drained boiled gnocchi with ¼ to ⅓ cup of prepared gluten-free pesto sauce and serve at once.

Polenta Gnocchi with Blue Cheese and Tomato-Cream Sauce

(EGG-FREE)

This easy dish makes a quick and delicious weeknight supper, as the polenta can be cooked and firmed in the refrigerator 24 hours ahead of cutting into shapes and baking. While most blue cheeses made today are gluten-free, check the label carefully before purchasing. Gluten-free crumbled Gorgonzola or goat cheese can replace the domestic blue variety, if desired.

MAKES 6 SERVINGS

4 cups water
1 cup quick-cooking polenta or regular polenta (coarse-ground yellow cornmeal)
½ tablespoon extra-virgin olive oil
1 teaspoon dried oregano
½ teaspoon garlic salt
Freshly ground black pepper, to taste
1 teaspoon extra-virgin olive oil
1¾ cups tomato sauce
¼ cup heavy whipping cream, light cream, or half-and-half
1 cup gluten-free crumbled domestic blue cheese

Lightly oil an 11 × 7-inch baking dish and set aside.

If using quick-cooking polenta: In a medium stockpot, bring the water, polenta, oil, oregano, garlic salt, and pepper to a boil over high heat. Immediately reduce the heat to medium and cook, stirring often with a long-handled spoon (polenta will sputter), 5 minutes. Immediately spoon polenta into the prepared dish, pressing down with the back of a large spoon or spatula (dampen slightly, if necessary) to form a smooth surface. Let stand about 15 minutes to cool. Cover and refrigerate 1 hour, or up to 1 day, before continuing with the recipe.

If using regular polenta: In a medium stockpot, bring the water, oil, oregano, garlic salt, and pepper to a boil over high heat. Slowly add the polenta, stirring constantly with a long-handled spoon. Reduce the heat to low and cook, covered, stirring occasionally, until the polenta is tender, about 15 minutes. Immediately spoon polenta into the prepared dish, pressing down with the back of a large spoon or spatula (dampen slightly, if necessary) to form a smooth surface. Let stand about 15 minutes to cool. Cover and refrigerate 1 hour, or up to 1 day, before continuing with the recipe.

Preheat oven to 350F (175C). Lightly oil a 9 × 13-inch baking dish.

Cut the firmed polenta into small cubes or triangles. In a small bowl, stir together the tomato sauce and cream until thoroughly blended (you will have 2 cups). Spread 1 cup of the tomato mixture into the prepared dish. Arrange the cut polenta attractively over the tomato mixture. Drizzle the remaining 1 cup of tomato mixture evenly over the polenta. Sprinkle the polenta evenly with the blue cheese. Bake, uncovered, about 25 minutes, or until hot and bubbly. Let cool 5 minutes before serving.

PER SERVING: Calories 237; Protein 8g; Total Fat 11g; Sat Fat 6g; Cholesterol 28mg; Carbohydrate 27g; Dietary Fiber 4g; Sodium 871mg

Ricotta Cheese Gnocchi and Peas with Spinach–Sunflower Seed Pesto

(LACTO-OVO)

Just about everyone enjoys this mild-tasting and filling gnocchi dish—store-bought gluten-free basil pesto can be used in a pinch, if necessary. For best results, reheat leftovers in the microwave.

MAKES 4 TO 6 MAIN DISH SERVINGS

Ricotta Cheese Gnocchi (page 121)
1 cup frozen peas, cooked according to
    package directions, drained
½ recipe Spinach–Sunflower Seed Pesto
    (about 6 tablespoons), or more to taste
    (page 122)
½ cup freshly grated gluten-free Parmesan
    cheese, divided
Salt and freshly ground black pepper, to taste

Place the hot cooked gnocchi in a large bowl and toss with the peas and pesto sauce. Add ¼ cup Parmesan cheese, salt, and pepper and toss again. Transfer equal amounts of gnocchi to each of 4 to 6 serving plates (about 8 to 12 each). Sprinkle each with 2 to 3 teaspoons of the remaining ¼ cup cheese. Serve at once.

PER SERVING: Calories 438; Protein 24g; Total Fat 23g; Sat Fat 11g; Cholesterol 101mg; Carbohydrate 34g; Dietary Fiber 4g; Sodium 723mg

Ricotta Cheese Gnocchi

(LACTO-OVO)

Cheese gnocchi harken back to medieval times, long before the potato was introduced in Italy from the Americas. Feel free to toss with any of your favorite gluten-free pasta or pesto sauces, or pair with peas and Spinach–Sunflower Seed Pesto, page 122, for a positively postmedieval option.

MAKES 4 SERVINGS (ABOUT 4 DOZEN GNOCCHI)

1 large egg

1 cup gluten-free whole-milk ricotta cheese, well drained

2 tablespoons finely chopped chives or the green parts of scallions

¾ cup gluten-free all-purpose flour, plus additional, for dusting, etc.

½ cup packed finely grated gluten-free Parmesan cheese (about 1 ounce)

¼ teaspoon xanthan gum

¼ teaspoon salt

Freshly ground black pepper, to taste

Olive oil or butter (optional)

About 2 cups gluten-free pasta sauce, heated, or 6 tablespoons gluten-free pesto (or to taste), to serve (optional)

In a small bowl, beat the egg with a fork, then add the ricotta and chives, stirring well with a spoon to thoroughly combine. In a large bowl, whisk together the flour, Parmesan, xanthan gum, salt, and pepper until thoroughly blended. Make a well in the center of the dry mixture and fill with the ricotta mixture. Stir the wet mixture into the dry mixture until combined and a dough forms, about 20 to 30 strokes. Lightly knead in the bowl (being careful not to overwork the dough, as this will result in a tougher dumpling) and shape into a ball.

Transfer the dough ball to a lightly floured work surface and divide into 4 equal balls. Roll each ball into a 6-inch long cylinder about 1-inch wide. Using a sharp knife, cut each cylinder crosswise into ½-inch-wide pieces, for a total of about 48 gnocchi. (At this point, gnocchi can be held at room temperature up to 1 hour, or refrigerated, covered, up to 24 hours before continuing with the recipe. Alternatively, gnocchi can be frozen individually on a covered baking sheet for 2 hours, then placed in a resealable freezer bag up to 3 months.)

To cook the gnocchi, bring a large stockpot of salted water to a boil over high heat. Working in batches so as not to crowd the pot, drop the gnocchi into the boiling water. As soon as they have all risen to the surface, about 2 minutes (about 3 minutes, if frozen), reduce heat to medium-high and simmer briskly 1 minute, or until cooked through the center; remove with a slotted spoon and transfer to a shallow holding dish with a lid. Toss the cooked gnocchi gently with a little oil or butter (or pasta sauce or pesto) to keep them from sticking together; cover while you cook the remaining gnocchi. When all gnocchi are cooked, toss gently with pasta sauce or pesto, or use as otherwise directed in the recipe. For best results, serve at once.

PER SERVING (about 12 gnocchi, or ¼ of recipe, without extra oil, butter, or sauce, etc.): Calories 269; Protein 16g; Total Fat 13g; Sat Fat 8g; Cholesterol 94mg; Carbohydrate 21g; Dietary Fiber 1g; Sodium 436mg

Spinach–Sunflower Seed Pesto

(VEGAN/LOW-CARB)

This engaging pesto is also tasty tossed with gluten-free pastas, zucchini "noodles," strands of "spaghetti" squash, or as a topping for grilled eggplant, Portobello mushrooms, and broiled tomatoes. If unsalted sunflower seeds are used, double the amount of coarse salt.

MAKES ABOUT ¾ CUP

3 cups fresh baby spinach leaves
1 cup packed fresh basil leaves
3 tablespoons shelled roasted sunflower seeds, preferably salted
3 tablespoons extra-virgin olive oil
1 tablespoon fresh lemon juice, or to taste
3 large cloves garlic, finely chopped
¼ teaspoon coarse salt, or to taste
Freshly ground black pepper, to taste

In a food processor fitted with the knife blade, process all ingredients until smooth. Serve at room temperature. Mixture can be refrigerated, covered, up to 3 days before using.

PER SERVING (about 1 tablespoon, or ¹⁄₁₂ of recipe): Calories 51; Protein 1g; Total Fat 5g; Sat Fat 1g; Cholesterol 0mg; Carbohydrate 2g; Dietary Fiber 1g; Sodium 51mg

Roman-Style Polenta Gnocchi

(EGG-FREE)

In a pinch, use 1 (26-ounce) jar of gluten-free tomato-basil pasta sauce in lieu of the crushed tomatoes; reduce the oregano, salt, and simmering time by half.

MAKES 4 SERVINGS

1 (16-ounce) tube polenta, sliced into ½-inch-thick half-rounds
1 tablespoon extra-virgin olive oil
1 large clove garlic, finely chopped
1 (28-ounce) can crushed tomatoes
½ teaspoon dried oregano
¼ teaspoon salt, or to taste
¼ cup chopped fresh basil, plus additional for garnish
4 ounces fresh mozzarella, drained, coarsely chopped
½ cup gluten-free freshly grated Parmesan cheese

Preheat oven to 400F (205C). Lightly oil an 11 × 7-inch baking dish. Arrange the polenta slices in a single layer and set aside.

In a medium saucepan, heat the oil over medium-low heat. Add the garlic and cook, stirring often, until fragrant and softened, 2 to 3 minutes. Add the tomatoes, oregano, and salt; bring to a boil over medium-high heat. Reduce the heat and simmer gently, uncovered, until mixture is thickened, about 10 minutes, stirring occasionally. Stir in the basil and remove from heat. Spoon evenly over the polenta and top evenly with the mozzarella cheese. Bake about 20 minutes, or until hot and bubbly, sprinkling evenly with the Parmesan cheese the last 5 minutes or so of cooking. Garnish with fresh basil and serve warm.

PER SERVING: Calories 271; Protein 13g; Total Fat 14g; Sat Fat 7g; Cholesterol 33mg; Carbohydrate 25g; Dietary Fiber 2g; Sodium 843mg

Grain-Free Sweet Potato Gnocchi

(DAIRY-FREE)

Consisting primarily of almond and tapioca starch flour, these protein-packed, chewy dumplings partner nicely with marinara or pesto sauce.

MAKES 6 SERVINGS (ABOUT 6 DOZEN GNOCCHI)

1 large sweet potato
  (about 10 ounces), unpeeled and
  cut into chunks
½ teaspoon salt
Freshly ground black pepper,
  to taste
2½ cups almond flour or meal
1 cup tapioca starch flour
1 large egg
¼ teaspoon xanthan gum
Olive oil or butter (optional)
About 3 cups gluten-free pasta sauce,
  heated, or 6 tablespoons
  gluten-free pesto (or to taste),
  to serve (optional)
Freshly shredded gluten-free Parmesan
  cheese, to serve (optional)

In a small saucepan, bring the potato and enough salted water to cover to a boil over high heat. Reduce the heat slightly and cook until the potato is very tender, 15 to 20 minutes. Drain well; when cool enough to handle, remove skins. Transfer to a 2-cup glass measuring cup and mash well. You will need on average between 1⅛ and 1¼ cups; remove any excess and save for another use. Transfer the remaining mashed sweet potatoes to a large mixing bowl and add the salt and pepper; mash well with a fork to remove any lumps and set aside to cool to room temperature.

Meanwhile, in a small bowl, whisk together the flours until thoroughly blended; set aside.

Add the egg and xanthan gum to the cooled mashed potatoes; mash well, then stir with a spoon to thoroughly combine. Gradually add the flour mixture by the ½ cup, mixing well after each addition. Using your fingers, knead in the bowl until a smooth dough forms. Mold dough into a ball and place on a flat work surface lightly dusted with almond or tapioca flour.

Divide the dough ball into 6 equal balls. Roll each dough ball into a 6-inch-long cylinder about 1 inch in diameter. Cut each cylinder crosswise into ½-inch-thick pieces (for about 6 dozen pieces total). Press each piece gently against the inside curve of a fork and gently roll so that the decorative rib marks appear on the dough. Or flatten each piece gently with your thumb into an indented disk. Alternatively, shape each piece into an oval. (At this point, gnocchi can be held at room temperature up to 1 hour, or covered and refrigerated up to 24 hours before continuing with the recipe. Alternatively, gnocchi can be frozen individually on the covered baking sheet for 2 hours, then placed in resealable freezer bags up to 3 months.)

Bring a large stockpot of salted water to a boil over high heat. Working in batches so as not to crowd the pot, drop the gnocchi into the boiling water. As soon as they have all risen to the surface, about 2 minutes (longer, if frozen), reduce heat to medium-high and simmer briskly 3 minutes, or until cooked through the center; remove with a slotted spoon and transfer to a holding dish with a lid. Toss the cooked gnocchi gently with a little oil or butter (or pasta sauce or pesto) to keep them from sticking together, as necessary; cover while you cook the remaining gnocchi. When all gnocchi are cooked, toss gently with pasta sauce or pesto, or use as otherwise directed in the recipe. For best results, serve at once, with the Parmesan, if using, passed separately.

PER SERVING (without oil, butter, sauce, etc.): Calories 378; Protein 25g; Total Fat 12g; Sat Fat 1g; Cholesterol 35mg; Carbohydrate 48g; Dietary Fiber 2g; Sodium 200mg

RISOTTO AND OTHER RICE DISHES

Artichoke and Spinach Risotto

(VEGAN)

Artichokes and spinach are a popular duo in Italy—in this creamy risotto, they shine.

MAKES 4 TO 6 SERVINGS

4 cups low-sodium vegetable broth, plus additional, as necessary

1 cup water

2 tablespoons extra-virgin olive oil

¼ cup finely chopped onion

1½ cups white Arborio rice

½ cup dry white wine

4 ounces baby spinach, finely chopped, divided

½ cup chopped and drained artichoke hearts in brine

Salt and freshly ground black pepper, to taste

¼ to ½ cup gluten-free freshly grated Parmesan cheese (optional)

¼ cup chopped fresh basil leaves

Bring the broth and water to a simmer in a large pot. In a large deep-sided nonstick skillet, heat the oil over medium heat. Add the onion and cook, stirring, until softened but not browned, about 2 to 3 minutes. Add the rice and cook, stirring, 2 minutes.

Add the wine and cook, stirring constantly, until almost all the wine has been absorbed. Add ½ cup of the simmering broth and 2 ounces spinach; cook, stirring constantly, until almost all the liquid has been absorbed. Continue adding the simmering broth by the ½ cup, cooking and stirring after each addition until it is almost completely absorbed and the rice begins to soften, about 15 minutes after the first addition of broth. Add the artichokes, remaining spinach, salt, pepper, and another ½ cup of broth, stirring constantly until almost all the liquid has been absorbed. Add remaining broth by ½ cup as needed, continuing to stir constantly until the mixture is creamy, the rice is tender yet firm to the bite, and almost all the liquid has been absorbed. Remove from the heat and stir in the Parmesan, if using, and basil. Serve at once.

PER SERVING: Calories 400; Protein 18g; Total Fat 7g; Sat Fat 1g; Cholesterol 0mg; Carbohydrate 62g; Dietary Fiber 5g; Sodium 574mg

One-Pot Risotto with Assorted Vegetables

(VEGAN)

My go-to risotto for company, this easy one-pot wonder dispenses with the continual stirring of conventional recipes. Feel free to substitute the suggested vegetables with your favorites.

MAKES 6 SERVINGS

2 tablespoons extra-virgin olive oil

1 cup finely chopped onion

1½ cups white Arborio rice

½ cup dry white wine

4½ cups low-sodium broth

2 cups fresh or frozen broccoli florets, thawed

2 cups fresh cubed butternut squash or 1 (10-ounce) package frozen cooked winter squash, thawed

1 cup fresh or frozen peas, thawed

1 cup chopped yellow summer squash

1 cup chopped zucchini

½ teaspoon salt

Freshly ground black pepper, to taste

¼ cup chopped fresh basil or flat-leaf parsley

¼ to ½ cup freshly shredded gluten-free Parmesan cheese (optional)

In a medium stockpot, heat the oil over medium heat. Add the onion and cook, stirring, until softened but not browned, about 2 minutes. Add the rice and cook, stirring, 2 minutes.

Add the wine and cook, stirring constantly, until almost all the wine has been absorbed, about 2 minutes. Stir in the remaining ingredients except the basil and cheese, if using; bring to a boil over high heat. Reduce heat to between low and medium-low, cover, and simmer without stirring for 25 minutes, or until rice is tender yet firm to the bite. If mixture is too soupy, cook, uncovered, stirring often, until desired consistency. Stir in the basil and cheese, if using. Remove pot from heat and let stand, covered, 10 minutes. Stir and serve at once.

PER SERVING: Calories 352; Protein 17g; Total Fat 5g; Sat Fat 1g; Cholesterol 0mg; Carbohydrate 58g; Dietary Fiber 8g; Sodium 588mg

Microwave Cabbage Risotto with Basil

(VEGAN)

The marriage of cabbage and basil is an unexpectedly flavorful one in this quick and easy microwave risotto. Based on a 1,000-watt microwave, the following recipe's cooking time may be adjusted as necessary.

MAKES 4 SERVINGS

¼ cup canola oil

¼ cup finely chopped onion

1 cup white Arborio rice

2¾ cups plus 2 tablespoons low-sodium vegetable broth, plus additional, as necessary

1¼ cups shredded coleslaw mix

4 tablespoons chopped fresh basil, divided

1 tablespoon chopped fresh flat-leaf parsley

¼ teaspoon salt, or to taste

Freshly ground black pepper, to taste

¼ cup freshly grated gluten-free Parmesan cheese (optional)

In a 2½-quart baking dish with a lid, combine the oil and onion. Microwave, covered, on high 3 minutes. Remove cover (and continue next cooking steps uncovered). Add rice and stir well to coat; microwave on high 2 minutes. Stir in broth and microwave on high 9 minutes. Add coleslaw mix, 2 tablespoons basil, parsley, salt, and pepper and stir well to combine. Microwave on high 9 minutes, or until rice is cooked al dente and most of the liquids have been absorbed. If rice is not al dente but the liquid has been absorbed, cook on high in additional 1-minute increments and add broth by the tablespoonful. Stir in cheese, if using, and remaining 2 tablespoons basil. Serve at once.

PER SERVING: Calories 333; Protein 12g; Total Fat 14g; Sat Fat 1g; Cholesterol 0mg; Carbohydrate 40g; Dietary Fiber 3g; Sodium 652mg

Black and White Risotto with Tuscan Kale and Cannellini Beans

(VEGAN)

"Black" Tuscan kale and "white" cannellini beans star in this creamy risotto, which can also be prepared with success using standard green kale and any white bean.

MAKES 4 TO 6 SERVINGS

- 4 cups low-sodium vegetable broth, plus additional, as necessary
- 1 cup water
- 2 tablespoons extra-virgin olive oil
- ¼ cup finely chopped onion
- 1½ cups white Arborio rice
- 1 teaspoon dried rosemary
- ½ cup dry white wine
- 4 ounces Tuscan kale, green kale, or collard greens, washed and stemmed, thick ribs removed, and cut crosswise into thin ribbons
- 1 cup rinsed and drained canned cannellini beans, or other white beans
- Salt and freshly ground black pepper, to taste
- ¼ to ½ cup gluten-free freshly grated Parmesan cheese (optional)

Bring the broth and water to a simmer in a large pot. In a large deep-sided nonstick skillet, heat the oil over medium heat. Add the onion and cook, stirring, until softened but not browned, about 2 to 3 minutes. Add the rice and rosemary and cook, stirring, 2 minutes.

Add the wine and cook, stirring constantly, until almost all the wine has been absorbed. Add the kale and cook, stirring, until wilted. Continue to cook, stirring constantly, until rice has absorbed almost all of the released liquids. Add ½ cup of the simmering broth and cook, stirring constantly, until almost all the liquid has been absorbed. Continue adding the simmering broth by the ½ cup, cooking and stirring after each addition until it is almost completely absorbed and the rice begins to soften, about 15 minutes after the first addition of broth. Add the beans, salt, pepper, and another ½ cup of broth, stirring constantly until almost all the liquid has been absorbed. Add remaining broth by ½ cup as needed, continuing to stir constantly until the mixture is creamy, the rice is tender yet firm to the bite, and almost all the liquid has been absorbed. Remove from the heat and stir in the Parmesan, if using. Serve at once.

PER SERVING: Calories 460; Protein 22g; Total Fat 7g; Sat Fat 1g; Cholesterol 0mg; Carbohydrate 72g; Dietary Fiber 8g; Sodium 547mg

Baked Risotto with Peas, Roasted Red Pepper, and Mushrooms

(VEGAN)

This tasty risotto is creamy without the cheese—if you opt to include it, use half the amount of salt called for in the recipe.

MAKES 4 SERVINGS

2 tablespoons extra-virgin olive oil

8 ounces medium button mushrooms, stemmed and quartered

2 tablespoons finely chopped onion

1 teaspoon dried whole rosemary leaves

2 cloves garlic, finely chopped

1 cup uncooked white Arborio rice

2 cups low-sodium vegetable broth, plus additional, if necessary

¼ cup dry white wine, water, or additional broth

½ teaspoon salt, or to taste

Freshly ground black pepper, to taste

1½ cups frozen green peas, thawed

1 (7-ounce) jar roasted red bell peppers, drained, cut into strips

½ to 1 cup freshly grated gluten-free Parmesan cheese (optional)

Preheat oven to 400F (205C). Lightly oil a 2½-quart baking dish with a lid and set aside.

In a large nonstick skillet, heat oil over medium heat. Add mushrooms, onion, and rosemary and cook, stirring often, until mushrooms begin to soften, about 4 minutes. Add the garlic and cook, stirring constantly, 1 minute. Add rice and cook, stirring constantly, 2 minutes. Add broth, wine, salt, and black pepper; bring to a boil over medium-high heat. Quickly remove from heat and immediately pour into prepared baking dish. Cover and bake 15 minutes. Stir in the peas and bell pepper; cover and bake an additional 10 minutes. Uncover and stir, adding the cheese, if using. Cover and cook an additional 5 to 10 minutes, or until the liquids are absorbed and the rice is cooked al dente. If rice is cooked but liquids remain, cook, uncovered, 5 minutes. Alternatively, if rice is undercooked but no liquids remain, add an additional ¼ cup of broth or water and cook, covered, an additional 5 min-

utes. Remove from the oven and stir gently. Serve at once.

PER SERVING: Calories 335; Protein 14g; Total Fat 7g; Sat Fat 1g; Cholesterol 0mg; Carbohydrate 52g; Dietary Fiber 6g; Sodium 598mg

Quick-Cooking Brown Rice Risotto with Peas and Artichokes

(VEGAN)

Though it requires the same amount of stirring as traditional risotto made with white Arborio rice, this whole-grain recipe made with quick-cooking brown rice is more healthful and equally delicious. Use it as a model to showcase your favorite vegetables.

MAKES 5 TO 6 SERVINGS

2 tablespoons extra-virgin olive oil

¼ cup finely chopped onion

2 cups quick-cooking brown rice

2 cloves garlic, finely chopped

⅔ cup dry white wine (or low-sodium vegetable broth)

½ teaspoon dried thyme leaves

¼ teaspoon salt, or to taste

6 cups low-sodium vegetable broth, heated to a simmer

1 cup frozen peas, thawed

1 (4-ounce) jar marinated artichoke hearts, drained and sliced

Freshly ground black pepper, to taste

½ cup freshly shredded gluten-free Parmesan cheese (optional)

In a large, deep-sided nonstick skillet, heat the oil over medium heat. Add the onion and cook, stirring, until softened but not browned, 2 to 3 minutes. Add the rice and garlic and cook, stirring, 2 minutes.

Add the wine, thyme, and salt; cook, stirring constantly, until almost all the wine has been absorbed. Add ½ cup of broth and cook, stirring constantly, until almost all the liquid has been absorbed. Continue adding the broth by the ½ cup, cooking and stirring after each addition until it is almost completely absorbed. When 1 cup of broth remains, add the peas, artichokes, pepper, and ½ cup broth; cook, stirring constantly, until almost all the liquid has been absorbed. Add the remaining ½ cup broth and cook, stirring, until mixture is creamy and slightly soupy. Remove from heat and let stand, covered, 5 minutes. Add the Parmesan, if using, stirring well to combine. Serve at once.

PER SERVING: Calories 312; Protein 19g; Total Fat 6g; Sat Fat 1g; Cholesterol 0mg; Carbohydrate 42g; Dietary Fiber 7g; Sodium 786mg

Brown Arborio Rice Risotto with Fresh Pumpkin and Sage

(VEGAN)

This lovely and fragrant risotto is ideal to serve in the fall, when winter squash is readily available. Precooking the rice makes for easy entertaining. If possible, use a Sugar Pie or other cooking variety of pumpkin—fresh cubed butternut squash can easily be substituted.

MAKES 4 SERVINGS

1 cup brown Arborio or other short- to medium-grain brown rice

2 tablespoons extra-virgin olive oil

¼ cup finely chopped onion

1 large clove garlic, finely chopped

3 cups peeled and cubed pumpkin (20 ounces)

2 tablespoons chopped fresh sage leaves

¼ teaspoon salt, or to taste

½ cup dry white wine or low-sodium vegetable broth

4 cups low-sodium vegetable broth, heated to simmering, plus additional broth or water, as necessary

½ cup freshly shredded gluten-free Parmesan cheese (optional)

½ cup chopped fresh flat-leaf parsley

Freshly ground black pepper, to taste

Bring a medium stockpot filled two-thirds full with salted water to a boil; add the rice and cook, pasta style, until tender halfway through, about 10 to 15 minutes. Drain well and set briefly aside. (At this point, mixture can be held at room temperature 1 hour, or covered and refrigerated up to 24 hours before continuing with the recipe.)

In a large, deep-sided nonstick skillet, heat the oil over medium heat. Add the onion and cook, stirring, until softened but not browned, 2 to 3 minutes. Add the drained rice and garlic and cook, stirring, 2 minutes. Stir in the pumpkin, sage, and salt, then add the wine; cook, stirring constantly, until almost all the wine has been absorbed.

Add ½ cup of the simmering broth to the rice mixture; cook, stirring constantly, until almost all the liquid has been absorbed. Continue adding the broth by the ½ cup, cooking and stirring after each addition until it is almost completely absorbed. When the rice is tender yet firm to the bite and the mixture is creamy (typically after 4 cups total broth has been added), remove from the heat and stir in the Parmesan, if using, parsley, and pepper. Serve at once.

PER SERVING: Calories 346; Protein 17g; Total Fat 8g; Sat Fat 1g; Cholesterol 0mg; Carbohydrate 49g; Dietary Fiber 7g; Sodium 660mg

Variation

To make Butternut Squash Risotto with Sage, substitute white Arborio rice for the short-grain variety and do not pre-boil; substitute fresh butternut squash for the pumpkin. Proceed as otherwise directed in the recipe.

Red Wine Risotto with Radicchio, Peas, and Pearl Onions

(VEGAN)

A full-bodied red wine, preferably Barolo, is recommended for the success of this pretty risotto. Red Belgian endive can replace the radicchio, if desired.

MAKES 5 TO 6 SERVINGS

4 cups low-sodium vegetable broth, plus
  additional, as necessary
1 cup water
2 tablespoons extra-virgin olive oil
¼ cup finely chopped onion
1½ cups white Arborio rice
1 teaspoon dried thyme
½ cup full-flavored red wine, such as a
  Barolo
1 medium head radicchio (about 6 ounces),
  chopped

1½ cups frozen peas and pearl onions,
  thawed
½ teaspoon salt, or to taste
Freshly ground black pepper, to taste
¼ to ½ cup freshly grated gluten-free
  Parmesan cheese (optional)

Bring the broth and water to a simmer in a large pot. In a large deep-sided nonstick skillet, heat the oil over medium heat. Add the onion and cook, stirring, until softened but not browned, about 2 to 3 minutes. Add the rice and thyme; cook, stirring, 2 minutes.

Add the wine and cook, stirring constantly, until almost all the wine has been absorbed. Add ½ cup of the simmering broth and cook, stirring constantly, until almost all the liquid has been absorbed. Continue adding the simmering broth by the ½ cup, cooking and stirring after each addition until broth is almost completely absorbed and the rice begins to soften, about 15 minutes after the first addition of broth. Add radicchio, peas and pearl onions, salt, pepper, and another ½ cup of broth, stirring constantly until almost all the liquid has been absorbed. Add remaining broth by the ½ cup as needed, continuing to stir constantly until the mixture is creamy, the rice is tender yet firm to the bite, and almost all the liquid has been absorbed. Remove from the heat and stir in the Parmesan, if using. Serve at once.

PER SERVING: Calories 342; Protein 15g; Total Fat 6g; Sat Fat 1g; Cholesterol 0mg; Carbohydrate 53g; Dietary Fiber 4g; Sodium 693mg

Sun-Dried Tomato and Pesto Risotto

(VEGAN)

Leftovers of this flavorful risotto make an excellent stuffing for bell peppers (see Stuffed Peppers with Sun-Dried Tomato and Pesto Risotto, page 153).

MAKES 4 TO 6 SERVINGS

   4 cups low-sodium vegetable broth, plus
      additional, as necessary
   1 cup water
   2 tablespoons extra-virgin olive oil
   ¼ cup finely chopped onion
   1½ cups white Arborio rice
   ½ cup dry white wine
   ½ cup drained and chopped marinated sun-
      dried tomatoes
   Salt and freshly ground black pepper, to taste
   3 to 4 tablespoons Rustic Pesto Sauce, page
      92, Classic Basil Pesto Sauce, page 97, or
      prepared gluten-free pesto
   ¼ to ½ cup freshly grated gluten-free
      Parmesan cheese (optional)
   ¼ to ½ cup chopped fresh basil leaves
      (optional)

Bring the broth and water to a simmer in a large pot. In a large deep-sided nonstick skillet, heat the oil over medium heat. Add the onion and cook, stirring, until softened but not browned, about 2 to 3 minutes. Add the rice and cook, stirring, 2 minutes.

Add the wine and cook, stirring constantly, until almost all the wine has been absorbed. Add ½ cup of the simmering broth and cook, stirring constantly, until almost all the liquid has been absorbed. Continue adding the simmering broth by the ½ cup, cooking and stirring after each addition until liquid is almost completely absorbed and the rice begins to soften, about 15 minutes after the first addition of broth. Add the sun-dried tomatoes, salt, pepper, and another ½ cup of broth, stirring constantly until almost all the liquid has been absorbed. Add remaining broth by ½ cup as needed, continuing to stir constantly until the mixture is creamy, the rice is tender yet firm to the bite, and almost all the liquid has been absorbed. Remove from the heat and stir in the pesto, Parmesan, if using, and basil, if using. Serve at once.

PER SERVING: Calories 472; Protein 18g; Total Fat 14g; Sat Fat 2g; Cholesterol 0mg; Carbohydrate 64g; Dietary Fiber 4g; Sodium 734mg

Risotto Croquettes with Marinara

(LACTO-OVO)

Serve these amazing croquettes atop heated marinara sauce and accompanied with a tossed green salad, for a simple yet elegant supper. For easy entertaining, the croquettes can be assembled a day ahead of sautéing and serving.

MAKES 8 CROQUETTES

   ½ tablespoon canola oil
   3 scallions, white and green parts separated,
      thinly sliced
   1 cup uncooked white Arborio rice
   1½ cups low-sodium vegetable broth
   ¾ cups water
   ¼ teaspoon salt
   Freshly ground black pepper
   1 tablespoon finely chopped fresh basil or
      flat-leaf parsley
   ½ cup gluten-free shredded mozzarella
      cheese

¼ cup gluten-free freshly grated Parmesan
   cheese

1 egg plus 2 egg whites, divided

1 to 1½ cups gluten-free Italian seasoned dry
   bread crumbs

2 tablespoons extra-virgin olive oil

About 2 cups gluten-free marinara sauce,
   heated (optional)

Shredded fresh basil leaves, for garnish
   (optional)

In a medium saucepan, heat the canola oil over medium heat. Add the white parts of the scallions and cook, stirring, until softened and fragrant, 1 to 2 minutes. Add the rice and cook, stirring, 1 minute. Add the broth, water, salt, and pepper and bring to a boil over high heat. Reduce the heat to between low and medium-low, cover, and simmer about 15 minutes, or until rice is tender yet firm to the bite. If liquids remain, cook uncovered, stirring, until liquids evaporate. Stir in the basil and scallion greens; let rice mixture cool in the pan. When cooled, add the mozzarella, Parmesan, and egg whites, stirring well to thoroughly combine.

Line a baking sheet or tray with wax paper. Whisk the remaining whole egg in a small wide bowl and place the bread crumbs on a deep-welled plate. Shape the rice-egg white mixture into 8 ovals (about ½ cup each). Dip each oval into the egg mixture, turning to coat all sides, letting excess run off back into the bowl. Gently roll each egg-coated oval into the bread crumbs. Transfer each croquette to the prepared baking sheet. Cover with plastic wrap and refrigerate a minimum of 1 hour, or up to 1 day.

In a large nonstick skillet, heat the olive oil over medium heat. Add the croquettes and cook, gently turning to brown on all sides, about 7 to 10 minutes. Serve at once, with the heated marinara, if using, and garnished with some shredded basil, if using.

PER SERVING (per croquette, or ⅛ of recipe): Calories 238; Protein 11g; Total Fat 8g; Sat Fat 3g; Cholesterol 36mg; Carbohydrate 30g; Dietary Fiber 1g; Sodium 676mg

Cremini Mushroom and Brown Rice Timbales

(EGG-FREE)

Cooking brown rice pasta style makes quick work of these molded delights, which are ideal for company, as the timbales can be held in a warm oven (about 200F/95C) up to 1 hour before inverting and serving. Cultivated white mushrooms can replace all or part of the cremini variety, if desired.

MAKES 4 SERVINGS

¾ cup uncooked long-grain brown rice

1 tablespoon extra-virgin olive oil

½ cup chopped onion

8 ounces sliced fresh cremini mushrooms

1 teaspoon dried thyme

¼ teaspoon salt, or to taste

1 to 2 cloves garlic, finely chopped

1 tablespoon Marsala wine or dry sherry

¼ cup (1 ounce) freshly shredded gluten-free
   Parmesan cheese

Freshly ground black pepper, to taste

2 cups gluten-free prepared pasta sauce or
   marinara sauce, heated

Fresh thyme sprigs, for garnish (optional)

Bring a medium stockpot filled with salted water to a boil. Add the rice and cook, pasta style, until al dente, 20 to 25 minutes. Transfer to a colander and drain. Lightly oil 4 (6-ounce) ramekins or custard cups and set aside.

Meanwhile, in a large nonstick skillet, heat the oil over medium heat. Add the onion and cook, stirring, until softened, about 3 minutes. Add the mushrooms, dried thyme, and salt; cook, stirring, until mushrooms release their liquids, about 5 minutes. Add the garlic and cook, stirring constantly, 30 seconds. Add the Marsala and cook, stirring constantly, until all of the liquids have evaporated. Add the cooked rice and toss well to combine. Remove skillet from heat and stir in the cheese and pepper. Transfer equal amounts of the rice-mushroom mixture (about ¾ cup unpacked) to the prepared ramekins; tightly pack, pressing down with your palm. (At this point, timbales can be covered and held in a warm (200F/95C) oven up to 1 hour before continuing with the recipe.) Ladle ½ cup heated sauce onto each of 4 serving plates. Invert a ramekin onto each plate and serve at once, garnished with the fresh thyme sprigs, if using.

PER SERVING: Calories 342; Protein 8g; Total Fat 12g; Sat Fat 2g; Cholesterol 4mg; Carbohydrate 52g; Dietary Fiber 6g; Sodium 840mg

Baked Tomatoes Stuffed with Arborio Rice and Basil

(VEGAN)

This is an excellent buffet dish, as the baked stuffed tomatoes are delicious at room temperature. Unlike the long-grain variety, Arborio rice retains its softness as it cools. Serve on a bed of fresh or slightly wilted baby spinach for a pretty presentation.

MAKES 4 GENEROUS OR 8 SMALL MAIN-DISH SERVINGS

8 large ripe yet firm tomatoes (8 to 10 ounces each)

Table salt

1 cup white or brown Arborio rice

4 tablespoons plus 4 teaspoons extra-virgin olive oil, divided

½ cup chopped fresh basil leaves

3 large cloves garlic, finely chopped

Salt, preferably the coarse variety, and freshly ground black pepper, to taste

Fresh basil leaves, for garnish (optional)

Cut a ½-inch-thick slice from the top of each tomato and reserve. Gently squeeze out the seeds from each tomato. Using a small, sharp knife or a melon baller, scoop out the pulp and reserve, discarding any white core. Lightly salt the inside of each tomato shell. Turn the shells upside down on several layers of paper towels and drain 30 minutes.

Meanwhile, preheat oven to 350F (175C). Lightly oil a shallow baking dish just large enough to comfortably hold the tomatoes in a single layer. Set aside.

Bring a medium stockpot filled two-thirds full with salted water to a boil over high heat. Add the rice and cook, pasta style, until just al dente, about 12 minutes for white Arborio and 20 minutes for brown Arborio. Drain well.

Chop the reserved tomato pulp and place in a medium bowl. Add the rice, 4 tablespoons of oil, chopped basil, garlic, salt, and pepper; stir well to combine. Fill the tomatoes evenly with the rice mixture (do not pack down). Cover with the reserved tops. Arrange upright in the prepared dish. Brush ½ teaspoon of the remaining oil over the tops and sides of each tomato. Bake, uncovered, 25 minutes. Remove the lids and bake 5 to 10 more minutes, or until the tomatoes are soft but not falling apart and the tops are lightly browned.

Let the tomatoes cool slightly and serve warm or at room temperature, garnished with the basil leaves, if using.

PER SERVING (per stuffed tomato): Calories 210; Protein 4g; Total Fat 10g; Sat Fat 1g; Cholesterol 0mg; Carbohydrate 29g; Dietary Fiber 2g; Sodium 23mg

POLENTA DISHES

Roasted Asparagus, Mushrooms, and Chickpeas over Creamy Parmesan Polenta

(EGG-FREE)

Tender asparagus, succulent mushrooms, and crispy chickpeas are a delightful contrast to their bed of creamy Parmesan polenta in this hearty main dish. For optimal timing, instant polenta is recommended.

MAKES 4 TO 6 SERVINGS

- 1½ pounds medium-thick asparagus, tough ends trimmed
- ½ pound medium cremini or cultivated white mushrooms, stemmed and quartered
- 1 (15-ounce) can chickpeas, rinsed and drained
- 3½ tablespoons extra-virgin olive oil, divided
- 1 tablespoon dried rosemary leaves
- Salt, preferably the coarse variety, and freshly ground black pepper, to taste
- 2 tablespoons balsamic vinegar
- 2 cups low-sodium vegetable broth
- 1 cup water
- ¾ cup quick-cooking polenta
- ¾ cup (3 ounces) gluten-free freshly shredded Parmesan cheese
- Fresh rosemary sprigs, for garnish (optional)

Preheat oven to 425F (220C). In a nonstick rimmed baking sheet, toss the asparagus, mushrooms, and chickpeas with 2½ tablespoons of the oil. Sprinkle with the rosemary, coarse salt, and pepper and toss again. Spread in a single layer and roast for 12 to 15 minutes, or until asparagus and mushrooms are browned and tender, and chickpeas are slightly crispy, stirring and turning the vegetables and chickpeas once or twice. Remove the baking sheet from the oven; turn off the oven. Drizzle the roasted vegetables and chickpeas with the vinegar; toss gently to combine. Cover with foil and place on the bottom rack of the oven to keep warm while you make the polenta.

In a medium stockpot, bring the broth, water, polenta, remaining 1 tablespoon of oil, salt, and pepper to a boil over high heat. Reduce the heat to medium and cook, stirring constantly with a long-handled wooden spoon (polenta will sputter), until the mixture is the consistency of porridge, about 5 minutes. Remove from the heat and immediately add the cheese, stirring well to thoroughly incorporate. Let stand, uncovered, about 5 minutes, stirring occasionally, until mixture is the consistency of mashed potatoes.

To serve, quickly spoon equal portions of the polenta mixture into the centers of 4 to 6 deep-welled serving plates or shallow bowls. Arrange equal portions of roasted asparagus around the polenta, and then spoon equal portions of mushrooms and chickpeas over top. Drizzle equally with any remaining accumulated juices. Garnish with fresh rosemary sprigs, if using, and serve at once.

PER SERVING: Calories 447; Protein 23g; Total Fat 20g; Sat Fat 5g; Cholesterol 15mg; Carbohydrate 46g; Dietary Fiber 7g; Sodium 617mg

Caramelized Cabbage and Red Bean–Polenta Pie

(VEGAN)

Cabbage and red kidney beans are a dependable duo during the cold winter months in northern Italian country kitchens. Caramelized, with a touch of balsamic vinegar, the lowly green crucifer transforms an otherwise humble polenta-bean pie into food fit for kings.

MAKES 6 SERVINGS

  3 tablespoons extra-virgin olive oil, divided

  3 cups low-sodium vegetable broth

  4 cloves garlic, finely chopped, divided

  2 teaspoons dried rosemary, divided

  ¼ teaspoon fennel seeds, crushed

  2 to 2¼ pounds green cabbage, outer leaves discarded, washed, quartered, cored, and shredded

  1 teaspoon salt, divided, plus additional, to taste

  Freshly ground black pepper, to taste

  ½ to 1½ teaspoons balsamic vinegar, or to taste

  1¼ cups water, plus additional, as necessary

  1 cup polenta or coarse-ground yellow cornmeal

  1 (15-ounce) can red kidney beans, rinsed and drained

  ½ cup freshly grated gluten-free Asiago, Pecorino Romano, or Parmesan cheese (optional)

In a large stockpot, heat 2 tablespoons of the oil over medium heat. Reserve 2 cups of the broth and set aside; keep the remaining 1 cup nearby. Add 2 cloves garlic, 1 teaspoon rosemary, and the crushed fennel to the heated pot; cook, stirring constantly, 1 minute, or until fragrant. Add the cabbage, ¼ cup broth, ½ teaspoon salt, and pepper, tossing well to combine. Cover and cook about 1 hour, stirring from the bottom every 5 minutes or so, and adding broth by the tablespoons from the remaining ¾ cup to prevent sticking and drying out (if all the broth has been used, add water, as necessary). When finished, cabbage should be medium-brown and very tender. Remove from heat and stir in ½ teaspoon vinegar, adding more by the ¼ teaspoon, to taste. Season with additional salt and pepper, if necessary; cover and set aside until needed.

Preheat oven to 350F (175C). Lightly oil a 9 or 10-inch pie plate or quiche dish and set aside.

In a medium stockpot, bring the reserved 2 cups of broth and water to a boil over high heat. Slowly add the polenta, stirring constantly with a long-handled wooden spoon (mixture will sputter). Reduce the heat to low and add the beans, remaining 1 tablespoon oil, remaining 2 cloves of garlic, remaining 1 teaspoon rosemary, remaining ½ teaspoon salt, and pepper, stirring well to combine. Cover and cook, stirring occasionally, until polenta is tender, about 15 minutes. Remove from heat and let stand, covered, 5 minutes.

Immediately spread the polenta mixture evenly in the prepared pie plate, pressing down with the back of a large spoon to form a smooth surface. Spoon the caramelized cabbage mixture on top, leaving a ½-inch border on polenta. Cover loosely with foil and bake for 10 minutes. Uncover and sprinkle evenly with the cheese, if using. Bake an additional 5 minutes, or until cheese is melted and all is heated through. Serve warm.

PER SERVING: Calories 281; Protein 14g; Total Fat 8g; Sat Fat 1g; Cholesterol 0mg; Carbohydrate 41g; Dietary Fiber 10g; Sodium 643mg

Roman Beans with Polenta

(VEGAN)

This rustic and colorful casserole is incredibly easy to make and festive enough for company. Red kidney beans can replace the Roman variety, also known as cranberry or borlotti beans, if desired. I like to use Trader Joe's 18-ounce ready-cooked tube of organic polenta here.

MAKES 5 TO 6 SERVINGS

1 (26-ounce) jar gluten-free marinara sauce, preferably the tomato-basil variety

1 (18-ounce) tube polenta, cut into ½-inch-thick slices

2 tablespoons extra-virgin olive oil, divided

1 large red bell pepper (about 10 ounces), chopped

4 large cloves garlic, finely chopped

1 (15-ounce) can Roman beans, rinsed and drained

¼ cup chopped fresh basil

¼ cup chopped fresh flat-leaf parsley

Salt and freshly ground black pepper, to taste

Crushed red pepper flakes, to taste (optional)

Preheat oven to 425F (220C).

Lightly oil an 11 × 8-inch baking dish; pour in the marinara sauce. Arrange the polenta slices in a single layer on top of the sauce, without pressing down, so that the tops of the polenta slices are completely exposed. Gently brush the tops of the polenta with ½ tablespoon of oil. Bake 25 minutes, or until mixture is bubbly and polenta is lightly browned. Remove from oven and let cool slightly. (At this point, mixture can be held in a low, 225F/105C, oven up to 1 hour before continuing with the recipe.)

Meanwhile, in a large nonstick skillet, heat the remaining 1½ tablespoons oil over medium-high heat. Add the bell pepper and cook, stirring often, until softened, about 2 to 3 minutes. Reduce the heat to medium and add the garlic; cook, stirring constantly, 1 minute. Add the beans, basil, parsley, salt, black pepper, and red pepper flakes, if using; cook, stirring, until heated through, about 2 minutes. Spoon evenly over the polenta-marinara mixture and serve at once.

PER SERVING: Calories 296; Protein 9g; Total Fat 11g; Sat Fat 2g; Cholesterol 0mg; Carbohydrate 45g; Dietary Fiber 4g; Sodium 930mg

Herbed Polenta Dumplings with Broccoli-Marinara Sauce

(EGG-FREE)

These easy polenta dumplings and quick-cooking pantry marinara are both staples in my household—feel free to mix and match them with your own favorite recipes and ingredients.

MAKES 6 SERVINGS

20-Minute Marinara Sauce (page 136), heated

2 cups frozen chopped broccoli, cooked according to package directions, well drained, finely chopped

Herbed Polenta Dumplings, page 136

Freshly shredded gluten-free Parmesan cheese, to serve (optional)

In a large deep-sided skillet over medium-low heat, combine the marinara sauce and broccoli; cook, stirring, until heated through, about 3 minutes. Gently stir in the dumplings and cook, covered, 5 minutes, or until heated through, stirring occasionally. Serve at once, with the Parmesan passed separately, if using.

PER SERVING: Calories 261; Protein 12g; Total Fat 8g; Sat Fat 2g; Cholesterol 3mg; Carbohydrate 40g; Dietary Fiber 9g; Sodium 970mg

20-Minute Marinara Sauce

(VEGAN/LOW-CARB)

With these handy ingredients in your pantry, there's no excuse not to enjoy homemade marinara sauce in just about 20 minutes. The recipe yields enough sauce to coat 10 to 12 ounces of cooked gluten-free pasta.

MAKES ABOUT 2½ CUPS

1 (28-ounce) can crushed tomatoes
1½ tablespoons extra-virgin olive oil
1 teaspoon dried oregano
1 teaspoon onion powder
1 teaspoon sugar
¼ teaspoon garlic salt
Freshly ground black pepper, to taste
Cayenne red pepper, to taste
    (optional)

In a medium deep-sided skillet, bring all ingredients to a simmer over medium-high heat, stirring occasionally. Reduce the heat to between low and medium-low; simmer, uncovered, stirring occasionally, until the sauce is thickened, about 20 minutes. Use as directed in recipe.

PER SERVING (about ½ cup, or ⅕ of recipe): Calories 107; Protein 3g; Total Fat 4g; Sat Fat 1g; Cholesterol 0mg; Carbohydrate 17g; Dietary Fiber 4g; Sodium 736mg

Herbed Polenta Dumplings

(EGG-FREE)

These delectable dumplings are delicious immersed in soups and stews, or tossed with your favorite pasta sauces and pesto. Feel free to replace the Italian seasoning with your own favorites, or omit altogether, if desired.

MAKES 2 TO 2½ DOZEN DUMPLINGS

2 cups low-sodium vegetable broth
1 cup water
1 cup quick-cooking polenta or regular
    polenta (coarse-ground yellow cornmeal)
1 tablespoon canola oil
½ teaspoon Italian seasoning
¼ teaspoon garlic salt
Freshly ground black pepper, to serve
¼ cup nonfat half-and-half
¼ cup freshly grated gluten-free Parmesan
    cheese

If using quick-cooking polenta: In a medium stockpot, bring the broth, water, polenta, oil, Italian seasoning, garlic salt, and pepper to a boil over high heat. Immediately reduce the heat to medium; cook, stirring often with a long-handled wooden spoon (mixture will sputter), 5 minutes. Remove from heat and immediately stir in half-and-half and cheese. Let stand, uncovered, at room temperature about 10 minutes to firm slightly.

If using regular polenta: In a medium stockpot, bring the broth, water, oil, Italian seasoning, garlic salt, and pepper to a boil over high heat. Slowly add the polenta, stirring constantly with a long-handled wooden spoon. Reduce the heat to low and cook, covered, stirring occasionally, until tender and thickened, about 15 minutes. Remove from heat and immediately stir in the half-and-half and cheese. Let stand, covered, 5 minutes. Uncover and let stand at room temperature about 10 minutes to firm slightly.

Line a baking sheet with wax paper. Using a small melon baller or similar spoon, form the polenta mixture into balls, for a total of 2 to 2½ dozen dumplings. Use as directed in recipe, or cover and refrigerate up to 1 day.

PER SERVING (about 4 dumplings, or ⅙ of recipe): Calories 240; Protein 10g; Total Fat 7g; Sat Fat 2g; Cholesterol 3mg; Carbohydrate 35g; Dietary Fiber 7g; Sodium 870mg

Polenta Gratin with Creamy Mushroom Sauce and Fontina Cheese

(EGG-FREE)

This easy yet elegant dish can be made in two stages for stress-free entertaining.

MAKES 4 SERVINGS

1 (16-ounce) tube polenta, sliced into ½-inch-thick half-rounds

1½ tablespoons canola oil, divided

1 small onion (about 4 ounces), chopped

1 pound cremini or white mushrooms, trimmed and sliced

¼ teaspoon salt, or to taste

Freshly ground black pepper, to taste

½ cup dry white wine

2 teaspoons finely chopped fresh tarragon, or ½ teaspoon dried tarragon

½ cup gluten-free reduced-fat sour cream

1 cup gluten-free shredded Fontina cheese

Preheat oven to 425F (205C). Lightly oil an 11 × 7-inch baking dish.

Arrange the polenta slices in a single layer in the prepared baking dish. Brush the tops evenly with ½ tablespoon oil. Bake until the tops are lightly browned, about 20 minutes. Remove from oven and reduce heat to 375F (190C). (At this point, polenta can be held up to 1 hour at room temperature before continuing with the recipe.)

Meanwhile, in a large nonstick skillet, heat the remaining 1 tablespoon oil over medium-high heat. Add onion and cook, stirring often, until lightly browned, about 3 minutes. Add mushrooms and salt; cook, stirring often, until the mushrooms are browned and most of the liquid has evaporated, about 8 minutes. Add the wine and dried tarragon (if not using fresh tarragon); let come to a boil, scraping up any browned bits from the bottom of the skillet. Reduce until most of the liquids have evaporated, 2 to 3 minutes. Remove the skillet from the heat and stir in sour cream, fresh tarragon (if not using dried tarragon), and pepper. (At this point, mixture can be held, covered, up to one hour before continuing with the recipe.)

Spread the mushroom mixture evenly over the polenta in the baking dish. Sprinkle evenly with the cheese. Return the baking dish to the oven and cook until cheese is melted and bubbly, 12 to 15 minutes. Serve at once.

PER SERVING: Calories 292; Protein 12g; Total Fat 15g; Sat Fat 6g; Cholesterol 35mg; Carbohydrate 24g; Dietary Fiber 2g; Sodium 374mg

Porcini Mushroom and Tomato Ragu with White Bean Polenta

(VEGAN)

This rich mushroom and tomato ragu is also excellent tossed with gluten-free pasta. Alternatively, the white bean polenta can serve as a tasty foundation for countless toppings and sauces.

MAKES 6 SERVINGS

1 ounce dried porcini mushrooms

3 tablespoons extra-virgin olive oil, divided

1 medium onion (about 6 ounces), chopped

¼ teaspoon dried oregano

1 tablespoon chopped fresh rosemary or 1 teaspoon dried rosemary

½ tablespoon chopped fresh sage or ½ teaspoon crumbled dried sage

8 ounces sliced cremini or cultivated white mushrooms

4 large cloves garlic, finely chopped, divided

1 (14.5-ounce) can stewed tomatoes, juices included

2 tablespoons tomato paste

4 tablespoons chopped fresh flat-leaf parsley, divided

1 teaspoon salt, divided

¼ teaspoon sugar

Freshly ground black pepper, to taste

2 cups low-sodium vegetable broth

1¼ cups water

1 cup regular polenta (coarse-ground yellow cornmeal)

1 (15-ounce) can cannellini or other white beans, rinsed and drained

1 teaspoon Italian seasoning

½ cup gluten-free freshly shredded Parmesan cheese (optional)

Soak the mushrooms in 1 cup hot water for 15 minutes; drain, reserving the soaking liquid. Strain the soaking liquid through a coffee filter or paper towel–lined strainer and set aside. Rinse the mushrooms thoroughly; chop coarsely and set aside.

In a large nonstick skillet, heat 2 tablespoons of the oil over medium heat. Add the onion, oregano, and dried rosemary and dried sage (if not using fresh herbs); cook, stirring, until onion is softened, about 3 to 4 minutes. Increase the heat to medium-high; add the fresh mushrooms, reserved porcini mushrooms, and 2 cloves garlic. Cook, stirring constantly, until the mushrooms soften, 3 to 4 minutes. Stir in the reserved soaking liquid, tomatoes and their juices, tomato paste, 2 tablespoons parsley, fresh rosemary and fresh sage (if not using dried herbs), ½ teaspoon salt, sugar, and pepper. Bring to a boil, breaking up the tomatoes as necessary with a wooden spoon. Reduce the heat to medium-low and simmer, uncovered, 10 minutes, stirring occasionally, or until the juices have slightly thickened. Remove from the heat and stir in the remaining 2 tablespoons of parsley. Cover and keep warm until needed.

Preheat oven to 350F (175C). Lightly oil a 9 × 13-inch baking dish and set aside. In a medium stockpot, bring the broth and water to a boil over high heat. Slowly add the polenta, stirring constantly with a long-handled wooden spoon. Reduce the heat to low and add the beans, remaining 1 tablespoon oil, remaining 2 cloves garlic, Italian seasoning, remaining ½ teaspoon salt, and pepper, stirring well to combine. Cover and cook, stirring occasionally, until polenta is tender, about 15 minutes. Remove from heat and let stand, covered, 5 minutes.

Immediately spread the polenta mixture evenly in the prepared baking dish. Using the bottom of a small rounded bowl, make 6 evenly spaced indentations in the polenta mixture. Let stand about 5 minutes to firm. Spoon the reserved ragu into the indentations. Bake about 15 minutes, or until mixture is heated through, sprinkling with the cheese, if using, during the last 5 minutes of cooking. Cut into 6 squares and serve at once.

PER SERVING: Calories 299; Protein 13g; Total Fat 8g; Sat Fat 1g; Cholesterol 0mg; Carbohydrate 47g; Dietary Fiber 11g; Sodium 753mg

Creamy Pumpkin Polenta
(EGG-FREE)

Prepared with plain yellow cornmeal, this creamy polenta dish makes a satisfying fall supper served with a tossed spinach and mushroom salad, or a tasty Thanksgiving side dish in lieu of standard mashed potatoes.

MAKES 4 TO 5 MAIN-COURSE OR 6 TO 8 SIDE-DISH SERVINGS

3 cups low-sodium vegetable broth
2⅓ cups water
1⅓ cups yellow cornmeal
1 tablespoon extra-virgin olive oil
½ teaspoon salt

¾ cup canned pumpkin puree
½ cup gluten-free light cream cheese with chives, in chunks
Chopped chives or the green parts of scallions, for garnish (optional)

In a large stockpot, bring the broth and water to a boil over high heat. Slowly add the cornmeal, stirring constantly with a long-handled wooden spoon. Reduce the heat to low and stir in the oil and salt; cover and cook, stirring occasionally, until the polenta is tender, about 15 minutes. Stir in the pumpkin and cream cheese; cook, stirring constantly, until thoroughly incorporated and mixture is heated through, about 3 minutes. Remove from heat and let stand, covered, 5 minutes. Stir again and serve at once, sprinkled with the chopped chives, if using.

PER SERVING: Calories 341; Protein 16g; Total Fat 9g; Sat Fat 4g; Cholesterol 16mg; Carbohydrate 49g; Dietary Fiber 10g; Sodium 817mg

Sweet and Sour Root Vegetable Ragu over Herbed Polenta
(VEGAN)

Ideal for fall and winter suppers, this fragrant polenta dish is one of my favorites. Both the ragu and polenta can be prepared a day ahead of assembling and serving for easy entertaining. The tangy stewed root vegetables can be served over brown rice in lieu of the polenta, if desired. For a heartier meal, stir in 1 to 2 cups of rinsed and drained canned red kidney beans along with the apple.

MAKES 6 SERVINGS

4 cups low-sodium vegetable broth, divided

1 cup polenta or coarse-ground yellow cornmeal

3½ tablespoons extra-virgin olive oil, divided

2 large cloves garlic, finely chopped

2 teaspoons chopped fresh thyme or ½ teaspoon dried thyme

2 teaspoon chopped fresh sage or ½ teaspoon crumbled dried sage

2 teaspoon chopped fresh rosemary or ½ teaspoon dried rosemary

½ teaspoon salt, plus additional, to taste

Freshly ground black pepper, to taste

1 medium red onion (about 6 ounces), coarsely chopped

4 ounces beets (about 2 small), peeled and coarsely chopped

4 ounces carrots (about 2 small), peeled and coarsely chopped

4 ounces parsnips (about 1 large), peeled and coarsely chopped

4 cups thinly sliced red cabbage

1 large bay leaf, halved

1 medium tart apple (about 6 ounces), such as a Granny Smith, coarsely chopped

½ cup water

1 to 2 tablespoons tomato paste

1 tablespoon sugar

¼ cup cider vinegar

¼ cup balsamic vinegar

6 tablespoons gluten-free crumbled goat cheese (optional)

6 tablespoons chopped walnuts, toasted, if desired

Lightly oil 9 × 5-inch loaf pan and set aside.

In a large stockpot, bring 3½ cups of broth to a boil over high heat. Slowly add the polenta, stirring constantly with a long-handled wooden spoon. Reduce the heat to low and stir in 1 tablespoon of the oil, garlic, half the thyme (1 teaspoon fresh, or ¼ teaspoon dried), half the sage (1 teaspoon fresh, or ¼ teaspoon dried), half the rosemary (1 teaspoon fresh, or ¼ teaspoon dried), salt, and pepper. Cover and cook, stirring occasionally, until the polenta is tender, about 15 minutes. Remove from heat and let stand, covered, 5 minutes. Spread the polenta mixture along the bottom of the prepared pan. Let stand until firm, about 20 minutes. (At this point, completely cooled polenta can be refrigerated, covered, up to 1 day before continuing with the recipe.) Unmold onto an ungreased baking sheet; cut into 12 slices. Brush the tops with ½ tablespoon oil and set aside.

Meanwhile, in a large deep-sided skillet, heat the remaining 2 tablespoons of oil over medium heat. Add the onion and cook, stirring, until softened, about 3 minutes. Add the beets, carrots, parsnip, cabbage, remaining thyme, sage, and rosemary (1 teaspoon fresh, or ¼ teaspoon dried), bay leaf, salt, pepper, and remaining ½ cup broth; cook, covered, stirring occasionally, until cabbage is tender, about 10 minutes. Add the apple and water; cook, covered, stirring occasionally, until all the vegetables are tender, about 10 more minutes. Reduce the heat to low and add the tomato paste, sugar, and both vinegars; cook, stirring constantly, until thoroughly incorporated and heated through. Turn off heat, cover, and keep warm. (At this point, completely cooled ragu can be refrigerated, covered, up to 1 day before reheating over low heat and proceeding with the recipe.)

Preheat the oven to broil. Broil the polenta slices 6 to 8 inches from the heat source until lightly browned, about 5 minutes. Place 2 polenta slices on each of 6 serving plates; top evenly with the vegetable ragu and accumulated cooking juices. Sprinkle each serving with 1 tablespoon of goat cheese, if using, followed with 1 tablespoon of walnuts. Serve at once.

PER SERVING: Calories 329; Protein 14g; Total Fat 13g; Sat Fat 2g; Cholesterol 0mg; Carbohydrate 43g; Dietary Fiber 10g; Sodium 570mg

OTHER ENTRÉES

Stuffed Artichokes with Kalamata Olives and Sun-Dried Tomatoes

(VEGAN)

All the rich flavors of the Mediterranean are captured in these beautiful globe artichokes. Though time-consuming to prepare, they can be assembled in stages and served warm or at room temperature for stress-free entertaining.

MAKES 4 MAIN-DISH OR 8 FIRST-COURSE OR SIDE-DISH SERVINGS

2 large lemons

8 large globe artichokes (about 12 ounces each)

3 tablespoons extra-virgin olive oil

1 large onion (about 8 ounces), finely chopped

¼ cup drained and chopped marinated sun-dried tomatoes, 1 tablespoon marinade reserved

¼ cup chopped kalamata olives

4 large cloves garlic, finely chopped

¼ cup finely chopped fresh flat-leaf parsley

2 tablespoons finely chopped fresh basil

Salt and freshly ground black pepper, to taste

3 cups fresh gluten-free bread crumbs, including crusts (about 4 ounces), preferably from day-old Gluten-Free Brown Ciabatta Bread, page 83 (vegan), or Gluten-Free Italian Bread, page 86 (contains eggs)

¼ cup freshly grated gluten-free Parmesan cheese (optional), divided

Gluten-free pasta sauce, heated (optional)

Fill a large bowl with water and add the juice from one of the lemons. Cut off the stem of each artichoke flush to the base so that the artichoke can stand upright. Cut about 2 inches from the top. Bend back and pull off the tough, dark green outer leaves to expose the pale green leaves. Trim the edges of the base, if necessary. Drop each artichoke into the lemon water as you finish.

Fill a medium stockpot with about 1 inch of water. Slice remaining lemon into thin rounds and place in the pot. Insert a steaming basket into the pot. Drain the artichokes in a colander and rinse briefly under running water. Arrange the artichokes, upside down, in the steaming basket. Bring to a boil over high heat. Cover tightly, reduce heat to medium, and steam until artichoke bottoms are just tender, about 20 minutes. Remove steaming basket from the pot and let artichokes cool slightly. Strain the cooking liquid into a glass measuring container and reserve.

Preheat the oven to 400F (205C). Lightly oil a baking dish large enough to accommodate the stuffed artichokes in a single layer; set aside.

In a large nonstick skillet, heat the oil over medium heat. Add the onion and cook, stirring, until just softened, about 2 minutes. Add the tomatoes, reserved marinade, olives, garlic, and ⅓ cup of reserved cooking liquid. Cook, stirring often, until onions are softened, about 2 minutes. Remove from heat and stir in the parsley, basil, salt, and pepper. Add the bread crumbs and 2 tablespoons of the cheese, if using, stirring well to combine. Add ½ cup of the reserved cooking liquid, stirring well to combine. With a wooden spoon, push stuffing into 8 equal mounds; set aside.

With your fingers, spread open the center of each cooled artichoke; twist out the inner purple-tinged leaves. Remove any hairy fibers in the center by scraping them out with a melon baller or sharp grapefruit spoon. Fill the center of each artichoke with an equal portion of the stuffing, pushing the leaves gently apart to accommodate filling. (At this point, artichokes can be covered and refrigerated up to 6 hours before proceeding.)

Place stuffed artichokes in the prepared baking dish; spoon 1 tablespoon of the remaining cooking liquid over each. Bake, covered, 20 minutes, or until artichokes are very tender when pierced near the base with the tip of a sharp knife. Spoon another 1 tablespoon of the reserved cooking liquid over each; sprinkle evenly with the remaining 2 tablespoons of cheese, if using. Bake, uncovered, until cheese (if used) is melted, and tops are lightly browned and crusty, 5 to 10 minutes. Serve warm, accompanied with pasta sauce, if using, or at room temperature, without the sauce.

PER SERVING (per 2 stuffed artichokes without sauce): Calories 372; Protein 13g; Total Fat 16g; Sat Fat 2g; Cholesterol 0mg; Carbohydrate 53g; Dietary Fiber 17g; Sodium 721mg

Cabbage Strata with Ricotta and Roman Beans

(EGG-FREE)

This cozy, comforting casserole is ideal to serve in the cold-weather months. For easy slicing, make sure to pre-boil the cabbage leaves until tender.

MAKES 4 SERVINGS

8 large outer green cabbage leaves
2 tablespoons extra-virgin olive oil
3 scallions, white and green parts separated, thinly sliced
2 large cloves garlic, finely chopped
8 ounces tomato sauce
1 tablespoon tomato paste
½ teaspoon sugar, or to taste
Salt and freshly ground black pepper, to taste
¼ cup chopped fresh basil
1 (15-ounce) can Roman, kidney, or cannellini beans, rinsed and drained, divided
1 tablespoon water
1 cup gluten-free part-skim ricotta cheese, well drained
½ teaspoon dried oregano
1 tablespoon gluten-free Italian seasoned dry bread crumbs

Preheat oven to 350F (175C). Lightly oil an 8-inch-square baking dish and set aside.

Bring a large stockpot of salted water to a boil. Boil the cabbage leaves until tender but not falling apart, about 5 to 7 minutes. Drain in a colander; pat dry with paper towels. Set aside.

In a small saucepan, heat 1 tablespoon oil over medium heat. Add the white parts of the scallions and cook, stirring, until just softened, about 2 minutes. Add the garlic and cook, stirring constantly,

30 seconds. Add the tomato sauce, tomato paste, sugar, salt, and pepper; bring to a simmer over medium-high heat. Reduce heat to low and cook, stirring occasionally, 2 minutes. Remove from heat and stir in the basil; set aside.

In a food processor fitted with the knife blade, puree half the beans and water. Transfer to a small bowl and add the whole beans, stirring to combine; set aside.

In a medium bowl, mix the ricotta, scallion greens, oregano, salt, and pepper until thoroughly blended. Place 2 cabbage leaves on bottom of prepared baking dish. Spread ¼ cup tomato sauce mixture over leaves; spread with half of the ricotta mixture, then top with half the bean mixture; repeat layering 2 more times. Top with a fourth layer of cabbage and remaining tomato sauce mixture (about ¼ cup). Drizzle evenly with the remaining 1 tablespoon of oil. Sprinkle evenly with the bread crumbs. Bake about 30 minutes, or until browned and hot through the center. Let stand 10 minutes before cutting and serving warm.

PER SERVING: Calories 274; Protein 15g; Total Fat 12g; Sat Fat 4g; Cholesterol 19mg; Carbohydrate 28g; Dietary Fiber 5g; Sodium 511mg

Cannellini Bean and Fennel Gratin

(EGG-FREE)

This homey and hearty casserole represents Italian peasant cooking at its finest. Though less convenient than canned, dried beans prepared from scratch lend it a superior texture as well as flavor.

MAKES 6 SERVINGS

1 pound dried cannellini or other white beans, rinsed and picked over

6 sprigs plus 1½ tablespoons chopped fresh thyme, divided

3 sprigs plus 3 tablespoons chopped fresh flat-leaf parsley, divided

1 medium fennel bulb (about 12 ounces), stalks and fronds reserved, bulb cored, quartered, and chopped

6 cloves garlic, peeled and halved, plus 6 cloves garlic, finely chopped, divided

1 large bay leaf

½ teaspoon salt, plus additional, to taste

Freshly ground black pepper, to taste

3 tablespoons extra-virgin olive oil, divided

2 cups chopped carrots

1 large onion (about 8 ounces), chopped

1 teaspoon white wine vinegar

¾ cup freshly shredded gluten-free Parmesan cheese, divided

1½ cups fresh gluten-free bread crumbs

In a medium bowl, soak beans in cold water to cover overnight. Drain.

In a large stockpot, place the beans and enough water to cover by 2 inches. Tie together thyme and parsley sprigs with kitchen string, and add to pot. Add fennel stalks and fronds, halved garlic cloves, bay leaf, salt, and pepper. Bring to a boil over high heat; reduce heat to medium and simmer, uncovered, about 45 minutes, stirring occasionally, or until beans are just tender. Drain beans, reserving the cooking liquid. Remove and discard herb bundles, fennel fronds and stalks, and bay leaf.

Preheat oven to 375F (190C). Lightly grease a 2½-quart baking dish with a lid and set aside.

In a large deep-sided nonstick skillet, heat 2 tablespoons of oil over medium heat. Add carrot, onion, chopped fennel, and salt; cook, covered, stirring occasionally, until vegetables are beginning to brown, about 10 to 15 minutes. Add chopped garlic and cook, stirring constantly, 1 minute, or until fragrant. Add vinegar and cook 30 seconds, stirring constantly and scrapping the bottom of the pot with a spatula to loosen any browned bits. Add beans, chopped thyme, 2 tablespoons of chopped parsley, ½ cup Parmesan, 1½ cups of the reserved bean cooking liquid, and pepper; stir well to combine. Transfer to the prepared baking dish. Liquids should come to about 1½ to 2 inches below top of beans; add more if necessary.

In a small bowl, combine bread crumbs, remaining ¼ cup Parmesan, remaining 1 tablespoon of chopped parsley, salt, and pepper. Drizzle with remaining 1 tablespoon of oil; stir to moisten. Spread bread crumb mixture over bean mixture. Bake, covered, 20 minutes. Uncover and bake an additional 20 minutes, or until browned and liquids are greatly reduced. Let stand 15 minutes before serving warm.

PER SERVING: Calories 462; Protein 26g; Total Fat 12g; Sat Fat 4g; Cholesterol 10mg; Carbohydrate 66g; Dietary Fiber 16g; Sodium 530mg

Buckwheat Risotto with Spinach and Goat Cheese

(EGG-FREE)

Buckwheat groats, also known as kasha, lend an earthy flavor and chewy texture to this unusual and tasty risotto.

MAKES 5 TO 6 SERVINGS

2 tablespoons extra-virgin olive oil

¼ cup finely chopped onion

1½ cups buckwheat groats (kasha)

2 large cloves garlic, finely chopped

½ cup dry white wine (or low-sodium vegetable broth)

½ teaspoon dried thyme leaves

¼ teaspoon salt, or to taste

5 cups low-sodium vegetable broth, heated to simmering, plus additional broth or water as necessary

1 (10-ounce) package frozen chopped spinach, cooked according to package directions, drained and squeezed dry between kitchen towels

¼ to ½ cup gluten-free crumbled goat or feta cheese

¼ to ½ cup chopped fresh basil

2 to 4 tablespoons chopped kalamata or other good-quality black olives (optional)

Freshly ground black pepper, to taste

In a large, deep-sided nonstick skillet, heat the oil over medium heat. Add the onion and cook, stirring, until softened but not browned, 2 to 3 minutes. Add the groats and garlic and cook, stirring, 2 minutes.

Add the wine, thyme, and salt; cook, stirring constantly, until almost all the wine has been absorbed. Add ½ cup of broth and cook, stirring constantly, until almost all the liquid has been absorbed. Continue adding the broth by the ½ cup, cooking and stirring after each addition until liquid is almost completely absorbed. When 4½ cups of broth have been used, add the spinach and final measured ½ cup broth; cook, stirring, until groats are tender yet firm to the bite and the mixture is creamy, adding additional broth or water as necessary. Remove from heat and add the cheese, basil, olives, if using, salt, and pepper, stirring well to combine. Serve at once.

PER SERVING: Calories 328; Protein 20g; Total Fat 9g; Sat Fat 3g; Cholesterol 6mg; Carbohydrate 42g; Dietary Fiber 9g; Sodium 693mg

Eggplant Parmesan

(LACTO-OVO)

An Italian cookbook just wouldn't seem complete without including a recipe for this perennial favorite. The following variation dispenses with the traditional pan-frying for an easier, healthier dish. If you prefer your eggplant Parmesan saucier, add an extra ½ cup sauce or so with the final addition.

MAKES 8 SERVINGS

2 large eggs

1 cup plus 1 tablespoon gluten-free Italian seasoned dry bread crumbs, divided

2 medium eggplants, about 12 ounces each, cut into ½-inch thick rounds, sprinkled with salt and set in a colander to drain 30 minutes (salting is optional)

Salt and freshly ground black pepper, to taste

4 tablespoons extra-virgin olive oil, divided

1 (26-ounce) jar gluten-free pasta sauce (about 3 cups)

2 cups (8 ounces) gluten-free shredded light mozzarella cheese

½ cup chopped fresh basil

½ cup gluten-free freshly shredded Parmesan cheese

Preheat oven to 375F (190C). Lightly oil a 13 × 9-inch baking dish and set aside. Lightly grease 2 baking sheets and set aside.

Place the eggs in a small wide bowl and lightly beat with a fork; place 1 cup of the bread crumbs on a deep-welled plate. Rinse the eggplant slices under cold-running water and thoroughly dry with paper towels. Dip each eggplant slice in eggs, and then in bread crumbs; transfer to the prepared baking sheets and arrange in a single layer. Season lightly with salt and pepper. Drizzle evenly with 2 tablespoons oil. Bake in preheated oven 5 to 7 minutes, or until beginning to brown. Turn slices over, season lightly with salt and pepper, and drizzle evenly with remaining 2 tablespoons oil; bake an additional 5 to 7 minutes. Remove from oven (do not turn off oven) and set aside.

Spread a third of the pasta sauce (about 1 cup) along the bottom of prepared baking dish. Arrange half the eggplant slices in a single layer in the sauce. Sprinkle evenly with half the mozzarella cheese. Cover with another third of sauce, then top with the remaining eggplant slices. Sprinkle evenly with the remaining mozzarella cheese, then cover with the remaining sauce. Cover and bake 30 to 40 minutes, or until eggplant is easily pierced with a fork. Sprinkle evenly with the basil, then the Parmesan cheese, and then the remaining 1 tablespoon bread crumbs. Return to the oven and bake, uncovered, until cheese is melted and sauce is bubbly, about 5 minutes. Let stand about 5 minutes before cutting into wedges and serving warm.

PER SERVING: Calories 356; Protein 16g; Total Fat 20g; Sat Fat 6g; Cholesterol 73mg; Carbohydrate 31g; Dietary Fiber 5g; Sodium 961mg

3-Cheese Eggplant Lasagna

(LACTO-OVO)

Feed a hungry crowd with this yummy lasagna, which can be assembled a day ahead of baking for easy entertaining.

MAKES 8 SERVINGS

    2 medium eggplants (about 12 ounces each)
    Table salt
    2 tablespoons extra-virgin olive oil, divided
    1 (15-ounce) container gluten-free no-fat
        ricotta cheese
    2 eggs
    ½ cup freshly shredded gluten-free Parmesan
        cheese
    ¼ cup chopped fresh flat-leaf parsley
    1 teaspoon onion powder
    ½ teaspoon dried oregano
    ¼ teaspoon garlic salt
    Freshly ground black pepper, to taste
    3 cups prepared gluten-free pasta sauce or
        marinara sauce
    1½ cups no-salt-added tomato sauce
    1 cup shredded gluten-free part-skim
        mozzarella cheese

Trim both ends of each eggplant; stand one eggplant upright on its flattest end. Remove most of the skin in thin slices. Cut lengthwise into 2 equal halves. Place 1 half, cut side down, on a cutting board. With one hand resting on top of the eggplant, make 3 equal lengthwise cuts with a large sharp knife. Repeat with the other half, for a total of 6 slices. Stand the remaining eggplant upright on its flattest end; repeat the process. When finished, you should have a total of 12 slices, about ¼-inch in thickness. Sprinkle the eggplant slices with salt and

place in a colander to drain for 30 minutes. Rinse under cold-running water and pat dry with paper towels.

Meanwhile, preheat oven to broil. Lightly oil 2 baking sheets and set aside. Lightly oil a 13 × 9-inch baking dish and set aside.

Place the eggplant slices on the prepared baking sheets. Brush the tops evenly with 1 tablespoon of the oil. Broil about 4 inches from the heat source until lightly browned, 2 to 3 minutes. Turn the slices over; brush the tops with 1 tablespoon of oil, and broil until lightly browned, 2 to 3 minutes. Remove baking sheets from the oven; reduce oven temperature to 350F (175C).

In a medium bowl, combine the ricotta cheese, eggs, Parmesan, parsley, onion powder, oregano, garlic salt, and pepper in a separate bowl; set briefly aside. In another medium bowl, combine the pasta sauce and tomato sauce; set briefly aside.

Spread ½ cup of pasta sauce mixture along the bottom of the prepared baking dish. Arrange half the eggplant over the sauce. Spread half the ricotta mixture over the eggplant. Spread 2 cups of the sauce mixture over the ricotta mixture. Arrange remaining half of eggplant over the sauce, followed by remaining half of the ricotta mixture, then the final 2 cups of sauce mixture. Sprinkle evenly with the mozzarella. (At this point, lasagna can be refrigerated, covered, up to 24 hours before continuing with the recipe.)

Cover the baking dish tightly with foil (lightly oil the underside if it will touch the cheese); bake 45 minutes (add 10 to 15 minutes if refrigerated), or until eggplant is very tender. Uncover and bake an additional 5 minutes, or until top is lightly browned and bubbly. Let stand 15 minutes before cutting and serving warm.

PER SERVING: Calories 294; Protein 19g; Total Fat 14g; Sat Fat 4g; Cholesterol 74mg; Carbohydrate 26g; Dietary Fiber 6g; Sodium 853mg

Eggplant Lasagna with Spinach and Sun-Dried Tomatoes

(VEGAN)

Cheese lovers won't miss the cheese in this light yet eminently satisfying plant-based lasagna.

MAKES 6 SERVINGS

2 medium eggplants (about 12 ounces each)

Table salt

2 tablespoons extra-virgin olive oil, divided

2 (10-ounce) packages frozen chopped spinach, thawed and drained well

½ cup drained and chopped marinated sun-dried tomato pieces, 2 tablespoons marinade reserved

Salt and freshly ground black pepper to taste

1 (26-ounce) jar gluten-free pasta sauce, preferably the tomato-basil variety

2 (8-ounce) cans no-salt-added tomato sauce

Trim both ends of each eggplant; stand one eggplant upright on its flattest end. Remove most of the skin in thin slices. Cut lengthwise into 2 equal halves. Place 1 half, cut side down, on a cutting board. With one hand resting on top of the eggplant, make 3 equal lengthwise cuts with a large sharp knife. Repeat with the other half, for a total of 6 slices. Stand the remaining eggplant upright on

its flattest end; repeat the process. When finished, you should have a total of 12 slices, about ¼-inch in thickness. Sprinkle the eggplant slices with salt and place in a colander to drain for 30 minutes. Rinse under cold-running water and pat dry with paper towels.

Meanwhile, preheat oven to broil. Lightly oil 2 baking sheets and set aside. Lightly oil a 13 × 9-inch baking dish and set aside.

Place the eggplant slices on the prepared baking sheets. Brush the tops evenly with 1 tablespoon of the oil. Broil about 4 inches from the heat source until lightly browned, 2 to 3 minutes. Turn the slices over, brush the tops with 1 tablespoon of oil, and broil until lightly browned, 2 to 3 minutes. Remove baking sheets from the oven; reduce oven temperature to 375F (190C).

In a medium bowl, combine spinach, sun-dried tomatoes and reserved marinade, salt, and pepper; set briefly aside. In another medium bowl, combine the pasta sauce and tomato sauce; set briefly aside.

Spread about 1 cup of sauce mixture along the bottom of the prepared baking dish. Arrange 4 of the eggplant slices over the sauce. Arrange one-third of the spinach mixture over the eggplant. Pour 1 cup of sauce over the spinach mixture. Arrange 4 more eggplant slices over the sauce, followed by one-third of the spinach mixture. Pour another 1 cup of sauce over the spinach mixture. Repeat once, ending with remaining sauce. Cover tightly with oiled foil and bake for 1 hour, or until eggplant is very tender. Let stand 10 minutes before cutting and serving.

PER SERVING: Calories 280; Protein 8g; Total Fat 13g; Sat Fat 2g; Cholesterol 0mg; Carbohydrate 37g; Dietary Fiber 10g; Sodium 728mg

Eggplant "Meat" Balls

(LACTO-OVO)

Serve these delectable mock meatballs with your favorite pasta sauce, by themselves, atop gluten-free spaghetti, or inside a sub roll with melted mozzarella. Alternatively, shape the filling into patties or a loaf—chilled slices with a smear of mustard make a mean "meat loaf" sandwich.

MAKES 6 SERVINGS

> 4 tablespoons extra-virgin olive oil, divided
> 1 medium onion (about 6 ounces), finely chopped
> 1 (12-ounce) eggplant, unpeeled, coarsely chopped
> 3 large cloves garlic, finely chopped
> ½ tablespoon dried oregano
> Salt and freshly ground black pepper, to taste
> ¼ cup chopped walnuts
> 1 cup gluten-free Italian seasoned dry bread crumbs
> 1 cup gluten-free unseasoned dry bread crumbs
> 1 cup freshly grated gluten-free Parmesan cheese
> ¼ cup chopped fresh basil
> ¼ cup chopped fresh flat-leaf parsley
> 2 eggs, beaten
> Gluten-free marinara sauce, heated, to serve

In a large nonstick skillet, heat 1 tablespoon of the oil over medium heat. Add onion and cook, stirring, until softened, about 3 minutes. Add the eggplant and cook, stirring, until eggplant begins to soften, about 3 to 4 minutes. Reduce the heat to medium-low and stir in 1 tablespoon of oil, garlic, oregano, salt, and pepper; cook, covered, stirring a few times, until eggplant is tender, about 5 minutes. Remove from heat and stir in the walnuts and 1 tablespoon of oil. Let cool a few minutes. Working in batches, as necessary, transfer eggplant mixture to a food processor fitted with the knife blade; process until smooth and pureed. Transfer to a large bowl and add bread crumbs, cheese, basil, and parsley; stir well to thoroughly combine. Add the eggs, stirring well to thoroughly combine. Cover and refrigerate a minimum of 1 hour, or overnight.

Preheat oven to 375F (190C). Lightly oil a baking sheet and set aside.

With dampened fingers, shape the eggplant mixture into golf ball–sized balls, using about 2 tablespoons per ball. Place on the prepared baking sheet. (You should have about 2 dozen balls.) With a pastry brush, brush the tops and sides evenly with the remaining 1 tablespoon of oil.

Bake the eggplant "meat" balls in the center of the oven without turning until lightly browned, about 25 minutes, taking care not to overbake. Serve warm, with the heated marinara sauce.

PER SERVING (about 4 pieces, or ⅙ of recipe): Calories 387; Protein 16g; Total Fat 21g; Sat Fat 6g; Cholesterol 84mg; Carbohydrate 35g; Dietary Fiber 3g; Sodium 835mg

Eggplant Rolls with Spinach, Feta, and Kalamata Olives

(EGG-FREE)

Though typically associated with Greek cuisine, both feta cheese and kalamata olives are enjoyed throughout Italy. Crumbled gluten-free Gorgonzola or goat cheese can replace the feta, if desired.

MAKES 6 SERVINGS

2 medium eggplants (about 12 ounces each)

Table salt

3 tablespoons extra-virgin olive oil, divided

1 large onion (about 8 ounces), finely chopped

3 large cloves garlic, finely chopped

1 (10-ounce) bag baby spinach

1 cup gluten-free low-fat ricotta cheese

½ cup gluten-free crumbled feta cheese

½ cup fresh gluten-free plain bread crumbs

2 tablespoons finely chopped fresh flat-leaf parsley, plus additional, for serving (optional)

½ teaspoon whole fennel seed, crushed

Salt and freshly ground black pepper, to taste

Pinch ground nutmeg

2 cups gluten-free marinara sauce, plus additional heated sauce, to serve

6 kalamata olives, pitted and chopped

¼ cup freshly shredded gluten-free Parmesan cheese

Trim both ends of each eggplant; stand one eggplant upright on its flattest end. Remove most of the skin in thin slices. Cut lengthwise into 2 equal halves. Place 1 half, cut side down, on a cutting board. With one hand resting on top of the eggplant, make 3 equal lengthwise cuts with a large sharp knife. Repeat with the other half, for a total of 6 slices. Stand the remaining eggplant upright on its flattest end; repeat the process. When finished, you should have a total of 12 slices, about ¼-inch in thickness. Sprinkle the eggplant slices with salt and place in a colander to drain for 30 minutes. Rinse under cold-running water and pat dry with paper towels.

Meanwhile, preheat oven to broil. Lightly oil 2 baking sheets and set aside.

Place the eggplant slices on the prepared baking sheets. Brush the tops evenly with 1 tablespoon of the oil. Broil about 4 inches from the heat source until lightly browned, 2 to 3 minutes. Turn the slices over, brush the tops with 1 tablespoon of oil, and broil until lightly browned, 2 to 3 minutes. Remove baking sheets from the oven.

Preheat oven to 375F (190C). Lightly oil an 11 × 7-inch baking dish and set aside.

In a large nonstick skillet, heat the remaining 1 tablespoon oil over medium heat. Add the onion and cook, stirring, until softened, about 3 minutes. Add the garlic and cook, stirring constantly, 30 seconds. Add half the spinach and cook, tossing and stirring until wilted, about 2 minutes. Add the remaining spinach and cook, tossing and stirring until wilted, about 2 minutes. Reduce heat to medium-low and cook, stirring often, until spinach is shriveled and liquids have evaporated, about 5 minutes. Remove from the heat and let cool a few minutes. Add the ricotta, feta, bread crumbs, parsley, fennel, salt, pepper, and nutmeg; stir until thoroughly combined.

Place 3 to 4 tablespoons of the spinach filling at the narrow end of each eggplant slice. Roll up and place seam-side down in the prepared baking dish. Spoon the marinara sauce evenly over the eggplant rolls. Bake, uncovered, about 20 to 25 minutes, or until heated through, sprinkling evenly with the olives and Parmesan cheese the last 5 minutes or so of cooking. Serve warm, garnished with fresh chopped parsley, if desired, with additional marinara sauce passed separately.

PER SERVING: Calories 291; Protein 12g; Total Fat 18g; Sat Fat 6g; Cholesterol 26mg; Carbohydrate 24g; Dietary Fiber 4g; Sodium 892mg

Baked Stuffed Eggplant Parmesan

(EGG-FREE)

This simple and delicious recipe is a family favorite. Serve with a tossed green salad and Herbed Italian Bread Sticks, page 86, for a simply delicious meal.

MAKES 4 SERVINGS

2 large eggplants (about 1 pound each), halved lengthwise

3 tablespoons extra-virgin olive oil, divided

1 small onion (about 4 ounces), chopped

2 large cloves garlic, finely chopped

1 teaspoon dried oregano

Salt and freshly ground black pepper to taste

¼ cup gluten-free freshly shredded Parmesan cheese

¼ cup gluten-free Italian-seasoned dry bread crumbs

1 cup gluten-free pizza sauce

½ cup shredded gluten-free mozzarella cheese

Chopped fresh basil or flat-leaf parsley, for garnish (optional)

Preheat oven to 350F (175C). Lightly oil a baking sheet with sides.

Place eggplant halves on the prepared baking sheet, cut sides up, and make a few ½-inch-deep slashes in the white part. Brush the tops and sides evenly with 1½ tablespoons oil. Bake, uncovered, for 30 minutes. Remove from oven (do not turn off oven); let cool about 10 minutes.

Scoop out the pulp from each eggplant half (discard any tough pieces around the stem end), leaving a ¼-inch-thick shell; place the shells on the baking sheet. Coarsely chop the pulp and set aside.

In a large nonstick skillet, heat the remaining 1½ tablespoons of oil over medium heat. Add the onion

and cook, stirring, until softened, about 3 minutes. Add the garlic and oregano and cook, stirring constantly, 1 minute. Add the reserved eggplant pulp, salt, and pepper; cook, stirring, 1 minute.

Spoon equal amounts of the eggplant mixture into the reserved shells. Sprinkle each filled shell with 1 tablespoon Parmesan cheese, followed by 1 tablespoon of bread crumbs. Spoon ¼ cup pizza sauce evenly over the top of each filled shell. Return to the oven and bake 15 minutes. Sprinkle each stuffed shell evenly with 2 tablespoons mozzarella cheese; bake an additional 5 minutes, or until cheese is melted. Serve warm, garnished with the fresh basil, if using.

PER SERVING: Calories 290; Protein 11g; Total Fat 17g; Sat Fat 5g; Cholesterol 13mg; Carbohydrate 27g; Dietary Fiber 5g; Sodium 791mg

Goat Cheese and Ricotta Skillet Pie

(LACTO-OVO/LOW-CARB)

Serve warm portions of this crustless, protein-rich cheese pie over your favorite tomato-based pasta sauce for dinner, or with Italian Skillet Breakfast Potatoes with Peppers and Onions, page 196, for brunch. For an elegant first course, serve smaller portions at room temperature over mixed salad greens. For best results, use a 10-inch cast iron skillet for the recipe.

MAKES 6 SERVINGS

1 pound gluten-free nonfat ricotta cheese

8 ounces creamy goat cheese

4 ounces gluten-free light cream cheese, cut into chunks, at room temperature

4 large eggs

2 egg whites

½ teaspoon salt

Freshly ground black pepper, to taste

¼ cup all-purpose gluten-free flour

¾ cup skim milk

¼ cup chopped chives or the green parts of scallions (optional)

1 tablespoon chopped fresh thyme or rosemary, or 1 teaspoon dried thyme or rosemary

Heated gluten-free pasta sauce, to serve (optional)

Mixed salad greens (optional)

Preheat oven to 375F (190C). Lightly grease a 10-inch cast iron skillet and set aside.

In a large bowl, mix together all the cheeses until combined. With an electric mixer on low speed, beat in the eggs, egg whites, salt, and pepper, then add the flour and milk. Stir in the chives, if using, and thyme until thoroughly distributed. Pour batter into the prepared skillet. Bake until golden and a knife inserted in the center comes out clean, 30 to 40 minutes. Let cool 10 minutes before cutting into wedges and serving warm or at room temperature, over heated pasta sauce or mixed salad greens, if using.

PER SERVING: Calories 356; Protein 32g; Total Fat 20g; Sat Fat 13g; Cholesterol 205mg; Carbohydrate 12g; Dietary Fiber 0g; Sodium 639mg

Stuffed Portobello Mushrooms with Ricotta and Spinach

(EGG-FREE/LOW-CARB)

Serve these scrumptious stuffed mushrooms with a tossed green salad and Herbed Italian Bread Sticks, page 86, for a satisfying light supper. The delicious filling can be used to stuff smaller cremini or cultivated white mushrooms, if desired.

MAKES 4 SERVINGS

4 large Portobello mushroom caps (2 to 3 ounces each)

1 tablespoon extra-virgin olive oil

Salt and freshly ground black pepper

1 cup gluten-free nonfat ricotta cheese

1 cup finely chopped fresh spinach

½ cup freshly shredded gluten-free Parmesan cheese, divided

3 tablespoons finely chopped marinated sun-dried tomatoes

2 tablespoons finely chopped fresh basil

½ teaspoon Italian seasoning

Salt and freshly ground black pepper, to taste

1 cup prepared gluten-free pasta sauce or marinara sauce, heated

Preheat the oven to 450F (230C). Lightly oil a rimmed baking sheet.

Brush the mushrooms on all sides with the oil. Transfer to the prepared baking sheet, cut sides up; bake about 15 minutes, or until just tender. Remove baking sheet from oven and carefully drain off any accumulated liquids in the baking sheet.

Reduce the oven temperature to 375F (190C).

In a small bowl, mix the ricotta, spinach, ¼ cup Parmesan cheese, tomatoes, basil, Italian seasoning, salt, and pepper until thoroughly blended. Spoon equal amounts (about ⅓ cup) onto each cooked mushroom cap, spreading over the entire cap with the back of a small spoon. Bake about 15 minutes, or until hot, sprinkling evenly with the remaining ¼ cup Parmesan the last few minutes of baking. Serve at once, over the marinara sauce.

PER SERVING: Calories 216; Protein 16g; Total Fat 10g; Sat Fat 3g; Cholesterol 17mg; Carbohydrate 18g; Dietary Fiber 4g; Sodium 637mg

Bell Peppers Stuffed with Quinoa and Chickpeas

(VEGAN)

Here is a hearty and delicious, stress-free plant-based dish to serve guests, as the assembled stuffed peppers can be refrigerated overnight before baking.

MAKES 6 SERVINGS

- 1¼ cups low-sodium vegetable broth
- 1 (26-ounce) jar prepared gluten-free pasta sauce or marinara sauce (about 3 cups), divided
- 1 cup quinoa, rinsed well under cold-running water
- ¼ teaspoon salt
- ¼ teaspoon dried oregano
- ⅛ teaspoon dried thyme
- Freshly ground black pepper, to taste
- 1 (15-ounce) can chickpeas, rinsed and drained
- 2 scallions, green parts only, thinly sliced
- ½ cup chopped fresh basil, plus whole fresh basil leaves, for garnish (optional)
- 1½ tablespoons extra-virgin olive oil, divided
- 6 medium green bell peppers (6 ounces each)
- 3 teaspoons gluten-free Italian-seasoned dry bread crumbs
- 6 tablespoons freshly shredded gluten-free Parmesan cheese (optional)
- 6 to 12 grape or cherry tomatoes, halved, for garnish (optional)

Preheat the oven to 400F (205C).

In a medium heavy-bottomed saucepan, combine the broth, ¼ cup sauce, quinoa, salt, oregano, thyme, and black pepper; bring to a boil over high heat. Stir, reduce heat to medium-low, and cover; cook until the liquid is absorbed, 15 to 20 minutes. Remove from heat and let stand, covered, 5 minutes.

Transfer quinoa mixture to a medium mixing bowl; add the chickpeas, ¾ cup marinara sauce, scallions, chopped basil, and 1 tablespoon oil, tossing to thoroughly combine. (At this point, quinoa mixture can be held at room temperature up to 1 hour before continuing with the recipe. Alternatively, completely cooled mixture can be refrigerated, covered, 24 hours before returning to room temperature and proceeding.)

Cut the top off the stem end of each bell pepper and reserve. Remove the seeds and white membranes from each pepper shell. Brush the outsides of the shells evenly with the remaining ½ tablespoon of oil. Stuff each pepper lightly (do not pack) with equal amounts of the quinoa mixture; top with the corresponding lid (lids will not close). (At this point, stuffed peppers can be refrigerated, covered, overnight before returning to room temperature and baking.)

Place the stuffed peppers upright in a baking dish just large enough to accommodate their size. Add enough water to the dish, pouring down the side, to measure ½ inch. Cover tightly with foil and bake for 50 minutes. Uncover and remove lids (reserve for serving, if desired); sprinkle each with ½ teaspoon bread crumbs, followed by 1 tablespoon of cheese, if using. Bake for 10 minutes, or until cheese is melted, bread crumbs are lightly browned, and peppers are tender when pierced with the tip of a sharp knife.

Meanwhile, heat the remaining marinara sauce. Garnish each stuffed pepper with tomato halves and fresh basil leaves, if using. Serve at once, with the heated sauce passed separately.

PER SERVING: Calories 393; Protein 14g; Total Fat 12g; Sat Fat 2g; Cholesterol 0mg; Carbohydrate 61g; Dietary Fiber 9g; Sodium 852mg

Stuffed Peppers with Sun-Dried Tomato and Pesto Risotto

(VEGAN)

Though the Sun-Dried Tomato and Pesto Risotto, page 130, is my personal favorite leftover risotto filling for bell peppers, just about any risotto prepared with white or brown Arborio rice will work well here.

MAKES 4 SERVINGS

4 medium green or red bell peppers (about 6 to 7 ounces each)
½ tablespoon extra-virgin olive oil
½ recipe Sun-Dried Tomato and Pesto Risotto, page 130, at room temperature
Gluten-free tomato-basil marinara or pasta sauce, heated, to serve (optional)

Preheat oven to 400F (205C).

Cut the top off the stem end of each bell pepper and reserve. Remove the seeds and white membranes from each pepper shell. Brush the outsides of the shells evenly with the oil. Stuff each pepper shell lightly (do not pack) with equal amounts of the risotto and top with the corresponding lid (lids may not close).

Place the stuffed peppers upright in a baking dish just large enough to accommodate their size. Add enough water to the dish, pouring down the side, to measure ½ inch. Cover tightly with foil and bake for 50 minutes. Uncover (do not remove lids) and bake for 10 minutes, or until the tops are lightly browned and peppers are tender when pierced with the tip of a sharp knife. Serve warm, with the marinara sauce passed separately, if using.

PER SERVING: Calories 288; Protein 11g; Total Fat 9g; Sat Fat 2g; Cholesterol 0mg; Carbohydrate 40g; Dietary Fiber 4g; Sodium 326mg

Potato and Cottage Cheese Lasagna

(EGG-FREE)

This hearty lasagna is perfect to serve at a family-style gathering, accompanied by the Green Bean Salad with Tomato-Basil Dressing, page 62, and Herbed Italian Bread Sticks, page 86.

MAKES 6 SERVINGS

1½ pounds medium boiling potatoes, peeled and left whole
1 tablespoon extra-virgin olive oil
1 medium onion (about 6 ounces), chopped
2 large cloves garlic, finely chopped
1 (26-ounce) jar gluten-free prepared marinara or pasta sauce
2 tablespoons chopped fresh basil
Salt and freshly ground black pepper, to taste
1 cup gluten-free low-fat cottage cheese
2 egg whites, slightly beaten
2 tablespoons chopped fresh flat-leaf parsley
¼ cup gluten-free freshly shredded Parmesan cheese, divided
4 ounces (1 cup) gluten-free part-skim shredded mozzarella cheese

Preheat oven to 375F (190C). Lightly grease an 8-inch-square baking dish and set aside. Lightly oil a piece of foil large enough to cover the baking dish; set aside.

In a large saucepan or medium stockpot, place the potatoes in enough salted water to cover by 2 inches. Bring to a boil over high heat. Reduce the heat slightly and boil until just tender, 10 to 12 minutes. Drain well and let cool slightly. Cut the potatoes into ¼-inch-thick slices; set aside.

Meanwhile, in a large nonstick skillet, heat the oil over medium heat. Add the onion and cook, stirring, until softened, about 3 minutes. Add the garlic and cook, stirring constantly, 1 minute. Add the marinara sauce, basil, salt, and pepper; cook, stirring, until heated through, about 3 minutes. Remove from heat and let cool slightly.

In a small bowl, mix together the cottage cheese, egg whites, parsley, 2 tablespoons Parmesan, salt, and pepper; set aside.

Spoon about ½ cup of the pasta sauce mixture along the bottom of the prepared baking dish. Place half of the potatoes over the sauce, overlapping as necessary. Spread with half of the remaining pasta sauce mixture. Top with half the cottage cheese mixture, followed with half the mozzarella cheese. Repeat layers, beginning with the remaining potatoes and ending with remaining mozzarella. Cover tightly with the oiled foil and bake 45 minutes to 1 hour, or until potatoes are fork tender. Sprinkle with the remaining 2 tablespoons Parmesan cheese. Bake, uncovered, an additional 5 minutes, or until cheese is melted and top is beginning to brown. Let stand 10 minutes before cutting. Serve warm.

PER SERVING: Calories 333; Protein 17g; Total Fat 13g; Sat Fat 4g; Cholesterol 14mg; Carbohydrate 40g; Dietary Fiber 6g; Sodium 944mg

Potato Torta with Broccoli and Tomatoes

(VEGAN)

This comforting torta—Italian for tart, cake, or pie—is one of my favorite gluten-free entrées. Feel free to get creative with the topping—for added protein, I sometimes toss the broccoli and tomatoes with 1 cup of rinsed and drained canned cannellini beans.

MAKES 4 SERVINGS

1¾ pounds russet potatoes, peeled and cubed

1 (14.5-ounce) can diced Italian-style tomatoes, drained, ¼ cup liquid reserved

¼ cup gluten-free all-purpose flour

1 tablespoon extra-virgin olive oil, divided

¼ cup drained and chopped marinated sun-dried tomatoes, ½ tablespoon marinade reserved

¼ teaspoon garlic salt

Freshly ground black pepper, to taste

1 large egg (optional)

1½ cups chopped frozen broccoli, partially cooked and drained

2 large cloves garlic, finely chopped

¼ teaspoon dried oregano

Salt, to taste

1 cup gluten-free shredded part-skim mozzarella cheese (optional)

¼ cup gluten-free freshly shredded Parmesan cheese (optional)

2 tablespoons gluten-free, egg-free, dairy-free Italian-seasoned dry bread crumbs (see Cook's Tip, page 28)

Preheat oven to 425F (220C). Lightly oil a 9-inch-round cake pan and set aside.

In a large saucepan, bring the potatoes and salted water to cover to a boil over high heat. Reduce heat slightly and boil until tender, about 15 minutes. Drain and return potatoes to pan; add reserved tomato liquids, flour, ½ tablespoon oil, reserved marinade, garlic salt, and pepper. Mash with a potato masher until smooth. Add the egg, if using; mash well again. Add the sun-dried tomatoes; stir well to evenly distribute.

Transfer potato mixture to the prepared pan, spreading evenly with the back of a spoon or spatula. In a medium bowl, mix the canned tomatoes, broccoli, remaining ½ tablespoon of oil, garlic, oregano, salt, and pepper until thoroughly combined; spoon evenly over potato mixture. Sprinkle evenly with the mozzarella, if using, followed by the Parmesan, if using. Sprinkle evenly with the bread crumbs. Bake about 25 minutes, or until lightly browned. Let stand 15 minutes before cutting and serving.

PER SERVING: Calories 251; Protein 8g; Total Fat 6g; Sat Fat 1g; Cholesterol 0mg; Carbohydrate 45g; Dietary Fiber 6g; Sodium 439mg

Stuffed Baked Potatoes with Sun-Dried Tomatoes and Scallions

(LACTO-OVO)

Serve these creamy, twice-baked potatoes with a tossed green salad for a supremely satisfying supper.

MAKES 4 SERVINGS

4 large russet potatoes, about 8 ounces each, scrubbed and dried with paper towels

½ cup gluten-free part-skim ricotta cheese

3 tablespoons skim milk

¼ teaspoon salt

Freshly ground black pepper, to taste

1 egg, lightly beaten

¼ cup drained and chopped marinated sun-dried tomatoes

2 scallions, mostly green parts, thinly sliced

Preheat oven to 400F (205C). Prick the potatoes in several places with a fork and place on an ungreased baking sheet. Bake until potatoes are cooked through the center, about 1 hour. Remove baking sheet from oven and let potatoes cool slightly. (Do not turn off oven.)

When potatoes are cool enough to handle, working lengthwise, cut off the top third of each potato. With a melon baller, carefully scoop out potato pulp, leaving ¼-inch-thick shells. Scoop out pulp from tops of potatoes; discard tops. Transfer pulp to a large mixing bowl and add the ricotta, milk, salt, and pepper; mash well with a potato masher until thoroughly blended. Add the egg, mashing well to thoroughly blend. Add the tomatoes and scallions, stirring well with a spoon to thoroughly incorporate. Spoon potato mixture back into shells, mounding in center. Smooth tops with a slightly dampened spatula. (At this point, stuffed potatoes can be held up to 1 hour at room temperature before proceeding with the recipe. Alternatively, completely cooled stuffed potatoes can be refrigerated, covered, up to 24 hours before returning to room temperature and proceeding.)

Place stuffed potatoes back on the baking sheet and return to the 400F (205C) oven. Bake until tops are golden, about 25 minutes. Serve at once.

PER SERVING: Calories 217; Protein 10g; Total Fat 5g; Sat Fat 2g; Cholesterol 63mg; Carbohydrate 35g; Dietary Fiber 3g; Sodium 223mg

Spaghetti Squash with Roasted Red Pepper–Ricotta Pesto

(EGG-FREE)

Spaghetti squash has been the savior of many a cook in search of both a low-carb and gluten-free pasta alternative. For a vegan variation, serve with Roasted Red Pepper Sauce, page 117.

MAKES 4 SERVINGS

1 (4-pound) or 2 (2-pound) spaghetti squash
Roasted Red Pepper–Ricotta Pesto, below
¼ cup chopped fresh basil
Gluten-free freshly grated Parmesan cheese,
  to serve (optional)

Preheat oven to 375F (190C).

Prick the squash in several places with a large fork and place on an ungreased baking sheet. Bake 50 minutes to 1 hour, or until softened and easily pierced through the center, turning over halfway through cooking time. (Do not turn off the oven.)

While still hot, slice the squash in half lengthwise; carefully scoop out the seeds and discard. Twist out the flesh with a fork and transfer to a 2½-quart baking dish, separating any thick strands into thinner strands as necessary. Add the pesto and basil, tossing well until thoroughly combined. (At this point, mixture can be held at room temperature up to 1 hour before continuing with the recipe.) Cover and bake in the oven 15 minutes, or until heated through. Serve at once, with the Parmesan cheese passed separately, if using.

PER SERVING: Calories 254; Protein 6g; Total Fat 11g; Sat Fat 2g; Cholesterol 5mg; Carbohydrate 37g; Dietary Fiber 5g; Sodium 365mg

Roasted Red Pepper–Ricotta Pesto

(EGG-FREE/LOW-CARB)

Toss this pretty pale pink pesto with zucchini noodles, gluten-free pastas, and gnocchi, as well. It also makes an excellent topping for baked potatoes.

MAKES ABOUT ¾ CUP

1 (7.25-ounce) jar roasted red bell peppers,
  drained
½ cup fresh basil leaves
¼ cup gluten-free part-skim ricotta cheese
2 tablespoons extra-virgin olive oil
2 large cloves garlic, finely chopped
½ teaspoon salt, or to taste
¼ teaspoon sugar, or to taste
⅛ teaspoon crushed red pepper flakes, or to
  taste (optional)
Freshly ground black pepper, to taste

In a food processor fitted with the knife blade, or in a blender, process or blend all ingredients until smooth and pureed. Use as directed in recipe. Pesto can be stored, covered, in refrigerator up to 3 days before returning to room temperature.

PER SERVING (1 tablespoon, or ¹⁄₁₂ of recipe): Calories 33; Protein 1g; Total Fat 3g; Sat Fat 1g; Cholesterol 2mg; Carbohydrate 2g; Dietary Fiber 1g; Sodium 96mg

Zucchini Cakes with Pine Nuts and Basil

(LACTO-OVO)

These savory little dinner cakes are downright addictive. To create attractive appetizers, use half the amount of batter per cake, and serve with gluten-free sour cream in lieu of the pasta sauce, if desired.

MAKES 6 SERVINGS (ABOUT 12 CAKES)

4 cups grated zucchini (from about 2 pounds)
Table salt
2 eggs, beaten
½ cup chopped fresh flat-leaf parsley
3 tablespoons chopped fresh basil

3 tablespoons finely chopped scallion greens

1 clove garlic, finely chopped

Salt and freshly ground black pepper, to taste

½ cup gluten-free unseasoned dry bread crumbs

½ cup gluten-free Italian seasoned dry bread crumbs

¼ cup toasted pine nuts

2 to 4 tablespoons rinsed and drained capers (optional)

3 tablespoons extra-virgin olive oil, divided

¼ cup gluten-free freshly shredded Parmesan cheese

About 6 cherry or grape tomatoes, halved

3 cups gluten-free pasta sauce or marinara sauce, heated

Place the zucchini in a colander set over a sink and sprinkle generously with salt; toss and let drain 15 minutes.

Preheat oven to 250F (120C). Line a baking sheet with paper towels and set aside.

Rinse zucchini under cold-running water and squeeze out as much moisture as possible, pressing with paper towels. Transfer drained zucchini to a large bowl and toss with the eggs, parsley, basil, scallions, garlic, salt, and pepper. Stir in the bread crumbs, pine nuts, and capers, if using. Measure the batter; there should be about 4 cups. Divide by 12 to approximate the amount needed per cake (about ⅓ cup).

In a large nonstick skillet, heat 1½ tablespoons oil over medium heat. Working in two batches, add the batter in approximate ⅓-cup measures, spreading slightly with the back of a spoon. Cook until golden brown, about 2 to 3 minutes per side. Transfer the cakes to the prepared baking sheet and place in the preheated oven. Repeat cooking process with the remaining batter. When all zucchini cakes have been made, top each with about 1 teaspoon of the cheese and garnish with a cherry tomato half. Return to the oven briefly to melt the cheese. To serve, ladle ½ cup of heated pasta sauce on each of 6 serving plates; top with 2 cakes and serve at once.

PER SERVING: Calories 375; Protein 12g; Total Fat 20g; Sat Fat 4g; Cholesterol 73mg; Carbohydrate 41g; Dietary Fiber 8g; Sodium 834mg

Raw Zucchini Spaghetti with Sun-Dried Tomato Marinara Sauce

(VEGAN/LOW-CARB)

In addition to skipping the stovetop, you can bypass the refrigerator by preparing this superb no-cook summertime dish with vegetables picked straight from the garden, or purchased from your local farmer's market (as I do).

MAKES 2 TO 3 MAIN-COURSE OR 4 SIDE-DISH SERVINGS

2 large zucchini, about 8 ounces each

Sun-Dried Tomato Marinara Sauce, page 158

Using the larger holes of a grater and working in continuous end-to-end motions, shred each zucchini into long, thin strands and place in a large bowl. Add the Sun-Dried Tomato Marinara Sauce and toss well with a fork to combine. Serve at once.

PER SERVING: Calories 212; Protein 6g; Total Fat 15g; Sat Fat 2g; Cholesterol 0mg; Carbohydrate 20g; Dietary Fiber 6g; Sodium 399mg

Sun-Dried Tomato Marinara Sauce

(VEGAN/LOW-CARB)

The sun-dried tomatoes lend this raw marinara sauce a fullness of flavor and "cooked" texture—feel free to use it on cooked spaghetti squash or gluten-free pasta. While you can use cherry tomatoes in lieu of the grape variety, the latter will produce a less watery and sweeter sauce.

MAKES ABOUT 1½ CUPS SAUCE

1½ to 2 cups grape tomatoes

1 cup fresh basil leaves

¼ cup packed and drained marinated julienne-sliced sun-dried tomatoes

2 tablespoons extra-virgin olive oil

2 cloves garlic, finely chopped

¼ teaspoon coarse salt, or to taste

Freshly ground black pepper, to taste

Place all ingredients in a food processor fitted with the knife blade; pulse until smooth but still slightly chunky. For best results, serve at once.

PER SERVING (about ¼ cup, or ⅙ of recipe): Calories 60; Protein 1g; Total Fat 5g; Sat Fat 1g; Cholesterol 0mg; Carbohydrate 4g; Dietary Fiber 1g; Sodium 131mg

Zucchini-Rice Loaf with Chickpeas and Basil

(VEGAN)

Here is a great make-ahead dish to prepare with leftover Chinese takeout rice—a packed pint container typically yields about 3 cups of fluffed rice. For best results, finely chop the zucchini in a food processor fitted with the knife blade.

MAKES 6 SERVINGS

4 tablespoons extra-virgin olive oil, divided

1 pound medium zucchini, finely chopped, drained and patted dry with paper towels

3 cups cooked white rice, at room temperature, grains separated if clumped

1 cup loosely packed fresh basil leaves, finely chopped

Juice and zest of 1 medium lemon

2 large cloves garlic, finely chopped

Salt and freshly ground black pepper, to taste

¾ cup gluten-free Italian-seasoned dry bread crumbs

1 (15-ounce) can chickpeas, rinsed and drained

Garlic salt, to taste

1 (24-ounce) jar gluten-free pasta sauce, preferably the tomato-basil variety, ½ cup reserved, remaining sauce heated

Fresh basil sprigs, for garnish (optional)

Preheat oven to 350F (175C). Lightly grease a baking sheet and set aside.

In a large nonstick skillet, heat 2 tablespoons oil over medium-high heat. Add the zucchini and cook, stirring, until softened, 2 to 3 minutes. Add the rice and cook, stirring, until rice is heated through, about 2 minutes. Reduce the heat to medium and add the basil, lemon juice and zest, 1 tablespoon oil, garlic, salt, and pepper; cook, stirring, 1 minute. Remove from heat and add the bread crumbs, stirring well to thoroughly combine. Add the chickpeas, stirring well to combine.

When cool enough to handle, shape the rice mixture into a 7-inch-long loaf with a flat top. Let stand about 15 minutes to firm. (At this point, completely cooled loaf can be refrigerated, covered, up to 1 day before returning to room temperature and continuing with the recipe.)

Transfer loaf to the prepared baking sheet and brush evenly with the remaining 1 tablespoon of oil. Sprinkle lightly with the garlic salt. Bake on center oven rack 15 minutes. Remove from oven and brush evenly with ¼ cup of the reserved pasta sauce. Return to oven and bake an additional 15 minutes. Brush evenly with remaining ¼ cup of reserved pasta sauce and bake an additional 15 minutes. Remove from oven and let stand 15 minutes before slicing. Serve warm, garnished with fresh basil sprigs, if using, with heated pasta sauce passed separately.

PER SERVING: Calories 420; Protein 11g; Total Fat 15g; Sat Fat 2g; Cholesterol 0mg; Carbohydrate 63g; Dietary Fiber 4g; Sodium 838mg

Stuffed Zucchini Boats with Spinach and Parmesan

(EGG-FREE/LOW-CARB)

These delightful zucchini boats are as delicious to eat as they are attractive to look at. Shredded mozzarella can replace all or part of the Parmesan, if desired.

MAKES 3 MAIN-DISH OR 6 SIDE-DISH SERVINGS

3 large zucchini (8 ounces each), trimmed and halved lengthwise

1 tablespoon extra-virgin olive oil

1 small red onion (about 4 ounces), chopped

2 cloves garlic, finely chopped

1 cup chopped fresh spinach

¼ cup prepared gluten-free marinara sauce, plus additional heated sauce, to serve

3 tablespoons gluten-free Italian-seasoned dry bread crumbs, divided

Salt and freshly ground black pepper, to taste

1 cup gluten-free freshly grated Parmesan cheese, divided

12 grape or cherry tomatoes, halved (optional)

Preheat the oven to 350F (175C). Prepare a large bowl of ice water. Lightly oil a baking sheet and set aside.

Bring a large stockpot of salted water to a boil. Cook the zucchini until just fork-tender to the center, 2 to 3 minutes. Immediately plunge into the ice-water bath; let rest 5 minutes, or until cooled. Drain well and pat dry with paper towels. Scoop out the pulp, leaving a ¼-inch-thick shell. Coarsely chop the pulp and blot lightly with paper towels; set aside.

In a medium nonstick skillet, heat the oil over medium heat. Add the onion and cook, stirring, until softened, about 5 minutes. Add the garlic and cook, stirring constantly, 30 seconds. Add the spinach and cook, stirring, until spinach is wilted and most of the water released has evaporated, 1 to 2 minutes. Remove skillet from heat and add the reserved chopped zucchini pulp, ¼ cup marinara sauce, 2 tablespoons bread crumbs, salt, and pepper, tossing well to combine. Let cool a few minutes, then add ½ cup Parmesan cheese, tossing well to combine.

Stuff the shells with equal amounts of the filling and transfer to the prepared baking sheet. Bake 15 minutes. Sprinkle evenly with the remaining 1 tablespoon of bread crumbs (½ teaspoon per stuffed shell), followed with the remaining ½ cup of cheese (4 teaspoons per stuffed shell). Bake an additional 5 minutes, or until cheese is melted. Garnish with the tomato halves (4 per stuffed shell), if using, and serve at once, with additional heated marinara sauce passed separately.

PER SERVING: Calories 288; Protein 19g; Total Fat 16g; Sat Fat 7g; Cholesterol 27mg; Carbohydrate 20g; Dietary Fiber 4g; Sodium 978mg

Zucchini-Quinoa Lasagna

(EGG-FREE)

An ancient grain indigenous to South America, quinoa's unique status as a complete protein makes it an excellent high-fiber meat substitute. For stress-free entertaining, prepare the tasty quinoa filling a day ahead of serving. For a vegan variation, use a gluten-free non-dairy cream cheese substitute (mash in ½ tablespoon chopped and drained marinated sun-dried tomato pieces, if desired), and omit the Parmesan cheese.

SERVES 6

2 extra-large zucchini (about 12 ounces each and 8 inches long), each cut lengthwise into 6 slices

1 teaspoon salt, plus additional, to taste

1 tablespoon extra-virgin olive oil

1 small onion (about 3 ounces), chopped

2 large cloves garlic, finely chopped

1 cup low-sodium vegetable broth

1 cup water or low-sodium vegetable broth

1 cup quinoa, rinsed and drained

½ cup no-salt added tomato sauce

1 teaspoon dried oregano

¼ cup chopped fresh basil

¼ cup chopped fresh flat-leaf parsley

3 tablespoons gluten-free cream cheese, preferably the sun-dried tomato variety

Freshly ground black pepper, to taste

2 cups prepared gluten-free marinara or pasta sauce

½ cup freshly shredded gluten-free Parmesan cheese

Preheat oven to 425F (220C). Lightly oil a 9-inch baking dish and set aside. Place zucchini slices on bed of paper towels. Sprinkle with 1 teaspoon salt, cover with paper towels, and let stand to release moisture, 30 minutes.

In a medium saucepan, heat the oil over medium heat. Add the onion and cook, stirring, until softened, about 2 to 3 minutes. Add the garlic and cook, stirring constantly, 30 seconds. Add the broth, water, quinoa, tomato sauce, and oregano; bring to a boil over high heat. Reduce the heat to medium-low, cover, and simmer 20 to 25 minutes, or until liquids have been absorbed. Remove from heat and stir in the basil, parsley, and cream cheese; season with salt and pepper and set aside. (At this point, completely cooled mixture can be refrigerated, covered, up to 24 hours before returning to room temperature and continuing with the recipe.)

Spoon ½ cup of the marinara sauce along the bottom of the prepared baking dish. Blot remaining moisture and salt from zucchini slices; arrange 4 zucchini slices over marinara sauce (if necessary, trim zucchini to fit dish). Spoon half of the quinoa mixture over the zucchini, and cover with ½ cup marinara sauce. Repeat with 4 more zucchini slices, remaining quinoa, and ½ cup marinara sauce. Top with remaining 4 zucchini slices and remaining marinara sauce. Cover with foil (lightly oil the underside if foil will touch the sauce) and bake 35 to 40 minutes, or until zucchini is fork-tender. Remove foil and sprinkle evenly with the Parmesan cheese.

Bake, uncovered, 5 minutes, or until cheese is melted. Let stand about 10 minutes before cutting into wedges and serving warm.

PER SERVING: Calories 301; Protein 12g; Total Fat 11g; Sat Fat 3g; Cholesterol 9mg; Carbohydrate 41g; Dietary Fiber 7g; Sodium 757mg

SIX

Side Dishes

No Italian meal is complete without a side dish or two—or, oftentimes, three. In Italy, the options are naturally vast and varied for those on the gluten-free path. From artichokes to zucchini, fresh vegetables star, shining their goodness in the form of antioxidants, essential vitamins, and phytonutrients on partakers of any and all food persuasions. Indeed, many health experts agree that the emphasis on fresh vegetables is as responsible as olive oil for the particular healthfulness of the Italian brand of the miraculous Mediterranean diet. Starches such as potatoes and corn also get into the act, providing fiber, iron, and complex carbohydrates for energy. As you dig into the following recipes, consider serving some over rice, polenta, or millet, along with a cup or two of beans, for quick and easy complete-protein suppers.

Asparagus with Sun-Dried Tomato and Black Olive Sauce (vegan/low-carb)

Roasted Balsamic Beets (vegan/low-carb)

Steamed Broccoli with Toasted Pine Nuts (vegan/low-carb)

Roasted Broccoli with Walnuts (vegan/low-carb)

Lemon Broccolini (vegan/low-carb)

Sautéed Broccoli Rabe with Garlic (vegan/low-carb)

Brussels Sprouts with Italian-Seasoned Bread Crumbs (vegan/low-carb)

Steamed Butternut Squash with Cranberries and Sage (vegan/low-carb)

Oven-Roasted Carrots with Whole Garlic and Thyme (vegan/low-carb)

Roasted Cauliflower with Rosemary (vegan/low-carb)

Italian-Style Grilled Corn on the Cob (vegan)

Braised Belgian Endive with Garlic and Thyme (vegan/low-carb)

Roasted Fennel (vegan/low-carb)

Sicilian-Style Fennel with Tomatoes and Currants (vegan/low-carb)

Italian-Style Green Beans with Tomatoes, Red Onion, and Olives (vegan/low-carb)

Braised Kale with Raisins and Garlic (vegan/low-carb)

Grilled Portobello Mushroom Strips with Lemon Thyme (vegan/low-carb)

Herb-Roasted Potatoes (vegan/low-carb)

New Potatoes and Green Beans with Sage, Basil, and Walnut Pesto (vegan/low-carb)

Potato Gratin with Roasted Onion and Garlic (vegan)

Roasted Garlic Mashed Potatoes with Sour Cream (egg-free)

Fried Red Bell Peppers (vegan/low-carb)

Pesto-Rice Timbales (egg-free/low-carb)

Braised Romaine Lettuce with Garlic (vegan/low-carb)

Parmesan-Creamed Spinach (egg-free/low-carb)

Herbed Sweet Potato Oven Fries (vegan)

Braised Swiss Chard with Balsamic Vinegar (vegan/low-carb)

Chilled Stuffed Tomatoes with Rustic Pesto Sauce (vegan/low-carb)

Sicilian Turnip Gratin (vegan/low-carb)

Sautéed Zucchini with Parmesan and Lemon (egg-free/low-carb)

Roasted Lemon-Basil Zucchini and Summer Squash (vegan/low-carb)

Asparagus with Sun-Dried Tomato and Black Olive Sauce

(VEGAN/LOW-CARB)

Ready in minutes, this tasty side dish also makes a fine first course, served at room temperature on a bed of greens.

MAKES 4 TO 6 SERVINGS

¼ cup drained and finely chopped marinated sun-dried tomatoes, 1 tablespoon marinade reserved

2 tablespoons finely chopped kalamata olives

½ tablespoon extra-virgin olive oil

2 cloves garlic, finely chopped

Salt and freshly ground black pepper, to taste

1½ pounds medium asparagus, tough stem ends trimmed

In a small bowl, place the tomatoes and reserved marinade, olives, oil, garlic, salt, and pepper; stir well to combine. Set aside.

Bring a large stockpot of salted water to a boil. Cook the asparagus until crisp-tender, about 5 minutes, depending on thickness. Drain well and transfer to a shallow serving bowl. Add the tomato mixture, tossing gently to combine. Serve warm or at room temperature.

PER SERVING: Calories 82; Protein 3g; Total Fat 6g; Sat Fat 1g; Cholesterol 0mg; Carbohydrate 7g; Dietary Fiber 2g; Sodium 138mg

Roasted Balsamic Beets

(VEGAN/LOW-CARB)

These luscious beets are delicious warm or cold, by themselves, tossed into salads, or tucked into sandwiches.

MAKES 6 SERVINGS

3 pounds small beets (20 to 24), trimmed, scrubbed, and halved lengthwise

2 tablespoons extra-virgin olive oil, divided

½ tablespoon balsamic vinegar

Salt and freshly ground black pepper, to taste

Preheat oven to 425F (220C).

Place the beets on a baking sheet with a rim and toss with ½ tablespoon of the oil. Turn the halved beets cut side down. Cover the baking sheet tightly with foil. Bake for 30 minutes, or until the beets are very tender when pierced with the tip of a sharp knife. Remove from the oven, uncover, and let cool for 5 minutes.

Peel off the skins from the beets and cut into ½-inch cubes. Transfer to a medium serving bowl; while still warm, add the vinegar, salt, and pepper, tossing well to combine. Add the remaining 1½ tablespoons oil, tossing to thoroughly coat. Serve slightly warm or at room temperature. Alternatively, cover and refrigerate up to 3 days and serve chilled, or return to room temperature.

PER SERVING: Calories 105; Protein 2g; Total Fat 5g; Sat Fat 1g; Cholesterol 0mg; Carbohydrate 15g; Dietary Fiber 4g; Sodium 119mg

Steamed Broccoli with Toasted Pine Nuts

(VEGAN/LOW-CARB)

Frozen broccoli florets, slightly undercooked according to package directions, can replace the fresh variety, if desired.

MAKES 4 TO 5 SERVINGS

1 pound fresh broccoli florets

2 tablespoons pine nuts

2 tablespoons extra-virgin olive oil

1 to 2 cloves garlic, finely chopped

1 tablespoon fresh lemon juice, or to taste

Salt and freshly ground black pepper, to taste

Place the broccoli in a steaming basket set over boiling water; cover and steam over medium heat until broccoli is crisp-tender and bright green, 3 to 5 minutes. Drain and set aside.

Heat a large nonstick skillet over medium heat; add the pine nuts and cook, stirring often, until lightly toasted, 3 to 5 minutes. Transfer nuts to a holding plate and add the oil to the skillet, swirling to coat the bottom. Add the garlic and cook, stirring constantly, 1 minute. Add the broccoli and cook, stirring, until just heated through, about 2 minutes. Remove skillet from heat and add the lemon juice, pine nuts, salt, and pepper, tossing well to combine. Serve at once.

PER SERVING: Calories 120; Protein 5g; Total Fat 10g; Sat Fat 1g; Cholesterol 0mg; Carbohydrate 7g; Dietary Fiber 4g; Sodium 5mg

Roasted Broccoli with Walnuts

(VEGAN/LOW-CARB)

This scrumptious broccoli dish becomes a nutritious light supper served over brown rice.

MAKES 4 SERVINGS

1¼ pounds broccoli crowns, trimmed and cut into bite-size florets

2 tablespoons extra-virgin olive oil

Salt and freshly ground black pepper, to taste

2 tablespoons chopped walnuts

Preheat oven to 400F (205C).

On a rimmed baking sheet, toss the broccoli with the oil, salt, and pepper. Roast until broccoli is browned and tender, 25 to 30 minutes, adding the walnuts and tossing well to combine after 15 minutes. Serve warm or at room temperature.

PER SERVING: Calories 125; Protein 5g; Total Fat 9g; Sat Fat 1g; Cholesterol 0mg; Carbohydrate 8g; Dietary Fiber 5g; Sodium 24mg

Variation

To make Roasted Broccoli with Walnuts and Gorgonzola, toss the hot roasted broccoli and walnuts with 2 to 3 tablespoons gluten-free crumbled Gorgonzola cheese immediately after baking. Serve warm.

Lemon Broccolini

(VEGAN/LOW-CARB)

Broccolini, a hybrid of broccoli and Chinese chard and loaded with vitamin C and potassium, shines in this delicious recipe. Either broccoli or broccoli rabe can be substituted, as necessary.

MAKES 4 SERVINGS

1 pound broccolini (about 2 small bunches or 1 large), stem ends slightly trimmed
2 tablespoons extra-virgin olive oil
2 cloves garlic, finely chopped
¼ teaspoon lemon-pepper seasoning
½ teaspoon coarse salt, or to taste
1 to 1½ tablespoons fresh lemon juice
Freshly ground black pepper, to taste

Bring a large stockpot filled with salted water to a boil. Boil the broccolini 2 minutes. Drain and refresh under cold-running water until cool. Drain again.

In a large nonstick skillet, heat the oil over medium heat. Add the garlic and cook, stirring constantly, 30 seconds. Add the lemon-pepper seasoning and stir a few seconds. Add the well-drained broccolini and salt; cook, tossing and stirring often, 2 minutes. Remove skillet from heat and add the lemon juice and black pepper, tossing well to combine. Serve warm or at room temperature.

PER SERVING: Calories 95; Protein 4g; Total Fat 7g; Sat Fat 1g; Cholesterol 0mg; Carbohydrate 7g; Dietary Fiber 4g; Sodium 287mg

Sautéed Broccoli Rabe with Garlic

(VEGAN/LOW-CARB)

Pre-boiling the broccoli rabe takes some of the bite from this bitter, yet ever-so-healthy, non-heading variety of broccoli, whose long, thin, leafy stalks are topped with buds resembling tiny broccoli florets.

MAKES 4 SERVINGS

1 pound broccoli rabe, stem ends trimmed 1 inch
2 tablespoons extra-virgin olive oil
2 cloves garlic, thinly sliced
½ teaspoon coarse salt, or to taste

Bring a large stockpot filled with salted water to a boil over high heat. Prepare an ice-water bath and set aside. Add the broccoli rabe to the boiling water; cook, uncovered, until just tender, about 3 minutes. Drain and transfer to the ice-water bath; let cool a few minutes. Drain well in a colander.

In a large nonstick skillet, heat the oil over medium heat. Add the garlic and cook, stirring often, 2 minutes, or until just beginning to brown. Add the broccoli rabe and salt, tossing to coat with the oil; cook, tossing and stirring often, until broccoli rabe is tender, 2 to 3 minutes. Serve warm.

PER SERVING: Calories 94; Protein 4g; Total Fat 7g; Sat Fat 1g; Cholesterol 0mg; Carbohydrate 7g; Dietary Fiber 3g; Sodium 266mg

Brussels Sprouts with Italian-Seasoned Bread Crumbs

(VEGAN/LOW-CARB)

These delicious and nutritious miniature cabbages will grace any Thanksgiving table. For easy entertaining, precook the Brussels sprouts in the microwave up to 1 hour before quickly finishing the dish on the stovetop.

MAKES 5 TO 6 SERVINGS

1 tablespoon extra-virgin olive oil
2 (10-ounce) packages frozen Brussels
    sprouts, cooked according to package
    directions, drained
Salt and freshly ground black pepper, to taste
¼ cup low-sodium vegetable broth
1 tablespoon gluten-free, egg-free, dairy-free
    Italian seasoned dry bread crumbs
1 tablespoon finely chopped fresh flat-leaf
    parsley

In a large nonstick skillet, heat the oil over medium heat. Add the Brussels sprouts, salt, and pepper; cook, stirring, 1 minute. Add the broth and raise the heat to medium-high; cook, stirring often, until liquid has evaporated, about 2 minutes. Reduce the heat to low and sprinkle the Brussels sprouts with the bread crumbs and parsley; cook, tossing with a spatula, until thoroughly coated, about 30 seconds. Serve warm.

PER SERVING: Calories 79; Protein 5g; Total Fat 3g; Sat Fat 1g; Cholesterol 0mg; Carbohydrate 10g; Dietary Fiber 5g; Sodium 48mg

Steamed Butternut Squash with Cranberries and Sage

(VEGAN/LOW-CARB)

Packages of peeled and cubed butternut squash make quick work of this ideal Thanksgiving and winter holiday side dish.

MAKES 5 TO 6 SERVINGS

1¼ pounds (20 ounces) peeled and cubed
    butternut squash (3 cups)
2 tablespoons dried cranberries
1 tablespoon extra-virgin olive oil
¼ cup finely chopped red onion or shallots
1 tablespoon finely chopped fresh sage or
    ½ teaspoon crumbled, dried sage
½ teaspoon coarse salt, or to taste
Freshly ground black pepper, to taste

Place the squash and cranberries in a large steaming basket set over about 2 inches of water; bring water to a boil over high heat. Reduce heat to medium-high, cover, and steam squash about 5 minutes, or until tender. Carefully remove steaming basket and let cool a few minutes. (At this point, squash and cranberries can be held at room temperature up to 1 hour before continuing with the recipe.)

In a large nonstick skillet, heat the oil over medium heat. Add the onion and cook, stirring, until lightly browned, about 3 minutes. Add the squash and cranberries, sage, salt, and pepper; cook, tossing constantly with a spatula, until heated through, 1 to 2 minutes. Serve warm or at room temperature.

PER SERVING: Calories 71; Protein 1g; Total Fat 3g; Sat Fat 0g; Cholesterol 0mg; Carbohydrate 12g; Dietary Fiber 2g; Sodium 192mg

Oven-Roasted Carrots with Whole Garlic and Thyme

(VEGAN/LOW-CARB)

This flavorful carrot dish will perfume your home for hours with the heady scents of garlic and thyme.

MAKES 4 SERVINGS

1 pound baby carrots

12 cloves garlic, peeled and left whole

4 teaspoons extra-virgin olive oil, divided

1 teaspoon dried thyme leaves

¼ teaspoon coarse salt, or to taste

Freshly ground black pepper, to taste

1 teaspoon white wine vinegar

Preheat oven to 450F (230C).

In a large bowl, combine the carrots, garlic, 3 teaspoons of the oil, thyme, salt, and pepper; toss well to evenly coat. Transfer to an ungreased shallow baking dish large enough to comfortably hold the carrots in a single layer. Cover tightly with foil and bake 20 minutes; stir. Bake, uncovered, for an additional 10 minutes. Add the remaining 1 teaspoon of oil and the vinegar; stir well. Bake, uncovered, 5 to 10 more minutes, or until carrots are tender yet firm and mixture is lightly browned. Serve warm.

PER SERVING: Calories 97; Protein 2g; Total Fat 5g; Sat Fat 1g; Cholesterol 0mg; Carbohydrate 13g; Dietary Fiber 3g; Sodium 155mg

Roasted Cauliflower with Rosemary

(VEGAN/LOW-CARB)

I make copious amounts of this tasty recipe throughout the winter months when fresh cauliflower is abundant. For a scrumptious soup variation, see Roasted Cauliflower Soup with Rosemary, page 37.

MAKES 6 SERVINGS

1 extra-large cauliflower (about 3½ pounds), separated into bite-size florets

¼ cup extra-virgin olive oil

1 tablespoon dried whole rosemary leaves

½ teaspoon garlic salt, plus additional, to taste

Freshly ground black pepper, to taste

Preheat oven to 425F (220C).

In a large bowl, toss together the cauliflower, oil, rosemary, garlic salt, and pepper until thoroughly combined. Arrange in a single layer on a large ungreased baking sheet with sides. Bake 30 minutes, turning the cauliflower once halfway through cooking, or until lightly browned and tender. Sprinkle with additional garlic salt and pepper, as necessary. Serve warm.

PER SERVING: Calories 139; Protein 5g; Total Fat 10g; Sat Fat 1g; Cholesterol 0mg; Carbohydrate 12g; Dietary Fiber 6g; Sodium 239mg

Italian-Style Grilled Corn on the Cob

(VEGAN)

While Italians living in Italy typically don't eat fresh corn, fortunately, they do here. Parboiling the corn ensures that it will be grilled to perfection.

MAKES 4 SERVINGS

4 ears husked fresh corn

2 tablespoons plus 2 teaspoons extra-virgin olive oil, divided

1 tablespoon balsamic vinegar

2 cloves garlic, finely chopped

½ teaspoon Italian seasoning, plus additional, to taste

Crushed red pepper flakes, to taste (optional)

½ teaspoon coarse salt, or to taste

Freshly ground black pepper, to taste

Gluten-free freshly grated Parmesan cheese, to taste (optional)

Prepare a medium-hot charcoal or gas grill, or preheat a broiler. Position the grill rack or oven rack 4 to 6 inches from the heat source. If broiling, lightly oil a baking sheet with sides and set aside.

Meanwhile, bring a large stockpot filled with water to a boil over high heat. Add the corn and let return to a boil. Cover and immediately remove from the heat. Let stand, covered, 5 minutes.

In a small bowl, whisk together 2 tablespoons of the oil, vinegar, garlic, Italian seasoning, and red pepper, if using; set aside.

Drain the corn in a colander and rinse under cold running water until cool enough to handle. Rub each ear of corn with ½ teaspoon of the remaining 2 teaspoons oil. Sprinkle with the salt and pepper. Grill or broil, turning often, until golden and lightly charred, 5 to 10 minutes. Transfer the corn to a serving platter and brush corn evenly with the oil and vinegar mixture. Sprinkle with the Parmesan, if using, and serve at once.

PER SERVING: Calories 203; Protein 5g; Total Fat 11g; Sat Fat 2g; Cholesterol 0mg; Carbohydrate 28g; Dietary Fiber 4g; Sodium 256mg

Braised Belgian Endive with Garlic and Thyme

(VEGAN/LOW-CARB)

This fragrant, homey dish is my favorite way to enjoy the eminently elegant Belgian endive.

MAKES 4 SERVINGS

1 tablespoon extra-virgin olive oil

4 large cloves garlic, peeled and halved lengthwise

4 large heads Belgian endive (about 1¼ pounds), bottoms trimmed, cut lengthwise in half

¾ cup low-sodium vegetable broth

8 small sprigs fresh thyme, divided

Salt and freshly ground black pepper, to taste

2 tablespoons chopped fresh flat-leaf parsley, for garnish

In a large nonstick skillet with a lid, heat the oil over medium heat. Add the garlic and cook, stirring often, until softened and fragrant, 1 to 2 minutes. Remove skillet from heat. Place endive, cut sides down, in the skillet, interspersing the garlic evenly alongside the halves. Add the broth and arrange 4 sprigs of the thyme over the endive; season lightly with salt and pepper. Bring to a simmer over medium-high heat. Reduce heat to medium, cover, and cook until endive is tender, 7 to 10 minutes. Uncover and remove garlic and thyme. Raise heat to medium-high and cook without stirring until most of the liquid has evaporated, 2 to 3 minutes. Serve warm or at room temperature, garnished with the parsley and remaining 4 thyme sprigs.

PER SERVING: Calories 73; Protein 5g; Total Fat 4g; Sat Fat 1g; Cholesterol 0mg; Carbohydrate 6g; Dietary Fiber 4g; Sodium 205mg

Roasted Fennel

(VEGAN/LOW-CARB)

Roasting fennel concentrates its natural sweetness, while a sprinkling of gluten-free bread crumbs lends it a crunchy crust.

MAKES 4 TO 6 SERVINGS

- 2 tablespoons extra-virgin olive oil
- 1 tablespoon red wine vinegar
- 3 cloves garlic, finely chopped
- ½ teaspoon Dijon mustard
- ½ teaspoon salt, or to taste
- Freshly ground black pepper, to taste
- 3 medium fennel bulbs (about 12 ounces each), trimmed, cored and cut lengthwise into eighths
- 2 tablespoons gluten-free, dairy-free, egg-free Italian-seasoned dry bread crumbs
- ¼ cup grated gluten-free Parmesan cheese (optional)

Preheat oven to 425F (220C). Lightly oil a rimmed baking sheet and set aside.

In a large bowl, whisk together the oil, vinegar, garlic, mustard, salt, and pepper. Add the fennel and toss well to thoroughly coat. Add the bread crumbs and toss well to thoroughly coat.

Transfer the fennel mixture in a single layer to the prepared baking sheet. Bake about 30 to 40 minutes, or until fennel is fork-tender and browned, turning halfway through cooking, and sprinkling with the Parmesan, if using, the last 5 minutes. Serve at once.

PER SERVING: Calories 132; Protein 3g; Total Fat 7g; Sat Fat 1g; Cholesterol 0mg; Carbohydrate 16g; Dietary Fiber 6g; Sodium 465mg

Sicilian-Style Braised Fennel with Tomatoes and Currants

(VEGAN/LOW-CARB)

This is my favorite way to enjoy fennel, a mildly licorice-scented vegetable that is often mislabeled as anise at the supermarket. Raisins can replace the currants, if desired.

MAKES 6 SERVINGS

- 2 tablespoons extra-virgin olive oil
- 1 small onion (about 4 ounces), chopped
- 2 large fennel bulbs (about 1 pound each), trimmed and cored, each cut lengthwise into eighths
- 4 medium plum tomatoes (about 3 ounces each), chopped
- ¼ cup currants
- ¼ cup low-sodium vegetable broth
- ¼ cup water
- ½ teaspoon dried oregano
- Salt and freshly ground black pepper, to taste

In a large deep-sided nonstick skillet with a lid, heat the oil over medium heat. Add the onion and cook, stirring, until softened, about 3 minutes. Add the fennel and cook, stirring, until just softened, 4 to 5 minutes. Add the remaining ingredients and bring to a simmer over medium-high heat. Reduce the heat to medium-low and simmer, covered, stirring occasionally, until the fennel is easily pierced with the tip of a sharp knife, 7 to 10 minutes. Increase the heat to medium and cook, uncovered, stirring occasionally, until liquids are reduced by half, about 3 minutes. Serve warm.

PER SERVING: Calories 125; Protein 3g; Total Fat 5g; Sat Fat 1g; Cholesterol 0mg; Carbohydrate 20g; Dietary Fiber 6g; Sodium 106mg

Italian-Style Green Beans with Tomatoes, Red Onion, and Olives

(VEGAN/LOW-CARB)

Here is a quick and easy way to dress up fresh green beans that's elegant enough to serve company. If you're not a fan of olives, omit them and the dish will still be delicious.

MAKES 6 SERVINGS

1½ pounds fresh green beans, trimmed

1 tablespoon extra-virgin olive oil

1 small red onion (about 4 ounces), sliced into thin half-rounds

4 ounces plum tomatoes (about 2 small), chopped

3 to 4 tablespoons chopped kalamata olives

Garlic salt, to taste

Freshly ground black pepper, to taste

⅓ to ½ cup prepared gluten-free, dairy-free Italian dressing

Bring a large stockpot filled with salted water to a boil. Add the beans and boil until crisp-tender, about 5 minutes. Drain in a colander and refresh under cold-running water; set aside to drain. (At this point, green beans can be held at room temperature up to 1 hour before continuing with the recipe.)

In a large nonstick skillet, heat the oil over medium-high heat. Add the onion and cook, stirring, until softened and beginning to brown, about 3 minutes. Add the green beans, tomatoes, olives, garlic salt, and pepper; cook, stirring, until heated through, 1 to 2 minutes. Remove from heat and add the dressing, tossing well to combine. Serve warm or at room temperature.

PER SERVING: Calories 94; Protein 2g; Total Fat 6g; Sat Fat 1g; Cholesterol 0mg; Carbohydrate 10g; Dietary Fiber 4g; Sodium 231mg

Braised Kale with Raisins and Garlic

(VEGAN/LOW-CARB)

Widely considered to be among the world's most nutritious vegetables, kale is high in beta carotene and vitamins K and C, and is loaded with antioxidants to boot. Stir in a can of chickpeas or other beans and serve over rice or toss with gluten-free pasta for a delicious meal.

MAKES 4 SERVINGS

1 tablespoon extra-virgin olive oil

3 large cloves garlic, finely chopped

1 (10-ounce) bag fresh kale, coarsely chopped, or 1 pound bunch fresh kale, washed, thick ribs and stems discarded, and leaves coarsely chopped, divided

⅔ cup low-sodium vegetable broth or water,
   divided

¼ cup raisins

Salt and freshly ground black pepper, to taste

½ to 1 tablespoon balsamic vinegar

2 tablespoons toasted pine nuts (optional)

In a medium stockpot, heat the oil over medium heat. Add the garlic and cook, stirring constantly, 30 seconds. Add half the kale and half the broth; cook, tossing and stirring, until kale is just wilted, 1 to 2 minutes. Add remaining kale and broth, raisins, salt, and pepper, cook, tossing and stirring, until kale is just wilted, 1 to 2 more minutes. Reduce the heat to low, cover, and steam until kale is tender, about 20 minutes, stirring a few times. Remove from heat and add the vinegar, stirring well to combine. Serve warm, sprinkled with the pine nuts, if using.

PER SERVING: Calories 104; Protein 5g; Total Fat 4g; Sat Fat 1g; Cholesterol 0mg; Carbohydrate 15g; Dietary Fiber 1g; Sodium 118mg

Grilled Portobello Mushroom Strips with Lemon Thyme

(VEGAN/LOW-CARB)

These succulent strips of meaty mushrooms are excellent companions to just about any meal. At room temperature, they make a fine antipasto.

MAKES 4 SERVINGS

4 large Portobello mushroom caps (about
   3 ounces each)

2 tablespoons extra-virgin olive oil,
   divided

Salt, preferably the coarse variety, and
   freshly ground black pepper, to taste

1 tablespoon chopped fresh thyme leaves

1 tablespoon chopped fresh chives or green
   parts of scallions

Juice of 1 medium lemon (3 tablespoons)

1 tablespoon chopped fresh flat-leaf parsley

Heat a grill pan with ridges over medium-high heat. Brush the caps and rims of the mushrooms evenly with 1 tablespoon oil. Place on the grill, gill sides up; grill about 3 minutes, rotating clockwise with a metal spatula twice, until bottoms are browned and tender. Turn each mushroom over, gill sides down, and grill until tender, 1 to 2 minutes.

Transfer mushrooms to a rimmed baking sheet and cut into ½-inch-wide strips. Season with salt and pepper and toss to combine. Sprinkle with the thyme and chives, then drizzle with the lemon juice and remaining 1 tablespoon of oil; toss well to combine. Transfer mushrooms and accumulated juices to a serving platter. Sprinkle evenly with the parsley and serve warm or at room temperature.

PER SERVING: Calories 87; Protein 2g; Total Fat 7g; Sat Fat 1g; Cholesterol 0mg; Carbohydrate 6g; Dietary Fiber 1g; Sodium 5mg

Herb-Roasted Potatoes

(VEGAN/LOW-CARB)

Feel free to use your favorite combinations of dried Italian herbs in this fragrant, flavorful side dish.

MAKES 6 SERVINGS

1½ pounds small red potatoes, quartered

1½ tablespoons extra-virgin olive oil

1½ tablespoons dried parsley flakes

1 teaspoon dried rosemary leaves

1 teaspoon coarse salt (or ½ teaspoon garlic salt, if not using optional fresh garlic)

½ teaspoon dried oregano

Freshly ground black pepper, to taste

3 large cloves garlic, finely chopped (optional)

Preheat the oven to 400F (205C).

In a large bowl, toss all the ingredients except the optional fresh garlic until well combined. Arrange in a single layer on an ungreased large baking sheet with sides. Roast 30 minutes, or until potatoes are browned and tender, turning halfway through cooking. Remove baking sheet from oven and sprinkle the potatoes with the fresh garlic, if using; toss well to combine. Return to the oven and roast an additional 5 minutes, or until garlic is fragrant, taking care not to burn the garlic. Toss well and serve at once.

PER SERVING: Calories 100; Protein 2g; Total Fat 4g; Sat Fat 1g; Cholesterol 0mg; Carbohydrate 16g; Dietary Fiber 1g; Sodium 320mg

New Potatoes and Green Beans with Sage, Basil, and Walnut Pesto

(VEGAN/LOW-CARB)

This special side dish can become a casual supper when tossed with a can of chickpeas. Serve chilled, it also makes an unusual—and delicious—potato salad. If tiny new potatoes are not available, use the smallest ones you can find and cut into quarters.

MAKES 6 SERVINGS

1½ pounds tiny new potatoes, preferably red-skinned, halved

8 ounces fresh green beans, trimmed

1 recipe Sage, Basil, and Walnut Pesto (page 177)

Salt, preferably the coarse variety, to taste

Freshly ground black pepper, to taste

Bring a large stockpot filled with salted water to a boil over high heat; add the potatoes and green beans. When water returns to a boil, reduce heat to medium-high. Boil gently for 10 to 12 minutes, or until potatoes are cooked through yet still firm and the beans are tender. Drain, reserving 2 tablespoons of the cooking liquid. Return to the pot and toss gently with the pesto and reserved cooking liquid. Season with salt and pepper, if necessary. Serve at once.

PER SERVING: Calories 159; Protein 3g; Total Fat 8g; Sat Fat 1g; Cholesterol 0mg; Carbohydrate 19g; Dietary Fiber 3g; Sodium 164mg

Sage, Basil, and Walnut Pesto

(VEGAN/LOW-CARB)

Toss this tasty pesto with countless vegetables and gluten-free pastas, brush over polenta and gluten-free flatbreads, or stir into soups.

MAKES ABOUT ⅓ CUP

½ cup fresh sage leaves
½ cup fresh basil leaves
3 tablespoons extra-virgin olive oil
2 tablespoons chopped walnuts
½ teaspoon coarse salt, or to taste
2 large cloves garlic, finely chopped
Freshly ground black pepper, to taste

In a food processor fitted with the knife blade, process all ingredients until a smooth paste forms. Cover and refrigerate up to 2 days before using as directed in recipe.

PER SERVING (about 1 tablespoon, or ⅙ of recipe): Calories 80; Protein 1g; Total Fat 8g; Sat Fat 1g; Cholesterol 0mg; Carbohydrate 1g; Dietary Fiber 0g; Sodium 157mg

Potato Gratin with Roasted Onion and Garlic

(VEGAN)

You will never miss the milk or butter in this rich and creamy potato gratin.

MAKES 4 TO 6 SERVINGS

1 large head garlic
1 large onion (about 8 ounces), unpeeled, any papery skin removed
2 extra-large russet potatoes (about 12 ounces each)
⅓ to ½ cup low-sodium vegetable broth
1½ tablespoons extra-virgin olive oil, divided
½ teaspoon coarse salt, or to taste
Fresh ground black pepper, to taste
2 tablespoons gluten-free, egg-free, dairy-free Italian seasoned dry bread crumbs

Preheat oven to 425F (220C). Wrap the garlic in foil. Place the onion on a double sheet of foil and pull the sides halfway up, forming a bowl.

Prick the potatoes in several places with the tines of a fork. Place on an ungreased baking sheet, along with the garlic and onion. Roast about 1 hour, or until potatoes are tender through the center and the onion is soft and collapsed. Remove the baking sheet from the oven and set aside to cool about 10 minutes.

Reduce the oven temperature to 350F (175C). Lightly oil an 8 × 8-inch baking dish and set aside.

Unwrap the garlic head and cut crosswise in half; squeeze out the softened garlic into a large bowl. Discard the stem and root end of the onion and the first layer of skin. Finely chop the onion and add to the bowl. Slice the potatoes in half lengthwise and scoop out the pulp into the bowl. (Discard or reserve skins for another use.) Add ⅓ cup broth, 1 tablespoon of the oil, salt, and pepper; mash well with a potato masher. With a spoon, vigorously stir the potato mixture until creamy, adding the rest of the broth, if necessary. Transfer to the prepared baking dish and smooth with the back of a spoon. (At this point, mixture can be held at room temperature up to 1 hour before continuing with the recipe.) Using a pastry brush, brush the top with the remaining ½ tablespoon of oil. Sprinkle evenly with the bread crumbs and bake, uncovered, about 30 minutes, or until top is lightly browned. Serve warm.

PER SERVING: Calories 200; Protein 5g; Total Fat 5g; Sat Fat 1g; Cholesterol 0mg; Carbohydrate 34g; Dietary Fiber 4g; Sodium 389mg

Roasted Garlic Mashed Potatoes with Sour Cream

(EGG-FREE)

These outstanding mashed potatoes are ideal to serve at Thanksgiving. Roasting tames the garlic's strong flavor and imparts a subtle sweetness.

MAKES 8 SERVINGS

1 medium head garlic

4 pounds russet potatoes, peeled and cut into small chunks

½ cup low-fat milk, plus additional, to taste

½ cup plus 2 tablespoons gluten-free light sour cream

2 tablespoons butter

1 tablespoon extra-virgin olive oil

1 teaspoon salt, or to taste

Freshly ground black pepper, to taste

Preheat oven to 400 F (205C).

Wrap the head of garlic in aluminum foil and roast about 50 minutes, or until soft. Remove the foil and set the garlic aside to cool slightly.

Meanwhile, in a medium stockpot, place the potatoes in enough salted water to cover by a few inches; bring to a boil over high heat. Reduce the heat slightly and cook until potatoes are very tender, about 20 minutes. Drain well and return to the stockpot.

Cut the roasted garlic head crosswise in half and squeeze the softened cloves into the potatoes. Add the milk, sour cream, butter, oil, salt, and pepper;

mash well with a potato masher, adding additional milk for a creamier consistency, if desired. Serve at once.

PER SERVING: Calories 194; Protein 5g; Total Fat 5g; Sat Fat 2g; Cholesterol 9mg; Carbohydrate 33g; Dietary Fiber 3g; Sodium 319mg

Fried Red Bell Peppers

(VEGAN/LOW-CARB)

Quicker and less fussy than roasted red peppers, which require preheating the oven and peeling the skin, skillet-fried bell peppers are ready to eat in just about 10 minutes. Enjoy them as part of an antipasto platter, on sandwiches, over polenta, or tossed with rice and gluten-free pastas.

MAKES 6 SERVINGS

¼ cup extra-virgin olive oil

3 large red bell peppers (about 8 ounces each), halved lengthwise, cored, seeded, and ribs removed, and cut lengthwise into ½-inch-wide strips

½ teaspoon coarse salt

In a large nonstick skillet, heat the oil over medium heat. Add the peppers, skin sides down, and cook without stirring 7 to 10 minutes, or until nicely browned. Turn and cook without stirring until tender when pierced with the tip of a sharp knife, about 3 minutes. With a slotted spoon, transfer pepper strips to a serving platter and sprinkle with the salt. (Reserve cooking oil and let cool to room temperature.) Serve warm or at room temperature. Completely cooled peppers can be refrigerated in a covered dish containing the completely cooled cooking oil up to 5 days before returning to room temperature and serving.

PER SERVING: Calories 110; Protein 1g; Total Fat 9g; Sat Fat 1g; Cholesterol 0mg; Carbohydrate 7g; Dietary Fiber 3g; Sodium 159mg

Pesto-Rice Timbales

(EGG-FREE/LOW-CARB)

For stress-free entertaining, these pretty green-flecked timbales can be held in the muffin pan in a warm oven (about 200F/95C) up to 1 hour before inverting and serving. To create a picture-perfect holiday main course, serve them on top of gluten-free tomato-basil pasta sauce.

MAKES 6 SIDE-DISH OR 3 MAIN-DISH SERVINGS

⅔ cup white or brown Arborio rice

½ cup chopped fresh basil

3 ounces gluten-free light cream cheese, cut into 4 pieces, softened

3 tablespoons prepared gluten-free pesto

½ teaspoon salt, or to taste

Freshly ground black pepper, to taste

Cherry or grape tomatoes, for garnish (optional)

Fresh basil leaves, for garnish (optional)

Preheat oven to 350F (175C). Bring a medium stockpot filled with salted water to a boil over high heat. Lightly oil a 6-cup muffin pan and set aside.

Add the rice to the boiling water and cook, pasta style, until al dente, 12 to 15 minutes for white rice, 20 to 25 minutes for brown rice. Drain the rice in a colander and transfer to a large bowl. Add chopped basil, cream cheese, pesto, salt, and pepper, stirring until thoroughly combined.

Spoon the rice mixture into the prepared muffin pan, packing it lightly. Bake for about 10 minutes, or until heated through. Invert onto a platter and serve at once, garnished with the cherry tomatoes and basil leaves, if using.

PER SERVING (per timbale, or ⅙ of recipe): Calories 146; Protein 4g; Total Fat 6g; Sat Fat 3g; Cholesterol 10mg; Carbohydrate 18g; Dietary Fiber 0g; Sodium 313mg

Braised Romaine Lettuce with Garlic

(VEGAN/LOW-CARB)

Braising romaine lettuce is a marvelous way to get a more concentrated amount of a good thing. Served over brown rice and sprinkled with some pine nuts and Parmesan, this perennial salad favorite becomes dinner. Escarole or curly endive can replace the romaine, if desired.

MAKES 4 SERVINGS

2 medium heads Romaine lettuce (about 2 pounds), thick bottoms trimmed, leaves separated, washed, and drained well

1 tablespoon extra-virgin olive oil

1 small red onion (about 4 ounces), sliced into thin half-rounds

4 large cloves garlic, finely chopped

¼ cup low-sodium vegetable broth

Salt and freshly ground black pepper, to taste

Blot the lettuce with paper towel and cut crosswise into 1-inch wide strips; set aside. In a medium stockpot, heat the oil over medium heat. Add the onion and cook, stirring, until softened, about 2 minutes. Add the garlic and cook, stirring constantly, 30 seconds. Add the lettuce, broth, salt, and pepper; cook, stirring, 1 minute. Cover the pot and reduce the heat to medium-low; cook, stirring occasionally, until lettuce is tender, about 10 minutes. Uncover and raise the heat to medium-high; cook, stirring often, until all the liquid has evaporated. Remove from heat, transfer to a bowl, and serve warm.

PER SERVING: Calories 82; Protein 5g; Total Fat 4g; Sat Fat 1g; Cholesterol 0mg; Carbohydrate 9g; Dietary Fiber 4g; Sodium 51mg

Parmesan-Creamed Spinach

(EGG-FREE/LOW-CARB)

Delicious on its own, this luxurious creamed spinach can be a filling for Portobello mushrooms, dip for gluten-free Italian bread, or sauce for poached eggs and gluten-free pasta.

MAKES 4 TO 6 SERVINGS

1 tablespoon extra-virgin olive oil
2 cloves garlic, finely chopped
1 (10-ounce) package frozen chopped spinach, cooked according to package directions, well drained
3 ounce gluten-free reduced-fat Neufchâtel cream cheese, softened
2 tablespoons skim milk
2 tablespoons gluten-free freshly grated Parmesan cheese
Salt and freshly ground black pepper, to taste

In a large nonstick skillet, heat the oil over medium heat. Add the garlic and cook, stirring, 1 minute, or until softened and fragrant. Add the spinach and cook, stirring, 1 minute. Reduce the heat to medium-low and add the remaining ingredients; cook, stirring, until thoroughly blended and heated through, about 3 minutes. Serve at once.

PER SERVING: Calories 121; Protein 6g; Total Fat 10g; Sat Fat 4g; Cholesterol 19mg; Carbohydrate 5g; Dietary Fiber 2g; Sodium 200mg

Herbed Sweet Potato Oven Fries

(VEGAN)

These tasty oven fries pair well with pizza sauce for dipping. Feel free to use any combination of dried Italian herbs and substitute the sweet potatoes with the russet variety, if desired.

MAKES 5 TO 6 SERVINGS

2 tablespoons extra-virgin olive oil
1 teaspoon dried rosemary
½ teaspoon dried thyme
½ teaspoon garlic salt, plus additional to taste
Freshly ground black pepper, to taste
2 extra-large sweet potatoes (10 to 12 ounces), peeled, halved crosswise and cut lengthwise into thin French fry–style strips
2 tablespoons chopped fresh flat-leaf parsley (optional)

Preheat oven to 450F (230C). Lightly oil a large baking sheet and set aside.

In a large bowl, whisk together the oil, rosemary, thyme, garlic salt, and pepper until thoroughly blended. Add the potatoes and toss until thoroughly coated.

Arrange sweet potatoes in a single layer on the prepared baking sheet. Bake until sweet potatoes are tender and golden brown, about 30 minutes, turning halfway through baking time. Transfer sweet potatoes to a serving platter and sprinkle with the parsley, if using. Serve at once.

PER SERVING: Calories 169; Protein 2g; Total Fat 6g; Sat Fat 1g; Cholesterol 0mg; Carbohydrate 28g; Dietary Fiber 4g; Sodium 221mg

stirring, until most of the liquids have evaporated, 1 to 2 minutes. Remove pot from heat and stir in the vinegar. Cover the pot and let stand for 5 minutes. Stir well and serve warm or at room temperature.

PER SERVING: Calories 80; Protein 4g; Total Fat 4g; Sat Fat 1g; Cholesterol 0mg; Carbohydrate 10g; Dietary Fiber 4g; Sodium 462mg

Braised Swiss Chard with Balsamic Vinegar

(VEGAN/LOW-CARB)

For an attractive holiday dish, prepare with a mixture of red and green Swiss chard.

MAKES 4 SERVINGS

- 1 tablespoon extra-virgin olive oil
- ½ cup chopped onion
- 2 pounds Swiss chard, stems removed and leaves cut crosswise into 1-inch-wide strips, divided
- Salt, preferably the coarse variety, and freshly ground black pepper, to taste
- 2 tablespoons water
- 2 tablespoons low-sodium vegetable broth
- 2 tablespoons balsamic vinegar

In a medium stockpot, heat the oil over medium heat. Add the onion and cook, stirring, until softened, 2 to 3 minutes. Add half the Swiss chard, salt, and pepper; cook, stirring, until Swiss chard begins to wilt, 1 to 2 minutes. Add the remaining Swiss chard and water, cook, stirring, until Swiss chard begins to wilt, 1 to 2 more minutes. Add the broth, cover the pot, and cook, stirring often, until Swiss chard is tender, 5 to 8 minutes. Uncover and cook,

Chilled Stuffed Tomatoes with Rustic Pesto Sauce

(VEGAN/LOW-CARB)

Served atop a bed of mixed greens, these no-cook stuffed tomatoes make an ideal first course to serve in the summertime. Gluten-free prepared pesto sauce can be used in lieu of the Rustic Pesto Sauce; in this instance, the dish will invariably contain dairy.

MAKES 4 SERVINGS

- 4 medium vine-ripened tomatoes (about 6 ounces each)
- ½ recipe Rustic Pesto Sauce, page 92 (about ¼ cup)
- Salt and freshly ground black pepper, to taste

Cut a thin slice from the top of each tomato and discard. Gently squeeze out the seeds from each tomato. Using a small sharp knife or a melon baller, scoop out the pulp and reserve, discarding any white core. Chop the pulp and transfer to a small bowl. Add the pesto sauce, salt, and pepper, stirring well to combine.

Spoon equal portions of the pesto sauce mixture into each tomato (about 1½ tablespoons). Serve at room temperature, or cover and refrigerate a minimum of 3 hours, or overnight, and serve chilled.

PER SERVING: Calories 113; Protein 2g; Total Fat 9g;
Sat Fat 1g; Cholesterol 0mg; Carbohydrate 8g; Dietary
Fiber 2g; Sodium 132mg

Return the dish to the oven and broil until
lightly browned, about 5 minutes. Serve warm.

PER SERVING: Calories 115; Protein 3g; Total Fat 5g;
Sat Fat 1g; Cholesterol 0mg; Carbohydrate 17g; Dietary
Fiber 4g; Sodium 113mg

Sicilian Turnip Gratin

(VEGAN/LOW-CARB)

*Thinly slicing the turnips and onions results in a pleasingly
tender gratin, perfect for the cold-weather months.*

MAKE 6 SERVINGS

4 medium turnips (about 1¾ pounds total),
  peeled and sliced into ⅛-inch-thick rounds

1 large onion (about 8 ounces), sliced into
  ⅛-inch-thick half-rounds

6 medium plum tomatoes (about 3 ounces
  each), sliced into ¼-inch-thick rounds

2 tablespoons extra-virgin olive oil

Garlic salt, to taste

Freshly ground black pepper, to taste

Dried oregano, to taste

2 tablespoons gluten-free, egg-free, dairy-free
  Italian seasoned dry bread crumbs

Preheat oven to 375F (190C). Lightly oil a
9 × 13-inch ovenproof baking dish.

Arrange half the turnip rounds, overlapping as
necessary, in the prepared baking sheet. Top with
half the onions, followed by half the tomatoes.
Using a pastry brush, brush the tomatoes with half
the oil. Sprinkle lightly with garlic salt, pepper, and
oregano. Repeat with a second layer, ending with
the bread crumbs. Cover tightly with foil and bake
about 1 hour, or until turnips are tender when
pierced with the tip of a sharp knife. Remove the
dish from the oven. Set the oven to broil and position oven rack 6 to 8 inches from the heat source.

Sautéed Zucchini with Parmesan and Lemon

(EGG-FREE/LOW-CARB)

*This is one of my favorite ways to enjoy zucchini. For best
results, use canned grated Parmesan cheese—its powdery
consistency is preferred over the freshly shredded variety
here. Make sure to check the label carefully, however, as
some brands may contain harmful glutens.*

MAKES 4 SERVINGS

1½ tablespoons extra-virgin olive oil

1 large clove garlic, peeled, left whole,
  smashed with the flat side of a knife

⅛ teaspoon crushed red pepper flakes, or to
  taste

4 small zucchini (4 ounces each), trimmed
  and cut into 2 × ¼-inch lengths

1 tablespoon fresh lemon juice

Salt and freshly ground black pepper

2 tablespoons finely grated gluten-free
  Parmesan cheese, divided, plus additional,
  to serve

Lemon wedges, to serve

In a large nonstick skillet, heat the oil over medium-
high heat. Add the garlic clove and red pepper
flakes; cook, stirring constantly, 30 seconds. Remove garlic with a slotted spoon and discard; add
the zucchini, tossing until thoroughly coated with

the oil. Spread in a single layer (some overlap is okay) and cook without stirring until undersides are browned, about 2 minutes. Toss again and cook, stirring often, until crisp-tender and browned on all sides, 1 to 2 minutes more. Remove skillet from heat and add the lemon juice, salt, and black pepper; toss well to combine. Transfer zucchini to a serving platter and toss with half the cheese. Sprinkle evenly with the remaining 1 tablespoon of cheese and serve at once, with the lemon wedges and additional cheese passed separately.

PER SERVING: Calories 76; Protein 3g; Total Fat 6g; Sat Fat 1g; Cholesterol 2mg; Carbohydrate 4g; Dietary Fiber 1g; Sodium 62mg

Preheat oven to 425F (220C).

In a large bowl, toss all ingredients except the basil until well combined. Arrange in a single layer on an ungreased 9 × 13-inch glass baking dish. Bake about 15 minutes, or until lightly browned. Sprinkle evenly with the basil and serve warm or at room temperature. Alternatively, completely cooled squash can be covered and refrigerated up to 3 days and served chilled, or returned to room temperature.

PER SERVING: Calories 90; Protein 2g; Total Fat 7g; Sat Fat 1g; Cholesterol 0mg; Carbohydrate 7g; Dietary Fiber 3g; Sodium 4mg

Roasted Lemon-Basil Zucchini and Summer Squash

(VEGAN/LOW-CARB)

Simple yet delicious aptly describes this colorful recipe— all green zucchini or yellow summer squash can be used, if desired.

MAKES 4 TO 6 SERVINGS

2 medium zucchini squash (about 6 ounces each), sliced into ¼-inch-thick rounds

2 medium yellow squash (about 6 ounces each), sliced into ¼-inch-thick rounds

2 tablespoons extra-virgin olive oil

1 tablespoon fresh lemon juice

Salt, preferably the coarse variety, and freshly ground black pepper, to taste

2 tablespoons finely chopped fresh basil

SEVEN

Brunch and Egg Dishes

Frittatas, stratas, tortas, crepes, pancakes, muffins—Italians do up their brunches in style. With a few minor alterations, most can be tailored to suit gluten-free dietary needs. The following collection of recipes will get your gathering—or day—off to a great start with delicious and nutritious dishes featuring protein-rich eggs, vitamin-rich vegetables, and fiber-rich grains and potatoes. For stress-free entertaining—or for breakfast in bed without the preliminary fussing in the kitchen—some, such as Zucchini and Mushroom Egg Strata with Goat Cheese, page 200, can be prepared the night before, and then baked while you chat with your guests over coffee—or climb back into bed with the newspaper. Though most are brunch and breakfast classics, many are appropriate for lunch or dinner as well. In lieu of a gluten-free sandwich, consider tucking a wedge of leftover cold frittata—any of the recipes work—into your lunchbox. For a midday protein boost, pop a leftover Muffin Frittata, page 197, into your mouth. Your family will be pleasantly surprised when you whip up Creamy Scrambled Eggs with Sun-Dried Tomatoes, page 193, and fry up Italian Skillet Breakfast Potatoes, page 196, for supper. Go one step further, and wow them with Chocolate Chip–Ricotta Pancakes, page 192, for a protein-rich treat. For a sweet conclusion to a special brunch, check out the Chestnut Flour Crepes with Nutella, page 212, in the next chapter, "Desserts"—*delicioso!*

Asparagus and Rosemary Frittata with Asiago (lacto-ovo/low-carb)

Baked Eggs Florentine (lacto-ovo/low-carb)

Baked Polenta and Egg Casserole with Sun-Dried Tomatoes and Basil (lacto-ovo)

Cherry Tomato and Fresh Mozzarella Gratin (egg-free/low-carb)

Chocolate Chip–Ricotta Pancakes with Orange Sauce (lacto-ovo)

Creamy Scrambled Eggs with Sun-Dried Tomatoes and Chives (lacto-ovo/low-carb)

Fried Eggs and Stewed Tomatoes on Portobello Mushrooms (dairy-free/low-carb)

Goat Cheese and Hearts of Palm Omelet with Olives (lacto-ovo/low-carb)

Grape Tomato and Italian Herb Oven Frittata with Mozzarella and Parmesan
(lacto-ovo/low-carb)

Italian Skillet Eggs (dairy-free/low-carb)

Italian Skillet Breakfast Potatoes with Peppers and Onions (vegan/low-carb)

Mixed Bell Pepper and Potato Frittata with Fontina (lacto-ovo/low-carb)

Muffin Frittatas with Spinach and Sun-Dried Tomatoes (lacto-ovo/low-carb)

Poached Eggs on a Bed of Roasted Lemon-Basil Squash with Marinara (dairy-free/low-carb)

Herbed Tomato Eggs (dairy-free/low-carb)

Tuscan-Style Herbed Scrambled Eggs with Mesclun (dairy-free/low-carb)

Tuscan Spinach and Cheese Torta with Sun-Dried Tomatoes and Pine Nuts
(lacto-ovo/low-carb)

Zucchini, Red Pepper, and Mushroom Egg Strata with Goat Cheese and Parmesan
(lacto-ovo)

Asparagus and Rosemary Frittata with Asiago

(LACTO-OVO/LOW-CARB)

Celebrate spring with this fabulous frittata, finished under the broiler for stress-free entertaining.

MAKES 4 SERVINGS

2 tablespoons extra-virgin olive oil

1 small red onion (about 4 ounces), sliced into thin half-rounds

1 pound asparagus, tough ends snapped off, spears cut diagonally into 1-inch lengths

1 teaspoon dried rosemary

2 cloves garlic, finely chopped

6 large eggs, lightly beaten

½ teaspoon salt, or to taste

Freshly ground black pepper, to taste

1 cup shredded gluten-free Asiago or Italian-blend cheese (Parmesan, mozzarella, Asiago, etc.), divided

Preheat oven to broil.

In a 10-inch nonstick ovenproof skillet with a lid, heat the oil over medium heat. Add the onion and cook, stirring, until softened, about 3 minutes. Add the asparagus, rosemary, and garlic; cook, stirring, 1 minute. Reduce the heat to medium-low, cover, and cook 3 minutes, stirring a few times, or until asparagus is crisp-tender. Add the eggs, salt, pepper, and ½ cup cheese, stirring quickly to combine. Reduce the heat to low and cook, without stirring, until eggs begin to set, lifting the set edges with a spatula and tilting the pan to allow the uncooked mixture to flow underneath, about 5 minutes. Remove skillet from heat and sprinkle with the remaining ½ cup cheese.

Place the skillet in the oven 8 to 10 inches from the heating element. Broil until the cheese is melted and the eggs are lightly browned, about 5 minutes. Remove the skillet from the oven and let frittata stand for 5 minutes before cutting into wedges and serving at once.

PER SERVING: Calories 282; Protein 8g; Total Fat 20g; Sat Fat 7g; Cholesterol 333mg; Carbohydrate 8g; Dietary Fiber 2g; Sodium 703mg

Baked Eggs Florentine

(LACTO-OVO/LOW-CARB)

Baked, or shirred, eggs are virtually impossible to ruin—unless, of course, you inadvertently break the yolk during the cracking step. When eggs' wholeness contributes to the integrity of the recipe, I always break my eggs into a small custard cup first—and keep a spare egg or two at hand, just in case.

MAKES 6 SERVINGS

½ cup half-and-half

2 tablespoons gluten-free reduced-fat Neufchâtel cream cheese, softened

Salt and freshly ground black pepper, to taste

Pinch ground nutmeg or mace

1 (12-ounce) box frozen chopped spinach, cooked according to package directions, squeezed dry

6 eggs

2 tablespoons gluten-free freshly shredded Parmesan cheese

Preheat the oven to 350F (175C). Lightly oil a 7 × 11-inch baking dish and set aside.

In a medium saucepan over medium-low heat, heat the half-and-half, cream cheese, salt, pepper, and nutmeg until just hot, stirring often to thoroughly blend. Add the spinach and stir well to thoroughly incorporate.

Transfer the spinach mixture to the prepared baking dish, spreading in an even layer. With the back of a large spoon, make 6 evenly spaced indentations. Break an egg into a custard cup or similar small container; carefully slide the egg into an indentation. Repeat with remaining 5 eggs. Sprinkle each egg lightly with salt and pepper. Bake 20 to 25 minutes, or until the egg whites are set but the yolks are medium-soft, sprinkling each egg with 1 teaspoon of Parmesan the last few minutes of cooking. Serve at once.

PER SERVING: Calories 128; Protein 9g; Total Fat 9g; Sat Fat 4g; Cholesterol 223mg; Carbohydrate 4g; Dietary Fiber 2g; Sodium 151mg

Baked Polenta and Egg Casserole with Sun-Dried Tomatoes and Basil

(LACTO-OVO)

Present this attractive brunch casserole in the dish for everyone to admire before serving.

MAKES 6 SERVINGS

  2 cups low-sodium vegetable broth
  1 cup water
  1 cup quick-cooking or regular polenta (coarse-ground yellow cornmeal)
  1 tablespoon extra-virgin olive oil
  Salt and freshly ground black pepper, to taste
  ¾ cup gluten-free shredded Italian blend or part-skim mozzarella cheese

  ¼ cup chopped fresh basil or flat-leaf parsley, divided
  ⅓ cup drained and chopped marinated sun-dried tomatoes
  6 large eggs
  ¼ cup freshly shredded gluten-free Parmesan cheese
  3 cherry or grape tomatoes, halved
  Gluten-free marinara sauce, heated, to serve

Preheat oven to 350F (175C). Lightly oil a 9 × 13-inch baking dish and set aside.

If using quick-cooking polenta: In a medium stockpot, bring the broth, water, polenta, oil, salt, and pepper to a boil over high heat. Reduce the heat to medium and cook, stirring with a long-handled wooden spoon (polenta will sputter), 5 minutes. Remove from heat and quickly add the Italian-blend cheese, 2 tablespoons basil, and tomatoes, stirring until thoroughly combined.

If using regular polenta: In a medium stockpot, bring the broth, water, oil, salt, and pepper to a boil over high heat. Slowly add the polenta, stirring constantly with a long handled wooden spoon. Reduce the heat to low and cook, covered, stirring occasionally, until tender and thickened, about 15 minutes. Remove from heat and immediately add the Italian-blend cheese, 2 tablespoons basil, and tomatoes, stirring until thoroughly combined. Let stand, covered, 5 minutes.

Immediately transfer polenta mixture to the prepared baking dish. Let stand a few minutes to allow the polenta mixture to cool slightly and begin to set. With the bottom of a small custard cup or similar dish, make 6 equally spaced indentations in the polenta mixture; using your fingers, build up the sides slightly to form a rim. (At this point, the polenta mixture can be held at room temperature up to 1 hour before continuing with the recipe. Alternatively, completely cooled mixture can be refrigerated, covered, up to 24 hours.) Break an egg into a custard cup or similar small container; carefully slide into an indentation. Repeat with remaining 5 eggs. Sprinkle eggs lightly with salt and pepper. Bake uncovered 20 to 25 minutes, or until the whites are set and yolks are medium-soft. Top each egg with a tomato half, then sprinkle evenly with the Parmesan cheese; bake 2 to 3 more minutes, or until the cheese is melted. Sprinkle with the remaining 2 tablespoons of basil and serve at once, with the marinara sauce passed separately.

PER SERVING: Calories 279; Protein 18g; Total Fat 12g; Sat Fat 4g; Cholesterol 222mg; Carbohydrate 24g; Dietary Fiber 4g; Sodium 480mg

Cherry Tomato and Fresh Mozzarella Gratin with Pesto

(EGG-FREE/LOW-CARB)

This outstanding gratin is a great accompaniment to any variety of egg and brunch dishes. For a vegan option, simply omit the cheese and replace with additional tomatoes— just make sure the bread crumbs you use are egg-free and dairy-free.

MAKES 6 SERVINGS

½ cup (about 15 pieces/5 ounces) well-drained bite-size fresh mozzarella balls

2 to 2½ cups cherry or grape tomatoes

3 tablespoons Rustic Pesto Sauce, page 92, Classic Basil Pesto Sauce, page 97, or prepared gluten-free pesto

Salt and freshly ground black pepper, to taste

3 tablespoons gluten-free Italian-seasoned dry bread crumbs

Preheat oven to 425F (220C).

Place the mozzarella balls in an 8½ or 9-inch ceramic or glass pie plate. Select enough tomatoes to compactly cover the remaining bottom of the plate. Transfer cheese and tomatoes to a medium mixing bowl. Add the pesto, salt, and pepper; toss gently yet thoroughly to combine.

Lightly oil the pie plate and return the cheese and tomato mixture in a single layer, interspersing the cheese evenly among the tomatoes. Sprinkle evenly with the bread crumbs. Bake about 15 minutes, or until tomato skins have begun to split, cheese is melted (but not runny), and top is lightly browned. Let cool about 10 minutes before serving warm or slightly above room temperature.

PER SERVING: Calories 97; Protein 4g; Total Fat 6g; Sat Fat 3g; Cholesterol 11mg; Carbohydrate 7g; Dietary Fiber 1g; Sodium 126mg

Chocolate Chip–Ricotta Pancakes with Orange Sauce

(LACTO-OVO)

Although these delectable, high-protein pancakes are best freshly prepared, the batter can be held at room temperature up to 1 hour before frying, while the sauce can be made 3 days ahead before reheating.

MAKES 5 TO 6 SERVINGS (ABOUT 15 SMALL PANCAKES)

 4 large eggs, lightly beaten
 2 cups gluten-free reduced-fat ricotta cheese
 ½ cup white rice flour
 ¼ cup potato starch flour
 2 tablespoons canola oil
 1 tablespoon sugar
 ½ teaspoon gluten-free baking powder
 1 teaspoon grated fresh orange peel
 ¼ teaspoon gluten-free pure vanilla extract
 ½ cup mini-chocolate chips, 2 tablespoons reserved
 Orange Sauce, on the right

Place the eggs, cheese, flours, canola oil, sugar, baking powder, orange peel, and vanilla in a large mixing bowl. Using an electric mixer, beat on medium speed until the batter is smooth and well blended. (At this point, batter can be held at room temperature up to 1 hour before continuing with the recipe.) Stir in 6 tablespoons of the chocolate chips until evenly distributed.

Heat a large nonstick skillet over medium heat. Working in batches, pour about ¼ cup of the batter into the skillet and cook until light golden brown, 2 to 3 minutes per side. Serve at once, drizzled with equal amounts of the Orange Sauce (about 2½ to 3 tablespoons per serving) and sprinkled evenly with the reserved chocolate chips (about 1 teaspoon per serving).

PER SERVING (about 3 pancakes, or ⅕ of recipe, without sauce): Calories 354; Protein 21g; Total Fat 15g; Sat Fat 5g; Cholesterol 186mg; Carbohydrate 37g; Dietary Fiber 1g; Sodium 291mg

Orange Sauce

(VEGAN/LOW-CARB)

Spoon this delicious sauce over gluten-free pancakes and waffles, stir into ricotta cheese or plain yogurt, or enjoy as an ice cream topping.

MAKES ABOUT 1 CUP

 1½ cups orange juice
 ¼ cup orange marmalade
 2 tablespoons light brown sugar
 ½ tablespoon cornstarch mixed with ½ tablespoon water
 ½ teaspoon gluten-free pure vanilla extract

In a small saucepan, bring the orange juice to a boil over medium-high heat. Reduce heat to medium and cook, uncovered, until reduced by half, about 10 to 15 minutes. Add marmalade and sugar; cook, whisking, until dissolved and smooth. Add the cornstarch mixture and cook, whisking constantly, until slightly thickened, about 1 minute. Remove from heat and whisk in the vanilla. Let cool slightly before serving warm. Completely cooled sauce can be refrigerated, covered, up to 3 days; reheat gently over low heat.

PER SERVING (about 2 tablespoons, or ⅛ of recipe): Calories 62; Protein 0g; Total Fat 0g; Sat Fat 0g; Cholesterol 0mg; Carbohydrate 15g; Dietary Fiber 0g; Sodium 3mg

Creamy Scrambled Eggs with Sun-Dried Tomatoes and Chives

(LACTO-OVO/LOW-CARB)

These scrumptious scrambled eggs make a quick and easy weeknight supper. For a relaxed brunch, slightly undercook them, cover, and hold in a warm oven (about 200F/95C) up to 1 hour before serving.

MAKES 4 TO 6 SERVINGS

8 eggs
¼ cup skim milk
Salt and freshly ground black pepper, to taste
1 tablespoon extra-virgin olive oil
¼ cup gluten-free sun-dried tomato cream cheese, cut into chunks, softened
2 tablespoons gluten-free cream cheese with chives, in chunks, softened

In a large bowl, whisk together the eggs, skim milk, salt, and pepper until well-blended; set aside.

In a large nonstick skillet, heat the oil over medium heat, swirling to evenly coat the bottom of the skillet. Add the egg mixture and cook, whisking often, until it has thickened into small, soft curds but is still somewhat runny, 3 to 4 minutes. Add cream cheeses and cook, stirring, until thoroughly incorporated and mixture is firm but still moist, 2 to 3 more minutes. Serve at once.

PER SERVING: Calories 233; Protein 15g; Total Fat 17g; Sat Fat 6g; Cholesterol 437mg; Carbohydrate 4g; Dietary Fiber 0g; Sodium 254mg

Fried Eggs and Stewed Tomatoes on Portobello Mushrooms

(DAIRY-FREE/LOW-CARB)

These impressive brunch treats are easy to make and fun to eat. To ensure that the cooked eggs don't overwhelm the mushroom, select large, wide caps for this recipe.

MAKES 4 SERVINGS

4 large eggs
4 large Portobello mushroom caps (about 3 ounces each)
Salt and freshly ground black pepper, to taste
2 tablespoons extra-virgin olive oil, divided
1 (14.5-ounce) can Italian-seasoned stewed tomatoes, drained and chopped, heated
4 teaspoons chopped fresh flat-leaf parsley

Gently crack each egg into its own small cup and set aside. Season the mushrooms on both sides with salt and pepper.

In a large nonstick skillet with a lid, heat 1 tablespoon oil over medium heat. Place the mushrooms, gill sides down, in the skillet and cook for 3 minutes. Turn each mushroom over and cook until bottoms are nicely browned, 3 to 4 minutes. While the mushrooms are finishing cooking, fill each cap with about 1½ tablespoons of the stewed tomatoes. Transfer mushrooms to a baking sheet and cover loosely with foil while you prepare the eggs. (If not using within 15 minutes, hold in a 200F/95C warming oven up to 1 hour before continuing with the recipe.)

Add the remaining 1 tablespoon of oil to the skillet; heat over medium-low heat. Carefully pour each egg into the skillet; cook, covered, about 5 minutes for moderately soft-cooked eggs, or to desired doneness. Remove skillet from heat; quickly top each mushroom cap with an egg. Season the egg lightly with salt and pepper. Divide the egg-topped mushrooms among each of 4 serving plates. Spoon the remaining stewed tomatoes around the mushrooms. Sprinkle the eggs with the parsley and serve at once.

PER SERVING: Calories 182; Protein 9g; Total Fat 12g; Sat Fat 3g; Cholesterol 213mg; Carbohydrate 11g; Dietary Fiber 2g; Sodium 328mg

Goat Cheese and Hearts of Palm Omelet with Olives

(LACTO-OVO/LOW-CARB)

Serve this unusual omelet with Focaccia Bread with Rosemary and Coarse Salt, page 84, and Poached Figs with Honey, page 214, for a marvelous Mediterranean-style brunch. Hearts of palm are sold in cans next to the artichokes; if necessary, substitute the former with the latter.

MAKES 4 SERVINGS

¾ cup well-drained chopped hearts of
   palm
2 ounces (¼ cup) gluten-free crumbled goat
   cheese
Salt and freshly ground black pepper, to taste
6 eggs
2 teaspoons water
2 tablespoons extra-virgin olive oil, divided
2 tablespoons chopped kalamata or other
   good-quality black olives

In a small bowl, combine the hearts of palm, goat cheese, salt, and pepper; set aside. In a medium

bowl, whisk together the eggs, water, salt, and pepper until just blended; set aside.

Heat an omelet pan or 8-inch nonstick skillet over medium-high heat until a drop of water sizzles on its surface. Add 1 tablespoon of the oil and swirl to coat the pan. Quickly add half the egg mixture. Swirl pan with 1 hand while stirring eggs in a circular motion with a fork (tines should be parallel to but not touching bottom of pan). When the eggs begin to set, quickly push cooked egg toward center of the pan, allowing uncooked egg to run underneath. Arrange half of the hearts of palm mixture over one half of the surface. Fold plain half over filled half. Remove pan from heat, cover, and let stand for 1 minute. Slide onto an ungreased baking sheet and cover with foil to keep warm.

Wipe out the omelet pan, if necessary, and heat remaining 1 tablespoon of oil over medium-high heat. Repeat procedure with remaining ingredients. Divide each omelet crosswise in half and transfer to each of 4 serving plates. Garnish each with ½ tablespoon of olives and serve at once.

PER SERVING: Calories 301; Protein 15g; Total Fat 21g; Sat Fat 7g; Cholesterol 334mg; Carbohydrate 14g; Dietary Fiber 1g; Sodium 268mg

Grape Tomato and Italian Herb Oven Frittata with Mozzarella and Parmesan

(LACTO-OVO/LOW-CARB)

After the tomatoes are sautéed, this dense and delicious egg dish is baked completely in the oven for easy entertaining. Grape tomatoes, with their lower moisture content and higher concentration of flavor, are preferred over the cherry variety in this recipe.

MAKES 6 SERVINGS

9 large eggs, at room temperature

½ cup skim milk

1 tablespoon finely chopped fresh basil

1 tablespoon finely chopped fresh oregano or
¾ teaspoon dried oregano

1 teaspoon finely chopped fresh thyme or
¼ teaspoon dried thyme

½ teaspoon salt, or to taste

Freshly ground black pepper, to taste

1½ tablespoons extra-virgin olive oil

1½ cups grape tomatoes

2 cloves garlic, finely chopped

1 cup shredded gluten-free part-skim
mozzarella cheese

¼ cup freshly shredded gluten-free Parmesan
cheese

Shredded fresh basil, for garnish (optional)

Preheat oven to 400F (205C).

In a medium bowl, whisk together the eggs, milk, basil, oregano, thyme, salt, and pepper. Set aside.

In a 10-inch cast iron skillet (or other ovenproof skillet), heat the oil over medium heat. Add the tomatoes and cook, stirring, until softened but not splitting apart, about 5 minutes. Add the garlic and cook, stirring constantly, 30 seconds. Add the egg mixture and the mozzarella cheese, stirring well to combine. Immediately remove skillet from heat and transfer to center oven rack.

Bake 12 to 15 minutes, or until frittata is puffed and golden, sprinkling with the Parmesan the last few minutes of cooking. Garnish with the shredded basil, if using. Let stand 5 minutes before cutting into wedges and serving at once.

PER SERVING: Calories 229; Protein 17g; Total Fat 15g; Sat Fat 6g; Cholesterol 332mg; Carbohydrate 6g; Dietary Fiber 1g; Sodium 444mg

Italian Skillet Eggs

(DAIRY-FREE/LOW-CARB)

This brunch specialty couldn't be easier to make or more delicious to eat. I like to serve each egg atop a gluten-free English muffin half to catch the sauce and yolk. Add a tossed green salad, and you've got a simple yet superb weeknight supper.

MAKES 6 SERVINGS

2 cups gluten-free pasta sauce, preferably the
tomato-basil variety

6 eggs

Salt and freshly ground black pepper, to taste

3 tablespoons gluten-free shredded
mozzarella or Parmesan cheese (optional)

3 teaspoons chopped fresh basil

In a 12-inch nonstick skillet with a lid, heat the pasta sauce over medium heat until hot but not simmering, about 5 minutes, stirring occasionally. Carefully break each egg into a small custard cup, then gently slide into the skillet, spacing them evenly apart; do not stir. Cover and cook without stirring until egg whites are set and yolks have reached desired doneness, 5 to 8 minutes.

Remove skillet from heat and sprinkle each egg lightly with salt and pepper; top each with ½ tablespoon cheese, if using, followed with ½ teaspoon basil. If using cheese, cover and let stand until cheese is melted, 1 to 2 minutes. Serve at once.

PER SERVING: Calories 143; Protein 8g; Total Fat 9g; Sat Fat 3; Cholesterol 216mg; Carbohydrate 9g; Dietary Fiber 0g; Sodium 602mg

Italian Skillet Breakfast Potatoes with Peppers and Onions

(VEGAN/LOW-CARB)

This hearty and heart-friendly Italian version of home fries requires a cast iron skillet for best results.

MAKES 5 TO 6 SERVINGS

1 small onion (about 4 ounces), chopped
½ small green bell pepper (about 2 ounces), chopped
½ small red bell pepper (about 2 ounces), chopped
3 tablespoons extra-virgin olive oil, divided
½ teaspoon coarse salt, or to taste, divided
Freshly ground black pepper, to taste
1¼ pounds Yukon Gold or red potatoes, unpeeled and cut into 1-inch cubes
¼ cup chopped fresh parsley

Preheat oven to 450F (230C). Heat a 10-inch cast iron skillet over medium-high heat for 5 minutes. In a medium bowl, toss the onion and bell peppers with 1 tablespoon of the oil. Sprinkle with ¼ teaspoon coarse salt and black pepper; toss again and set aside.

When the skillet is hot, add the remaining 2 tablespoons of oil and swirl to coat. Add the potatoes and remaining ¼ teaspoon of salt, tossing well to thoroughly coat. Spread the potatoes in a single layer and cook without stirring until nicely browned on the bottom, about 5 to 7 minutes. Remove skillet from heat. Using a metal spatula, scrape underneath the potatoes and carefully turn over. Top the potatoes evenly with the reserved onion and bell pepper mixture.

Place skillet in the upper third of the oven and bake until potatoes are tender and top is browned,

about 10 minutes. Carefully remove the skillet from the oven and sprinkle with the parsley; toss with the metal spatula, scraping from the bottom, to combine. Serve at once.

PER SERVING: Calories 154; Protein 2g; Total Fat 8g; Sat Fat 1g; Cholesterol 0mg; Carbohydrate 19g; Dietary Fiber 2g; Sodium 221mg

Mixed Bell Pepper and Potato Frittata with Fontina

(LACTO-OVO/LOW-CARB)

I like to serve this savory frittata with Focaccia Bread with Rosemary and Coarse Salt, page 84, and a tossed mixed green salad for a satisfying supper.

MAKES 4 SERVINGS

3 tablespoons extra-virgin olive oil, divided
2 small red potatoes (about 3 ounces each), unpeeled and cut into ½-inch cubes
½ medium green bell pepper (about 3 ounces), chopped
½ medium red bell pepper (about 3 ounces), chopped
½ small red onion (about 2 ounces), chopped
4 eggs, beaten with 2 tablespoons of water
2 tablespoons chopped fresh flat-leaf parsley
2 tablespoons chopped fresh basil
Salt and freshly ground black pepper, to taste
¼ cup gluten-free shredded Fontina cheese

Preheat oven to broil.

In a 10-inch cast iron skillet, heat 2 tablespoons of the oil over medium heat. Add the potatoes and cook, stirring often, until tender but still firm, about 10 minutes. Add remaining 1 tablespoon of oil along with the bell peppers and onion; cook, stirring, until peppers and onions are softened and potatoes are tender and lightly browned, about 5 minutes. Add the eggs, parsley, basil, salt, and black pepper, stirring well to thoroughly combine. Reduce heat to medium-low; cook without stirring 2 minutes. Remove skillet from heat and sprinkle evenly with the Fontina cheese.

Place the skillet under the broiler on the center oven rack. Broil until cheese is melted and top is golden and set, about 5 to 8 minutes. Remove skillet from oven and let stand 5 minutes before cutting into wedges and serving warm or at room temperature.

PER SERVING: Calories 234; Protein 9g; Total Fat 18g; Sat Fat 4g; Cholesterol 221mg; Carbohydrate 10g; Dietary Fiber 2g; Sodium 124mg

Muffin Frittatas with Spinach and Sun-Dried Tomatoes

(LACTO-OVO/LOW-CARB)

If you're looking for a special yet easy brunch dish to serve company, these adorable muffin-like frittatas are the answer. Made predominately from egg whites, they are relatively low in cholesterol to boot.

MAKES 6 MINI FRITTATAS

1 tablespoon extra-virgin olive oil
¼ cup chopped onion
2 large cloves garlic, finely chopped
3 cups baby spinach leaves, torn
Salt and freshly ground black pepper
2 tablespoons finely chopped fresh basil
6 egg whites
2 egg yolks

6 tablespoons gluten-free shredded Fontina cheese
4 tablespoons drained and chopped marinated sun-dried tomatoes
2 tablespoons gluten-free freshly grated Parmesan cheese
Gluten-free marinara sauce, heated, to serve (optional)

Preheat oven to 350F (175C). Generously grease a standard-size 6-cup muffin tin and set aside.

In a medium nonstick skillet, heat the oil over medium heat. Add the onion and cook, stirring, until softened, about 2 minutes. Add the garlic and cook, stirring constantly, 30 seconds. Add the spinach, salt, and pepper; cook, stirring, until spinach is completely wilted and liquids have evaporated, about 3 minutes. Remove from heat and toss with the chopped basil; let cool a few minutes.

In a medium bowl, whisk together the egg whites, egg yolks, salt, and pepper; set aside.

Divide the spinach mixture equally among prepared muffin cups. Top each with 1 tablespoon of Fontina cheese, followed with ½ tablespoon sun-dried tomatoes, reserving 1 tablespoon for garnish. Pour in equal amounts of the egg mixture over the spinach-cheese mixture. Bake on the center oven rack 15 to 20 minutes, or until puffed and golden. Sprinkle each with 1 teaspoon Parmesan and top with ½ teaspoon sun-dried tomatoes; return to the oven until cheese is melted, about 1 minute. Let cool a minimum of 5 minutes before loosening the edges of each muffin cup with the tip of a sharp knife; transfer frittatas to a heated serving platter or individual serving plates. Serve at once, with marinara sauce passed separately, if using.

PER SERVING: Calories 107; Protein 8g; Total Fat 7g; Sat Fat 3g; Cholesterol 80mg; Carbohydrate 4g; Dietary Fiber 1g; Sodium 212mg

Poached Eggs on a Bed of Roasted Lemon-Basil Squash with Marinara

(DAIRY-FREE/LOW-CARB)

This simple yet delicious Italian take on eggs Benedict is not only more healthful, but more colorful.

MAKES 4 SERVINGS

4 large eggs
Roasted Lemon-Basil Zucchini and Summer
    Squash, page 183
1 cup gluten-free marinara sauce, heated
4 fresh basil leaves, for garnish (optional)

Lightly oil a baking dish large enough to hold the poached eggs in a single layer; set aside.

In a medium deep-sided skillet, pour enough water to measure 1 inch. Bring the water to a gentle simmer over medium-high heat. Meanwhile, crack each egg into its own small custard cup or similar container. When the water has reached a gentle simmer, quickly yet carefully slide each egg from its cup into the water. After about 30 seconds, using a slotted spoon and beginning with the first immersed egg, quickly yet gently push each egg white back toward the yolk to form a circular shape, taking care that the eggs do not touch one another. Lower the heat as necessary to maintain a gentle simmer. As the eggs begin to firm, use the slotted spoon to gently lift each egg so that it doesn't stick to the bottom. Poach until the egg whites are firm and the yolks are still soft, about 3 minutes. Using the slotted spoon, remove the eggs from the water and carefully transfer them to the prepared baking dish. If not using immediately, cover and keep warm in a very low oven up to 1 hour.

To assemble the dish, divide the roasted lemon-basil squash evenly among each of 4 serving plates. Gently place a poached egg over each serving and top with ¼ cup of heated marinara sauce. Garnish with a basil leaf, if using, and serve at once.

PER SERVING: Calories 207; Protein 9g; Total Fat 14g; Sat Fat 3g; Cholesterol 213mg; Carbohydrate 14g; Dietary Fiber 3; Sodium 460mg

Herbed Tomato Eggs

(DAIRY-FREE/LOW-CARB)

Select the ripest tomatoes possible for this recipe to ensure that they will be softened enough by the time the eggs are firm. For stress-free entertaining, the slightly undercooked tomato eggs can be held in a warm oven (about 200F/95C) for 1 hour before serving; in this case, however, the eggs will be cooked medium-hard.

MAKES 6 SERVINGS

6 large ripe tomatoes (about 8 ounces each)
1½ teaspoons extra-virgin olive oil
Garlic salt, to taste
Freshly ground black pepper, to taste
6 eggs, at room temperature
Dried oregano and/or thyme leaves
Baby spinach leaves
Chopped fresh flat-leaf parsley

Preheat oven to 350F (175C). Lightly oil an 8 × 8-inch glass baking dish and set aside.

Cut a thin slice off the top of each tomato. From the center of each tomato, cut out a hollow large enough to hold an egg (about ¼ cup size). Place the tomatoes in the prepared baking dish. Add ¼ teaspoon of oil to each hollow and sprinkle lightly with garlic salt and pepper. Carefully break an egg into each hollow. Lightly sprinkle the top of each egg with salt, pepper, and oregano. Bake 25 to 30 minutes, or until eggs are cooked to desired doneness (soft to medium-hard) and tomatoes are soft but still hold their shape. To serve, place some spinach leaves on each of 6 serving plates. Top each with a tomato egg. Garnish each with parsley and serve at once.

PER SERVING: Calories 128; Protein 8g; Total Fat 7g; Sat Fat 2g; Cholesterol 213mg; Carbohydrate 10g; Dietary Fiber 2g; Sodium 82mg

Variations

To make Pesto Tomato Eggs, omit the dried oregano and parsley. Top each cooked tomato egg with 1 teaspoon of Rustic Pesto Sauce, page 92, Classic Basil Pesto Sauce, page 97, or prepared gluten-free pesto sauce during the last few minutes of baking.

To make Parmesan Tomato Eggs, sprinkle each tomato egg with 1 teaspoon of gluten-free freshly shredded Parmesan cheese during the last few minutes of baking.

Tuscan-Style Herbed Scrambled Eggs with Mesclun

(DAIRY-FREE/LOW-CARB)

This unusual recipe is unexpectedly delicious—if you make it for guests, be prepared to pass out the recipe. If doubling the recipe, use a 12-inch nonstick skillet. Baby spinach can stand in for the Mesclun, if desired.

MAKES 3 SERVINGS

5 large eggs
1 tablespoon of mixed chopped fresh thyme, rosemary, and/or oregano, or 1 teaspoon of mixed dried herbs

½ teaspoon salt, divided
Freshly ground black pepper, to taste
2 tablespoons extra-virgin olive oil, divided
½ tablespoon balsamic vinegar
2 loosely packed cups (1½ to 2 ounces) Mesclun or mixed young greens
½ recipe Potato Croutons, page 68 (optional)

In a medium bowl, whisk together the eggs, herb mixture, ¼ teaspoon salt, and pepper until thoroughly blended. In another medium bowl, whisk together 1 tablespoon of the oil, vinegar, remaining ¼ teaspoon salt, and pepper; add Mesclun, tossing well to thoroughly coat.

In an omelet pan or 8-inch nonstick skillet, heat the remaining 1 tablespoon of oil over medium heat, swirling to coat the bottom. Add the egg mixture and scramble in a circular motion with a fork (tines should be parallel to but not touching bottom of pan), gradually adding the Mesclun mixture, until eggs are set but still moist, lifting the pan off the heat as necessary to avoid overcooking. Divide eggs among three plates and serve at once, garnished with the potato croutons, if using.

PER SERVING: Calories 210; Protein 11g; Total Fat 18g; Sat Fat 4g; Cholesterol 354mg; Carbohydrate 2g; Dietary Fiber 0g; Sodium 464mg

Tuscan Spinach and Cheese Torta with Sun-Dried Tomatoes and Pine Nuts

(LACTO-OVO/LOW-CARB)

Torta is a catch-all term for pie, cake, and tart in Italy. With its custard-like texture, this savory cheese and spinach pie, studded with bursts of sun-dried tomatoes and garnished with fragrant pine nuts, is reminiscent of a French quiche, only heartier. For easy entertaining, the crust can be prebaked the night before—after cooling, cover and refrigerate before returning to room temperature and using in the recipe.

MAKES 6 SERVINGS

3 eggs

2 egg whites

½ teaspoon onion powder

½ teaspoon garlic salt

½ teaspoon Italian seasoning

¼ teaspoon dried oregano

Freshly ground black pepper, to taste

1½ cups gluten-free shredded part-skim mozzarella cheese

6 ounces frozen chopped spinach, cooked according to package directions, drained and squeezed dry

¼ cup drained and chopped marinated sun-dried tomatoes, ½ tablespoon marinade reserved

1 (9-inch) Gluten-Free Savory Pastry Crust, page 224 (see Variation), prebaked and cooled

¼ cup gluten-free freshly shredded Parmesan cheese

1½ to 2 tablespoons pine nuts

Preheat oven to 350F (175C).

In a large bowl, beat the eggs, egg whites, onion powder, garlic salt, Italian seasoning, oregano, and pepper until thoroughly blended. Add the mozzarella cheese; stir well to combine. Add the spinach and tomatoes; stir well to combine.

Using a pastry brush, brush the bottom and sides of the prebaked pastry crust evenly with the reserved marinade. Spoon the egg mixture evenly into the crust. Bake on the center oven rack 20 minutes, or until filling is almost completely set (only the center should be slightly runny). Sprinkle evenly with the Parmesan cheese, followed with the pine nuts. Bake an additional 5 to 10 minutes, or until cheese is melted, pine nuts are toasted, and filling is puffed and golden. Let stand 10 minutes before cutting into wedges and serving warm, or at room temperature.

PER SERVING: Calories 336; Protein 16g; Total Fat 21g; Sat Fat 12g; Cholesterol 153mg; Carbohydrate 20g; Dietary Fiber 2g; Sodium 550mg

Zucchini, Red Pepper, and Mushroom Egg Strata with Goat Cheese and Parmesan

(LACTO-OVO)

This fragrant and flavorful brunch favorite can easily be doubled to feed a crowd; in this instance, select a 9 × 13-inch baking dish.

MAKES 6 SERVINGS

1 tablespoon plus 1 teaspoon extra-virgin olive oil, divided

½ medium red onion (about 3 ounces), finely chopped

½ small zucchini or summer squash (about 3 ounces), finely chopped

½ medium red bell pepper (about 3 ounces), finely chopped

3 ounces cremini or cultivated white mushrooms, thinly sliced

¼ teaspoon dried thyme

¼ teaspoon dried rosemary

¼ teaspoon salt

2 cloves garlic, finely chopped

Freshly ground black pepper, to taste

2 tablespoons finely chopped fresh basil

1 tablespoon finely chopped fresh flat-leaf parsley

½ recipe Gluten-Free Italian Bread (1 loaf), page 86, cut into 1-inch cubes, or about 8 ounces of other gluten-free Italian-style bread, divided

4 ounces (½ cup) gluten-free crumbled goat cheese, divided

1 cup plus 2 tablespoons shredded gluten-free Parmesan cheese, divided

4 large eggs

⅔ cup skim milk or rice milk

Pinch or more ground nutmeg

Grease an 8 × 8-inch baking dish with 1 teaspoon of the oil and set aside.

In a large nonstick skillet, heat the remaining 1 tablespoon of oil over medium heat. Add the onion, zucchini, bell pepper, mushrooms, thyme, rosemary, and salt; cook, stirring, until softened and most of the water released from the vegetables has evaporated, about 7 to 10 minutes. Add the garlic and black pepper; cook, stirring, 1 minute. Remove skillet from heat and add the basil and parsley, tossing well to combine; let cool to room temperature. (At this point, mixture can be held at room temperature up to 1 hour before continuing with the recipe.)

Arrange half the bread cubes in the prepared baking dish. Top with half the zucchini mixture, followed with ¼ cup goat cheese, then ½ cup Parmesan cheese. Repeat layers with remaining ingredients.

In a small bowl, whisk together the eggs, milk, and nutmeg; slowly pour over the bread mixture. Cover and refrigerate overnight.

Preheat oven to 350F (175C). Bake strata on the center oven rack, uncovered, about 45 minutes, or until set and a knife inserted near the center comes out clean. (If top is browning too quickly after about 40 minutes, cover loosely with foil until done.) Sprinkle with the remaining 2 tablespoons of Parmesan and return to the oven 1 minute, or until cheese is melted. Let stand for 15 minutes before cutting.

Serve at once.

PER SERVING: Calories 353; Protein 21g; Total Fat 19g; Sat Fat 9g; Cholesterol 173mg; Carbohydrate 25g; Dietary Fiber 2g; Sodium 688mg

EIGHT

Desserts

Ah, desserts—they bring joy to the Italian heart. Making spectacular Italian cakes, tarts, and cookies can be daunting enough for the average home cook; the stakes are even higher for those with celiac disease or gluten sensitivity, who must rise to the occasion without the clear advantages of wheat flour, the preferred grain of tradition. The following recipes meet the challenge, and more—from the rustic Tuscan Apple Cake, page 207, to the delicate Pignoli Cookies, page 219, to the glorious Italian Strawberry Tart with Pastry Cream, page 223, every bite is testimony that the extra time and effort was worth it. If you happen to have any leftovers, remember to set aside a keepsake for yourself—to the victor belong the spoils.

Tuscan Apple Cake (lacto-ovo)

Apricot Custard with Almonds (lacto-ovo/low-carb)

Grain-Free Cranberry-Walnut Biscotti (vegan/low-carb)

Almond-Orange Biscotti (lacto-ovo/low-carb)

Italian Bread Pudding with Apples and Dried Fruits (dairy-free)

Classic Italian Cheesecake (lacto-ovo)

Chestnut Cake with Pine Nuts and Rosemary (vegan)

Chestnut Flour Crepes with Nutella (lacto-ovo)

Chocolate-Espresso Soufflé Cake (dairy-free/low-carb)

Chocolate-Hazelnut Sundaes (lacto-ovo)

Chocolate *Sorbetto* (vegan)

Poached Figs with Honey (egg-free/dairy-free)

Grape and Mascarpone Pie (egg-free/low-carb)

Italian Lemon Pudding Cake with Raspberries (lacto-ovo)

Melon and Blueberry Salad (vegan)

Oranges in Spiced Red Wine (vegan)

Panforte (egg-free/dairy-free)

Baked Stuffed Peaches (vegan)

Stuffed Pears with Gorgonzola and Honey (egg-free/low-carb)

Pignoli Cookies (dairy-free/low-carb)

Tuscan Plum Pudding (lacto-ovo/low-carb)

Polenta Pound Cake (lacto-ovo)

Raspberries with Whipped Ricotta and Honey (egg-free)

Italian Rice Pudding (dairy-free)

Italian Strawberries (vegan/low-carb)

Italian Strawberry Tart with Pastry Cream (lacto-ovo)

Italian Strawberry Ice (vegan)

Tuscan Apple Cake

(LACTO-OVO)

Firm, crisp apples, such as Galas, Fujis, or Granny Smiths—I like to use one of each—work best in this rustic cake, delicious straight out of the oven or fridge the next day. For an extra indulgence, serve with gluten-free vanilla ice cream or whipped cream.

MAKES 1 CAKE (8-INCH ROUND OR SQUARE) TO SERVE 8

3 large eggs, at room temperature
1 cup sugar
½ cup gluten-free nonfat half-and-half
1½ tablespoons canola oil
1 tablespoon butter, melted
1½ cups gluten-free all-purpose flour
2 teaspoons gluten-free baking powder
½ teaspoon gluten-free pure vanilla extract
3 large apples (about 7 to 8 ounces each),
   preferably Gala, Fuji, or Granny Smith,
   peeled, if desired, cored, and cut into
   ¼-inch-thick slices
Confectioner's sugar

Preheat oven to 350 F (175C). Lightly grease and flour an 8-inch Springform pan or, alternatively, lightly grease an 8-inch-square baking dish; set aside.

In a large bowl, combine the eggs and sugar. Using an electric mixer, beat at medium speed for 5 minutes, or until pale yellow and creamy. Reduce speed to low and beat in the half-and-half, oil, and butter. Gradually add the flour, scraping down the sides of the bowl after each addition. Increase the speed to medium and beat for 3 minutes. Add the baking powder and vanilla; beat an additional 2 minutes on medium speed.

Transfer batter to the prepared baking pan. If using a round Springform pan, beginning with the outside edge of the pan, arrange the apple slices vertically, skin sides up, in the batter, forming concentric circles to resemble a rose. If using a square pan, arrange the slices in rows. Bake on the center oven rack 50 minutes, or until apples are lightly browned and toothpick inserted in the center comes out clean, covering the top loosely with foil after about 30 minutes.

Let cake cool 10 minutes. If using a Springform pan, carefully remove the sides. Serve warm or at room temperature, sprinkled with confectioner's sugar. Alternatively, completely cooled cake can be refrigerated, covered, up to 1 day and served chilled.

PER SERVING: Calories 207; Protein 3g; Total Fat 6g; Sat Fat 2g; Cholesterol 84mg; Carbohydrate 37g; Dietary Fiber 2g; Sodium 137mg

Apricot Custard with Almonds

(LACTO-OVO/LOW-CARB)

This silky custard can be made with other dried fruits—prunes and figs are good choices.

MAKES 4 SERVINGS

8 dried apricot halves
1 cup whole milk, half-and-half, or soy
   creamer
2 eggs
3 tablespoons sugar
½ teaspoon gluten-free almond extract
2 tablespoons slivered almonds

Preheat oven to 350F (175C).

Bring a small saucepan of water to a boil; add the apricots and boil until softened and plumped, about 3 minutes. Drain and coarsely chop. Divide equally among 4 ungreased 6-ounce ovenproof ramekins or custard dishes.

In a small bowl, whisk together the milk, eggs, sugar, and almond extract. Pour equal amounts of the milk mixture into the ramekins. Sprinkle each top with ½ tablespoon of almonds. Place ramekins on a baking sheet and bake on the center oven rack 25 to 30 minutes, or until custard is set. Let cool to room temperature before serving. Alternatively, completely cooled custard can be refrigerated, covered, up to 3 days before serving chilled.

PER SERVING: Calories 159; Protein 6g; Total Fat 7g; Sat Fat 2g; Cholesterol 115mg; Carbohydrate 20g; Dietary Fiber 1g; Sodium 63mg

Grain-Free Cranberry-Walnut Biscotti

(VEGAN/LOW-CARB)

Almond flour's natural suitability for creating a crunchy, slightly chewy, twice-baked cookie perfect for dunking into a cup of hot coffee or tea is apparent in this tasty vegan recipe.

MAKES 24 BISCOTTI

2½ cups almond flour or meal

2 tablespoons arrowroot powder or potato starch flour (not potato flour)

½ teaspoon baking soda

½ teaspoon salt

½ cup light corn syrup

½ tablespoon grated fresh orange zest or ½ teaspoon dried orange peel

½ teaspoon gluten-free vanilla extract

½ cup dried cranberries

½ cup coarsely chopped toasted walnuts

Preheat oven to 325F (165C). Line a baking sheet with parchment paper and set aside.

In a food processor fitted with the knife blade, combine almond flour, arrowroot powder, baking soda, and salt; pulse until well combined. Add the corn syrup, orange zest, and vanilla extract; pulse until dough forms a ball.

Turn dough out onto a flat work surface and knead in the cranberries and nuts. Form dough into 2 flat logs about 6 inches long; place on prepared baking sheet, about 4 inches apart. Bake on the center oven rack for 25 to 30 minutes, or until set and lightly browned. Place baking sheet on a wire rack to cool for 30 minutes. Reduce oven temperature to 300F (150C).

Using a sharp, serrated knife, cut logs crosswise at a slight diagonal into ½-inch-thick slices. Spread slices out on prepared baking sheet (if necessary, re-line with fresh parchment paper or transfer to another baking sheet lined with parchment paper), cut side down; bake until dry to the touch, 7 to 10 minutes per side. Lift biscotti on parchment paper and place on a wire rack to cool completely. Remove from parchment paper and serve at room temperature. Completely cooled biscotti can be stored in an airtight tin lined with wax paper for 1 week. Alternatively, freeze up to 2 months.

PER SERVING (per biscotti, or ¹⁄₂₄ of recipe): Calories 97; Protein 6g; Total Fat 4g; Sat Fat 0g; Cholesterol 0mg; Carbohydrate 10g; Dietary Fiber 0g; Sodium 76mg

Variation

To make Cherry-Almond Biscotti, replace the cranberries with dried cherries and replace the walnuts with toasted slivered almonds. Add ¼ teaspoon of gluten-free almond extract along with the vanilla extract. Proceed as otherwise directed in the recipe.

Almond-Orange Biscotti

(LACTO-OVO/LOW-CARB)

Traditional to Tuscany, these classic twice-baked biscuits are typically served with Vin Santo, a sweet dessert wine. They are equally delicious with a cup of espresso or cappuccino.

MAKES ABOUT 4 DOZEN BISCOTTI

⅓ cup unsalted butter, softened

¾ cup white sugar

2 large eggs

4 teaspoons grated fresh orange zest or
    1 teaspoon dried orange peel

1 tablespoon water, plus additional, if
    necessary

1 teaspoon gluten-free vanilla extract

¾ teaspoon gluten-free almond extract

1 cup soy flour

1 cup white rice flour

¼ cup tapioca starch flour

¼ cup potato starch (do not use potato flour),
    plus additional, as necessary

1 teaspoon xanthan gum

½ teaspoon salt

½ cup chopped toasted almonds

Preheat oven to 325F (165C). Line a baking sheet with parchment paper and set aside.

In a large bowl, using an electric mixer on medium speed, beat the butter and sugar until light and fluffy. Reduce speed to low and beat in the eggs, orange zest, water, and extracts until blended. In a medium bowl, whisk together the flours, potato starch, xanthan gum, and salt until thoroughly combined. Slowly add the dry mixture to the egg mixture, beating on low speed after each addition. Dough should be soft and slightly sticky; if necessary, stir in water by the ½ tablespoon. Using your hands, knead in the almonds. Lightly flour your fingers with potato starch flour; gather dough into a ball and transfer to a lightly floured work surface.

Divide the dough into 2 equal balls. With lightly floured fingers, roll each dough ball into a flat log about 12 inches in length. Transfer the dough logs to the prepared baking sheet, arranging them side by side, about 4 inches apart. Bake on the center oven rack for 25 minutes, or until set and lightly browned. Place baking sheet on a wire rack to cool for 5 minutes.

Using a sharp, serrated knife, cut biscotti loaves on the slight diagonal into ½-inch-thick slices. Place the slices, cut side down, on the baking sheet. Return to the oven and bake until lightly browned, about 5 to 8 minutes per side. Transfer biscotti to a wire rack to cool completely. Serve at room temperature. Completely cooled biscotti can be stored in an airtight tin lined with waxed paper for 1 week. Alternatively, freeze up to 2 months.

PER SERVING (per biscotti, or ¹⁄₄₈ of recipe): Calories 59; Protein 1g; Total Fat 3g; Sat Fat 1g; Cholesterol 13mg; Carbohydrate 8g; Dietary Fiber 0g; Sodium 26mg

Variation

To make Almond-Anise Biscotti, omit the orange zest and replace with 2 teaspoons ground anise seed.

Italian Bread Pudding with Apples and Dried Fruits

(DAIRY-FREE)

Prepared with dairy-free, gluten-free Italian bread and rice milk, this is a nutritious and delicious gluten-free dessert for those with milk allergies.

MAKES 6 TO 8 SERVINGS

> 3 cups 1-inch cubed day-old Gluten-Free Italian Bread, page 86 (5 or 6 ounces, or ⅓ of recipe), or commercially prepared gluten-free, dairy-free Italian bread
>
> 3 cups rice milk or skim milk
>
> ½ cup unsweetened apple juice
>
> ½ cup sugar, divided
>
> 3 large Golden Delicious apples (about 8 ounces each), peeled, cored, and cut into ½-inch cubes
>
> ½ cup raisins
>
> ½ cup dried apricots, coarsely chopped
>
> 3 eggs
>
> 2 teaspoons gluten-free vanilla extract
>
> 1 teaspoon ground cinnamon
>
> ⅛ teaspoon ground nutmeg
>
> Whipped cream (optional)

Preheat oven to 325F (165C). Lightly grease a 9 × 13-inch ovenproof baking dish and set aside. In a large bowl, combine the bread and milk; set aside to soak for 30 minutes, turning the bowl a few times to evenly distribute the liquid without turning or stirring the ingredients.

Meanwhile, in a large nonstick skillet, heat the apple juice and ¼ cup sugar over medium heat, stirring until the sugar is dissolved. Add the apples and raise the heat to medium-high; cook, stirring often, until apples are tender and most of the liquids have evaporated, about 10 minutes. Stir in the raisins and apricots and remove skillet from heat; set aside to cool.

In a medium bowl, whisk together the eggs, remaining ¼ cup of sugar, vanilla, cinnamon, and nutmeg until thoroughly blended.

When apple mixture has cooled, add the soaked bread-cube mixture and egg mixture to the skillet, stirring gently yet thoroughly to combine. Pour pudding mixture into the prepared dish. Bake 50 to 60 minutes, or until a knife inserted near the center comes out clean. Remove baking dish from oven.

Preheat oven to broil. Adjust oven rack so that the top of the pudding is 6 to 8 inches from heat source. Return baking dish to the oven and broil until the top is lightly browned, 1 to 2 minutes, taking care not to burn. Serve warm or at room temperature, with the whipped cream, if using. Alternatively, completely cooled pudding can be covered and refrigerated up to 3 days and served chilled, or returned to room temperature.

PER SERVING: Calories 335; Protein 11g; Total Fat 4g; Sat Fat 1g; Cholesterol 106mg; Carbohydrate 66g; Dietary Fiber 4g; Sodium 241mg

Classic Italian Cheesecake

(LACTO-OVO)

This extravagant Italian classic is, on special occasions, well worth the caloric splurge—for a less decadent cake, replace half the whole-milk ricotta with part-skim or, better still, nonfat ricotta.

MAKES 8 TO 12 SERVINGS

> 24 ounces (about 3 cups) gluten-free whole-milk ricotta cheese
>
> 1 cup sugar

6 tablespoons gluten-free all-purpose flour

1 teaspoon ground cinnamon

½ teaspoon salt

4 large eggs, at room temperature

¼ cup heavy cream, light cream, or half-and-half

1 teaspoon gluten-free lemon extract

1 teaspoon fresh lemon zest

Preheat oven to 350F (175C). Lightly grease a 9-inch Springform pan and set aside.

In a large bowl, using an electric mixer on medium speed, beat together the ricotta, sugar, flour, cinnamon, and salt until blended. In a medium bowl, on medium speed, beat together the eggs, cream, lemon extract, and lemon zest until blended. Gradually add the egg mixture to the cheese mixture, beating on low speed after each addition (do not overbeat). Transfer to prepared pan. Bake on the center oven rack about 40 minutes, or until a wooden pick inserted in the center comes out clean. Turn oven off and leave door slightly open. Let cheesecake remain in oven 1 hour. Remove cheesecake from oven and let cool 10 minutes; run the tip of a sharp knife around the edge to loosen. After about 45 minutes, remove the sides of the pan. Let cool completely before refrigerating, covered, a minimum of 3 hours or up to 3 days and serve chilled.

PER SERVING: Calories 332; Protein 14g; Total Fat 16g; Sat Fat 10g; Cholesterol 159mg; Carbohydrate 33g; Dietary Fiber 0g; Sodium 106mg

Chestnut Cake with Pine Nuts and Rosemary

(VEGAN)

Italian chestnut cake, also known as castagnaccio, is a Tuscan specialty that is often served with a rich lemon sauce. I prefer a simpler dusting of confectioner's sugar—for an extra-special treat, use the cocoa-flavored variety, which is typically gluten-free. Though traditional, both the pine nuts and rosemary can be omitted, if desired.

MAKES 8 SERVINGS

2 cups rice milk or skim milk

1 tablespoon extra-virgin olive oil

2 cups chestnut flour

2 tablespoons sugar

Pinch salt

¼ cup pine nuts or chopped walnuts

2 tablespoons chopped fresh rosemary leaves or ½ tablespoon dried rosemary

Confectioner's sugar, for dusting

Preheat oven to 350F (175C). Line a 12-inch-round cake pan with parchment paper; set aside. In a small bowl, combine the milk and oil; set aside.

In a large mixing bowl, whisk together the flour, sugar, and salt. Slowly whisk in the milk mixture until smooth and thoroughly blended. Add the nuts, stirring well to evenly distribute. Pour batter into prepared pan and scatter the rosemary evenly over the top. Bake on the center oven rack 35 to 45 minutes, or until a wooden pick inserted in the center comes out clean. (If cake is browning too quickly after about 30 minutes, cover loosely with foil.) Let cool completely in the pan before removing and serving warm or at room temperature, dusted with confectioner's sugar.

PER SERVING: Calories 208; Protein 12g; Total Fat 8g; Sat Fat 1g; Cholesterol 0mg; Carbohydrate 25g; Dietary Fiber 2g; Sodium 50mg

Chestnut Flour Crepes with Nutella

(LACTO-OVO)

These special dessert crepes are ideal for stress-free entertaining, as the entire recipe can be made a day ahead. To create a brunch-style crepe, see the Variation, on the right. Chestnut flour is available at specialty stores and Italian markets.

MAKES ABOUT 8 CREPES

⅔ cups gluten-free all-purpose flour mix

⅓ cup chestnut flour

½ cup whole milk

½ cup water, plus additional, if necessary

2 large eggs, at room temperature

½ tablespoon canola oil

½ tablespoon sugar

¼ teaspoon gluten-free vanilla extract

¼ teaspoon salt

Pinch ground cinnamon

8 teaspoons butter or gluten-free margarine

About 1 cup Nutella

Confectioner's sugar

Whipped cream (optional)

In a medium mixing bowl, beat together the flours, milk, water, eggs, oil, sugar, vanilla, salt, and cinnamon until smooth. Heat a large nonstick skillet over medium heat. Add 1 teaspoon of the butter, swirling to evenly coat. Using a ¼ cup measure, pour the batter into the hot skillet, turning to thinly and evenly distribute the batter into a circle about 8 inches in diameter. Cook until very lightly browned, about 30 seconds per side. Transfer crepe to a plate and repeat with remaining butter and batter, stacking the crepes as they finish cooking. Let cool to room temperature.

Spread each cooled crepe with about 2 tablespoons of the Nutella and roll up jelly-roll style. (At this point, filled crepes can be covered and refrigerated up to 24 hours before returning to room temperature.) Sprinkle each filled crepe with confectioner's sugar and garnish with the whipped cream, if using; serve at once.

PER SERVING (per filled crepe, or ⅛ of recipe): Calories 250; Protein 7g; Total Fat 11g; Sat Fat 4g; Cholesterol 68mg; Carbohydrate 32g; Dietary Fiber 1g; Sodium 142mg

Variation

To make Chestnut Flour Crepes with Strawberry Preserves, prepare the recipe as directed above, replacing the Nutella with about 1 cup strawberry preserves.

Chocolate-Espresso Soufflé Cake

(DAIRY-FREE/LOW-CARB)

While soufflés may be French, the espresso that lends this decadent dessert its intense flavor is most definitely Italian. Prepared instant espresso (or coffee) can be used, if necessary.

MAKES 4 SERVINGS

2 tablespoons plus 2 teaspoons sugar, divided

2 ounces bittersweet or semisweet chocolate, chopped, if necessary

1 tablespoon prepared espresso or very strong
   coffee

4 egg whites, at room temperature

Confectioner's sugar

Preheat oven to 350F (175C). Lightly oil 4 (4-ounce) ramekins; coat the insides of each with ½ teaspoon of sugar.

Place the chocolate in a medium microwave-safe mixing bowl; microwave on high power 1 to 2 minutes, stirring every 30 seconds, or until melted. Stir in the espresso. Alternatively, place chocolate in the top of a double-boiler over barely simmering water; gently stir until almost melted. Remove from heat and stir until completely melted; stir in the espresso.

In a clean and dry large stainless mixing bowl, using an electric mixer, beat the egg whites on medium speed until soft peaks form, about 2 to 3 minutes. Beat in the remaining 2 tablespoons of sugar, 1 tablespoon at a time, on high speed until stiff and glossy peaks form, about 2 to 3 minutes. With a rubber spatula, gently fold half the egg whites into the chocolate mixture. Gently fold the chocolate mixture back into the remaining beaten egg white mixture until no white streaks remain. Spoon equal amounts of the batter into the prepared ramekins. Place the ramekins on a baking sheet and bake about 10 to 15 minutes, or until soufflés are puffed and firm. Dust with confectioner's sugar and serve at once.

PER SERVING: Calories 123; Protein 5g; Total Fat 8g; Sat Fat 5g; Cholesterol 0mg; Carbohydrate 13g; Dietary Fiber 2g; Sodium 57mg

Chocolate-Hazelnut Sundaes

(LACTO-OVO)

The chocolate-hazelnut sauce also makes an excellent fondue for fresh and dried fruits, as well as gluten-free cookies and biscotti.

MAKES 6 SERVINGS

¼ cup water

¾ cup Nutella

3 cups (1½ pints) gluten-free vanilla ice
   cream, frozen yogurt, or nondairy frozen
   dessert

2 tablespoons toasted chopped hazelnuts (see
   Cook's Tip, Panforte recipe, page 218)

Whipped cream

6 maraschino cherries

In a small saucepan, heat the water over medium-low heat until just warm. Add the Nutella and cook, stirring, until thoroughly incorporated and hot. Remove from heat and let cool to slightly warm or room temperature.

Divide the ice cream evenly among 6 dessert dishes. Top each with about 2½ tablespoons of the sauce, then sprinkle with 1 teaspoon of the nuts. Serve at once, garnished with whipped cream and a cherry.

PER SERVING: Calories 316; Protein 8g; Total Fat 20g; Sat Fat 7g; Cholesterol 29mg; Carbohydrate 31g; Dietary Fiber 2g; Sodium 167mg

Chocolate *Sorbetto*

(VEGAN)

For adults only, this chocolate-intense dessert requires the addition of liqueur to achieve its smoother status of *sorbetto*, versus Italian ice or granita. To make the latter, follow the freezing instructions for Italian Strawberry Ice, page 224.

MAKES 6 SERVINGS

2¼ cups water, divided
1 cup sugar
½ cup unsweetened Dutch-process cocoa
2 tablespoons hazelnut, almond, coffee, or orange liqueur

In a medium saucepan, bring 1 cup of water and the sugar to a simmer over medium heat. Cook, stirring constantly, until the sugar is completely dissolved. Reduce the heat to low and whisk in the cocoa powder; whisk constantly until completely smooth, about 2 minutes. Remove from heat and whisk in the remaining 1¼ cups of water and liqueur. Transfer the cocoa mixture to a covered container and refrigerate until well chilled, about 2 to 3 hours.

Freeze mixture in an ice-cream maker according to the manufacturer's instructions. Alternatively, pour into 2 (16-cube) plastic ice cube trays and freeze until solid, 4 to 6 hours. Transfer the cubes to a food processor fitted with the knife blade; process until smooth, working in batches, as necessary. If not serving immediately, transfer to a covered plastic container and store in the freezer up to 3 days. Serve frozen.

PER SERVING: Calories 159; Protein 1g; Total Fat 1g; Sat Fat 0g; Cholesterol 0mg; Carbohydrate 39g; Dietary Fiber 2g; Sodium 2mg

Poached Figs with Honey

(EGG-FREE/DAIRY-FREE)

Though fresh figs are divine by nature, their dried counterparts require a little intervention to be transformed into a truly awesome dessert. For sheer decadence, spoon the poached figs and honey syrup over gluten-free vanilla ice cream or soy frozen dessert.

MAKES 6 SERVINGS

1½ cups unsweetened apple juice
3 tablespoons honey
1 cinnamon stick
8 ounces dried Calimyrna figs (about 12), stemmed and halved lengthwise
Whipped cream (optional)

In a large saucepan, bring the apple juice, honey, and cinnamon to a simmer over medium-low heat. Add the figs, reduce the heat to low, and simmer, partially covered, until figs are very soft, about 10 to 15 minutes, stirring a few times. Using a slotted spoon, transfer figs to a shallow serving bowl. Reduce the cooking liquids over high heat until about ½ cup remains. Strain the syrup over the figs, discarding the cinnamon stick. Let cool to room temperature before serving with whipped cream, if desired. Completely cooled figs can be refrigerated, covered, up to 3 days before returning to room temperature and serving.

PER SERVING: Calories 163; Protein 1g; Total Fat 1g; Sat Fat 0g; Cholesterol 0mg; Carbohydrate 42g; Dietary Fiber 5g; Sodium 7mg

Grape and Mascarpone Pie

(EGG-FREE/LOW-CARB)

This quintessential late-summer and early fall pie can be made with just about any grape—a combination of green, red, and black is always appealing. For a delightful spring to midsummer dessert, replace the grapes with assorted fresh berries.

MAKES 12 SERVINGS

8 ounces mascarpone cheese, at room
    temperature
¼ cup gluten-free Neufchâtel cream cheese,
    at room temperature
¼ cup sugar
1 tablespoon fresh lemon juice
¾ teaspoon gluten-free vanilla extract
1 cup gluten-free nonfat sour cream
Nut Pie Crust, on the right, baked and cooled
2 to 3 cups seedless grapes

In the medium bowl, using an electric mixer, beat the mascarpone cheese, Neufchâtel cheese, sugar, lemon juice, and vanilla on medium speed until smooth. On low speed, beat in the sour cream until just combined. Spoon the filling into the cooled pie crust, spreading evenly with a spatula. Cover lightly with plastic wrap; refrigerate for a minimum of 8 hours, or up to 1 day.

Just before serving, scatter the grapes in a single layer evenly over top. Serve at once.

PER SERVING: Calories 318; Protein 8g; Total Fat 27g; Sat Fat 5g; Cholesterol 46mg; Carbohydrate 14g; Dietary Fiber 2g; Sodium 50mg

Nut Pie Crust

(DAIRY-FREE/LOW-CARB)

Use this protein-packed crust for countless no-bake pies and tarts.

MAKES 1 (9-INCH) PIE CRUST

2 cups nuts, preferably walnuts or pecans
1 to 2 tablespoons sugar
Pinch salt
6 tablespoons unsalted butter, melted

Preheat oven to 350F (175C). Lightly grease a deep-dish 8½- or 9-inch pie plate, and set aside.

In a food processor fitted with the knife blade, pulse nuts, sugar, and salt until ground. Add the melted butter and pulse to combine. Transfer nut mixture to the prepared pie plate, spreading and pressing evenly with your fingers to promote even baking.

Bake on the center oven rack 12 to 15 minutes, or until crust is lightly browned. Transfer to a rack to cool completely before filling (crust will firm as it cools). Use as directed in recipe. Completely cooled crust can be stored in an airtight container at room temperature up to 24 hours, or refrigerated up to 3 days.

PER SERVING (⅛ of recipe): Calories 276; Protein 8g; Total Fat 27g; Sat Fat 7g; Cholesterol 25mg; Carbohydrate 5g; Dietary Fiber 2g; Sodium 18mg

Italian Lemon Pudding Cake with Raspberries

(LACTO-OVO)

For lemon lovers throughout the planet, this lip-smacking, lemony pudding cake is luxurious with fresh raspberries— or any seasonal berry, for that matter—and whipped cream.

MAKES 4 SERVINGS

⅓ cup sugar, plus additional, as necessary
2 tablespoons honey
1 large egg
1½ tablespoons butter, softened
2 teaspoons grated lemon zest
2 tablespoons all-purpose gluten-free flour
¼ cup skim milk
¼ cup buttermilk
¼ cup fresh lemon juice
3 large egg whites, at room temperature
Pinch salt
Fresh raspberries, to serve
Whipped cream, to serve (optional)

Preheat oven to 350F (175C). Set baking rack in lower third of oven. Lightly oil an 8-inch deep-dish pie dish and sprinkle with some sugar; set aside.

In a large bowl, using an electric mixer on medium speed, beat the ⅓ cup sugar, honey, egg, butter, and lemon zest for 2 minutes. Add the flour and beat until smooth. Add the milk, buttermilk, and lemon juice and beat until combined. In a clean and dry medium bowl, using clean and dry beaters, beat the egg whites with the salt on medium speed until soft peaks form, about 2 minutes. With a spatula, stir about one-third of the egg whites into the batter; gently fold in the remaining egg whites.

Spoon the batter into the prepared pie dish and place in a 9 × 13-inch baking dish. Add enough warm water to the baking dish to come halfway up the sides of the pie dish. Bake in the lower third of the oven for 35 to 40 minutes, or until lightly browned and set (pudding cake should be firm yet jiggly, like Jell-O). Transfer the pudding cake to a wire rack to cool 15 minutes. Serve slightly warm or at room temperature, garnished with the raspberries and whipped cream, if using. Completely cooled pudding cake can be stored, covered, in the refrigerator up to 1 day before serving chilled.

PER SERVING (without raspberries): Calories 196; Protein 6g; Total Fat 6g; Sat Fat 3g; Cholesterol 65mg; Carbohydrate 32g; Dietary Fiber 0g; Sodium 158mg

Melon and Blueberry Salad

(VEGAN)

While this super-easy fruit salad is delicious on its own, it's out of this world spooned over gluten-free vanilla ice cream or soy frozen dessert.

MAKES 4 TO 6 SERVINGS

2 cups cubed or balled fresh cantaloupe
2 cups cubed or balled fresh honeydew
2 cups fresh blueberries
2 tablespoons sugar
Fresh mint sprigs for garnish (optional)

Place the fruit in a large serving bowl and sprinkle with the sugar; toss gently to combine. Cover and refrigerate a minimum of 2 hours, or overnight. Toss gently and serve chilled, garnished with the mint, if using.

PER SERVING: Calories 127; Protein 2g; Total Fat 1g; Sat Fat 0g; Cholesterol 0mg; Carbohydrate 32g; Dietary Fiber 3g; Sodium 20mg

Oranges in Spiced Red Wine

(VEGAN)

Here is a light and lovely dessert to serve after a hearty meal around the holidays. For a festive touch, divide the orange segments among six wineglasses and pour equal amounts of the wine syrup over each.

MAKES 6 SERVINGS

1½ cups dry red wine, divided
½ cup sugar
2 cinnamon sticks
1 tablespoon grated orange zest
6 large navel oranges (about 8 ounces each), peeled, white pith and membranes removed, and oranges segmented

In a small saucepan, bring 1 cup of the wine, sugar, and cinnamon sticks to a brisk simmer over medium heat, stirring often until the sugar is dissolved. Reduce the heat slightly and simmer, stirring occasionally, until mixture is reduced to half (about ¾ cup), 10 to 15 minutes. Remove pan from heat and stir in the remaining ½ cup of wine and orange zest; let cool to room temperature.

Place orange segments in a serving bowl. Strain the wine syrup over the oranges; toss gently to thoroughly combine. Cover and refrigerate a minimum of 2 hours or overnight. Serve chilled.

PER SERVING: Calories 155; Protein 2g; Total Fat 0g; Sat Fat 0g; Cholesterol 0mg; Carbohydrate 30g; Dietary Fiber 1g; Sodium 39mg

Panforte

(EGG-FREE/DAIRY-FREE)

A specialty of Siena, panforte is a highly spiced fruitcake traditionally eaten at Christmastime. Feel free to substitute your favorite dried and candied fruits for those suggested in the recipe. Light corn syrup can be used in lieu of the honey, if desired.

MAKES 12 SERVINGS

½ cup gluten-free all-purpose flour
2 tablespoons unsweetened cocoa powder
½ tablespoon ground cinnamon
¼ teaspoon ground nutmeg
¾ cup coarsely chopped dried figs
½ cup coarsely chopped pitted dates
½ cup coarsely chopped walnuts
½ cup coarsely chopped blanched almonds
½ cup coarsely chopped toasted hazelnuts (see Cook's Tip, page 218)
1 cup coarsely chopped gluten-free candied citron
2/3 cup sugar
2/3 cup honey
Confectioner's sugar

Preheat oven to 300F (150C). Grease the bottom and sides of a 9-inch Springform pan. Cut a 9-inch circle of waxed paper or parchment paper; place in bottom of pan and grease. Set aside.

In a small bowl, whisk together the flour, cocoa, cinnamon, and nutmeg until thoroughly combined. In a large bowl, combine the figs, dates, nuts, and citron. Add the flour mixture, stirring well to break up any lumps.

In a small saucepan, combine the sugar and honey; cook over medium-low heat, stirring occasionally, until syrup forms a firm ball when dropped into cold water, about 10 minutes (do not let mixture boil). Immediately pour the syrup over the fruit mixture, stirring quickly until the flour is thoroughly moistened.

Spoon the batter into the prepared pan. Press into an even layer with the back of a large spoon. Bake for 45 minutes. (Do not test for doneness. Cake will be soft and firm as it cools.) Let cool completely in the pan on a rack.

Remove the sides of the Springform pan and invert the cake onto a plate lined with a piece of waxed paper. Remove the bottom and peel off the parchment circle. Set a cake plate over the top, and turn the cake right side up. Sprinkle with the confectioner's sugar. Cut into wedges and serve at room temperature. Completely cooled cake can be stored in an airtight container at room temperature up to 3 days, or refrigerated up to 1 week.

PER SERVING: Calories 327; Protein 4g; Total Fat 9g; Sat Fat 1g; Cholesterol 0mg; Carbohydrate 62g; Dietary Fiber 3g; Sodium 61mg

Cook's Tip

To toast hazelnuts, preheat oven to 375F (190C). Spread nuts in a single layer on an ungreased baking sheet; bake about 10 minutes, or until fragrant and lightly toasted. Let cool slightly before placing nuts between a clean kitchen towel and rubbing briskly to remove most of the brown papery skins.

Baked Stuffed Peaches

(VEGAN)

Everyone loves peaches, especially the Italians, who are fond of stuffing their favorite fruits and vegetables. For best results, select peaches that are ripe yet firm when gently pressed.

MAKES 4 LARGE OR 8 SMALL SERVINGS

4 ripe yet firm medium peaches (about
    6 ounces each), unpeeled, halved
    crosswise, and pitted
½ cup fresh gluten-free, egg-free, dairy-free,
    crust-free plain bread crumbs
½ cup white sugar
⅓ cup finely ground walnuts
2 tablespoons Dutch-process cocoa
1 tablespoon Marsala wine or sherry
½ cup dry white wine
½ cup apple or pear juice
1½ tablespoons light brown sugar

Preheat the oven to 350F (175C). Lightly oil a shallow baking dish just large enough to accommodate the peach halves in a single layer; set aside.

Scoop out about 1 teaspoon of peach flesh from the center of each peach half and set aside. In a small bowl, mix together the bread crumbs, white sugar, ground nuts, cocoa, and Marsala. Chop the peach flesh and add to the bread crumb mixture, stirring to combine.

Fill the peach halves evenly with the stuffing (do not pack down); transfer to the prepared baking dish. Combine the wine and juice in a small measuring cup and pour around the peaches. Sprinkle the peaches evenly with the brown sugar. Bake, uncovered, about 25 minutes, or until peaches are tender but not falling apart. Serve warm. Completely cooled baked stuffed peaches can be refrigerated, covered, up to 24 hours before reheating in a low oven (about 225F/105C) for about 25 minutes.

PER SERVING: Calories 293; Protein 5g; Total Fat 7g; Sat Fat 1g; Cholesterol 0mg; Carbohydrate 54g; Dietary Fiber 4g; Sodium 34mg

Chilled Stuffed Pears with Gorgonzola and Honey

(EGG-FREE/LOW-CARB)

This elegant, no-cook dessert is the perfect conclusion to a heavy meal. Any gluten-free domestic blue cheese can replace the Gorgonzola, if desired. The recipe easily doubles to serve 8 people.

MAKES 4 SERVINGS

2 small ripe yet firm pears (about 6 ounces each), unpeeled, halved lengthwise with stems intact

Juice of ½ medium lemon (about 1½ tablespoons)

2 teaspoons honey

2 tablespoons (1 ounce) gluten-free crumbled Gorgonzola cheese

4 teaspoons finely ground walnuts

Remove the cores and about 1 teaspoon of flesh from each pear half. Using a pastry brush, brush the entire cut side of the pears with the lemon juice. Fill each cavity with ½ teaspoon of honey; top the cavity with ½ tablespoon cheese. Sprinkle the entire cut side evenly with 1 teaspoon of ground nuts. Repeat with remaining 3 pear halves. Serve at once, or cover and refrigerate overnight and serve chilled.

PER SERVING: Calories 103; Protein 3g; Total Fat 4g; Sat Fat 1g; Cholesterol 5mg; Carbohydrate 17g; Dietary Fiber 2g; Sodium 99mg

Pignoli Cookies

(DAIRY-FREE/LOW-CARB)

These melt-in-your-mouth cookies are nice to serve around the holidays—or anytime, for that matter—with a cup of hot tea or coffee. Almond paste (not to be confused with almond filling or marzipan) can be located in most well-stocked supermarkets in the baking aisle. Check the label carefully, as some brands contain wheat starch.

MAKES ABOUT 3 DOZEN COOKIES

1 (8-ounce) can pure almond paste, broken into small pieces

1 cup sugar

2 egg whites

Pinch salt

¼ cup pine nuts

Preheat oven to 325F (165C). Line two baking sheets with parchment paper and set aside.

In a food processor fitted with the knife blade, process the almond paste until almost smooth. With the processor running, slowly add sugar through the feed tube until incorporated. Turn off food processor and add the egg whites and salt; process in on/off motions until a smooth batter forms.

Using a level tablespoon, drop the dough onto the prepared baking sheets, leaving a 2-inch space between each cookie. Gently press about 3 or 4 pine nuts into each cookie. Bake on the center oven rack 12 to 15 minutes, or until cookies are firm and lightly browned. Let cool on baking sheets for 5 minutes before carefully sliding parchment paper off of baking sheets and placing onto wire racks. When cookies are completely cooled, peel gently from parchment. Completely cooled cookies can be stored between wax paper in an airtight container up to 3 days for optimal freshness.

PER SERVING (per cookie, or 1/36 of recipe): Calories 56; Protein 1g; Total Fat 2g; Sat Fat 0g; Cholesterol 0mg; Carbohydrate 9g; Dietary Fiber 0g; Sodium 7mg

Tuscan Plum Pudding

(LACTO-OVO/LOW-CARB)

Dried figs or apricots can stand in for the prunes in this healthy, low-carb pudding, if desired.

MAKES 4 SERVINGS

1 cup gluten-free low-fat ricotta cheese

3 egg yolks

2 tablespoons sugar

½ teaspoon gluten-free vanilla extract

¼ teaspoon gluten-free almond extract (optional)

¼ teaspoon ground cinnamon

½ cup chopped pitted prunes, soaked in warm water to cover until plumped, drained well

2 teaspoons slivered almonds or pine nuts (optional)

Preheat oven to 350F (175C). Lightly oil 4 (½-cup) ovenproof custard cups and set aside.

In a large bowl, with an electric mixer on low speed, beat the ricotta cheese, egg yolks, sugar, vanilla extract, almond extract (if using), and cinnamon until thoroughly blended. Stir in the fruit until thoroughly incorporated. Spoon the custard mixture into the prepared custard cups and place on a baking sheet. Sprinkle each with ½ teaspoon almonds, if using. Bake on the center oven rack for 15 to 18 minutes, or until tops are firm to the touch but not browned. Let cool 15 minutes before serving warm or at room temperature. Alternatively,

completely cooled custard can be refrigerated, covered, up to 2 days and served chilled.

PER SERVING: Calories 115; Protein 9g; Total Fat 4g; Sat Fat 2g; Cholesterol 162mg; Carbohydrate 9g; Dietary Fiber 0g; Sodium 235mg

Polenta Pound Cake

(LACTO-OVO)

This lemon-scented pound cake is wonderful topped with fresh strawberries and whipped cream, or all by itself with a cup of tea. For best results, use stone-ground yellow cornmeal in lieu of the coarsely ground type, which is commonly used to make polenta.

MAKES 1 (9 × 5-INCH) POUND CAKE

4 ounces unsalted butter, softened

1 cup sugar

Finely grated zest of 1 medium lemon (about 1 tablespoon), or 2 teaspoons dried lemon peel

3 eggs, at room temperature

1 teaspoon gluten-free vanilla extract

½ teaspoon gluten-free almond extract

½ cup gluten-free light sour cream

1 cup all-purpose gluten-free flour

½ cup stone-ground yellow cornmeal

½ teaspoon gluten-free baking powder

¼ teaspoon salt

½ cup pine nuts or slivered almonds

Preheat oven to 350F (175C). Lightly grease a 9 × 5-inch loaf pan and set aside.

Place the butter, sugar, and lemon peel in a large bowl. Using an electric mixer on medium speed, beat until light and fluffy, about 3 minutes. Reduce speed to low; add the eggs, one at a time. Add the extracts and sour cream. Gradually add the flour, cornmeal, baking powder, and salt. Beat on medium speed 2 minutes.

Spoon the batter into the prepared loaf pan. Scatter the nuts over the top and gently press them into the batter. Bake on the center oven rack 1 hour or until golden brown and a knife inserted in the center comes out clean. (If top is browning too quickly, cover loosely with foil after about 30 minutes.) Remove from oven and allow to cool 15 minutes. Loosen the sides with the tip of a sharp knife and turn out onto a wire rack to cool to room temperature. Cake can be stored in an airtight container at room temperature up to two days, or frozen up to 3 months.

PER SERVING ($^1/_{12}$ of recipe): Calories 246; Protein 5g; Total Fat 13g; Sat Fat 6g; Cholesterol 75mg; Carbohydrate 30g; Dietary Fiber 1g; Sodium 81mg

Raspberries with Whipped Ricotta and Honey

(EGG-FREE)

This luscious and lovely dessert can be made with halved strawberries or whole blackberries, or a combination of all three. For a touch of elegance, present in red wineglasses.

MAKES 6 SERVINGS

1 cup gluten-free whole-milk ricotta cheese
1 cup gluten-free nonfat ricotta cheese
4 ounces gluten-free light cream cheese, room temperature
4 tablespoons sugar, divided
3 tablespoons honey
½ teaspoon gluten-free vanilla extract

¼ teaspoon gluten-free almond extract
2 pints/4 cups fresh raspberries
2 teaspoons fresh lemon juice

In a medium bowl, using an electric mixer on medium speed, beat ricotta cheeses, cream cheese, 2 tablespoons sugar, honey, and extracts until smooth and creamy (like frosting). Transfer mixture to a small bowl. Cover and refrigerate a minimum of 2 hours, or up to 1 day.

In a large bowl, combine raspberries, lemon juice, and remaining 2 tablespoons sugar; toss gently to coat. Let stand 30 minutes at room temperature; toss again.

To serve, stir the ricotta mixture and divide evenly among 6 wineglasses or dessert bowls. Top with equal amounts of raspberries and any accumulated juices. Serve at once.

PER SERVING: Calories 250; Protein 13g; Total Fat 9g; Sat Fat 6g; Cholesterol 38mg; Carbohydrate 31g; Dietary Fiber 4g; Sodium 221mg

Variation

To make Fresh Fruit with Whipped Ricotta and Honey Dip, omit 2 tablespoons of sugar and the lemon juice. Replace the raspberries with a mixture of fresh seasonal berries, grapes, pineapple spears, etc. Prepare the whipped ricotta mixture as directed in the recipe. Serve with the fresh fruit for dipping.

Italian Rice Pudding

(DAIRY-FREE)

This creamy rice pudding is the ultimate comfort food for all seasons and all reasons—it's sweet, soothing, and satisfying. Any dried fruit—currants, cranberries, cherries, apricots, dates—can replace the raisins, if desired.

MAKES 6 SERVINGS

½ cup long-grain white rice

½ cup water

3½ cups rice milk (or skim milk for dairy
    option), divided

1 cinnamon stick

2 eggs

½ cup sugar

¼ cup golden or black raisins

1 teaspoon gluten-free vanilla extract

Pinch ground nutmeg

Ground cinnamon, for garnish

In a medium stockpot, combine rice and water; bring to a boil over medium heat. Cover and reduce heat to low; cook, without stirring, until rice has absorbed all the water, about 4 to 5 minutes. Stir in 3 cups of the rice milk and cinnamon stick. Bring to a boil over medium heat, stirring a few times. Cover and reduce heat to between low and medium-low; cook, stirring occasionally, until rice is tender and most of the milk has been absorbed, about 25 minutes.

While rice is cooking, place eggs, sugar, and remaining ½ cup of rice milk in a small bowl; whisk well to combine. When rice is tender and most of the milk has been absorbed, very gradually add the egg mixture, stirring constantly over low heat, until pudding is thick and creamy, about 3 minutes. Stir in raisins and remove from heat; cover and let

stand 5 minutes. Remove cinnamon stick and stir in the vanilla extract and nutmeg. Serve at room temperature (pudding will thicken as it cools), sprinkled lightly with cinnamon. Alternatively, completely cooled pudding can be covered and refrigerated a minimum of 3 hours or up to 3 days, and served chilled.

PER SERVING: Calories 219; Protein 8g; Total Fat 2g; Sat Fat 1g; Cholesterol 73mg; Carbohydrate 42g; Dietary Fiber 0g; Sodium 96mg

Italian Strawberries

(VEGAN/LOW-CARB)

This simple dessert is beloved throughout Italy—sometimes, for good measure, a sliced banana is added just before serving.

MAKES 4 SERVINGS

4 cups strawberries, washed, hulled, and
    halved lengthwise

1 to 2 tablespoons sugar

⅔ cup orange juice, preferably freshly
    squeezed

1 tablespoon Grand Marnier or other orange
    liqueur (optional)

Place the strawberries in a medium-size serving bowl and sprinkle with the sugar; toss gently to combine. Add the juice and liqueur, if using; toss gently to combine. Cover and refrigerate a minimum of 3 hours or overnight and serve chilled.

PER SERVING: Calories 74; Protein 1g; Total Fat 1g; Sat Fat 0g; Cholesterol 0mg; Carbohydrate 18g; Dietary Fiber 3g; Sodium 2mg

Italian Strawberry Tart with Pastry Cream

(LACTO-OVO)

Don't be daunted by this spectacular strawberry dessert—both the pastry cream and crust can be made well ahead of assembling and serving the tart in just about 15 minutes. Raspberries can replace the strawberries, if desired.

MAKES 8 SERVINGS

> 3½ cups (about 2 pounds) whole small strawberries, or large strawberries, halved or quartered
> ¼ cup sugar
> Pastry Cream, on the right, well-chilled
> 1 Gluten-Free Sweet Pastry Crust, completely cooked and completely cooled (page 224)
> Confectioner's sugar

In a large bowl, toss the strawberries and sugar until combined; let stand at room temperature about 10 minutes.

Meanwhile, spread the cold pastry cream evenly over the bottom of the completely cooled crust. Toss the strawberries; drain off and discard the accumulated juices. Starting from the outer edge of the tart, arrange the drained strawberries in attractive concentric circles over the pastry cream. Dust with confectioner's sugar and serve immediately.

PER SERVING: Calories 341; Protein 6g; Total Fat 17g; Sat Fat 9g; Cholesterol 196mg; Carbohydrate 42g; Dietary Fiber 2g; Sodium 247mg

Pastry Cream

(LACTO-OVO/LOW-CARB)

Use this basic Italian cream as a filling for countless gluten-free tarts, pies, cakes, and other pastries, or serve as a pudding, garnished with fresh berries.

YIELDS ABOUT 2 CUPS

> 2 cups whole milk
> ¼ teaspoon salt
> 6 large egg yolks, at room temperature
> ½ cup sugar
> 3 tablespoons cornstarch
> 2 tablespoons cold, unsalted butter
> 1 tablespoon gluten-free pure vanilla extract

In a large saucepan, bring the milk and salt to a boil, take off the heat, and set aside.

In the bowl of an electric mixer with a paddle attachment, beat the egg yolks and sugar on medium-high speed until the mixture is thick and light yellow, about 3 minutes. Turn the speed to low, and beat in the cornstarch. Slowly pour the hot milk into the egg mixture and beat until well blended. Pour the mixture back into the saucepan.

Cook the mixture over medium heat, stirring constantly with a whisk or wooden spoon until the mixture becomes thick and starts to gently boil. Continue to cook for 1 to 2 minutes more. Remove from heat and stir in the cold butter and vanilla. If the mixture appears curdled, whisk vigorously until it comes together again. Strain the mixture through a fine sieve into a bowl. Cover with a piece of plastic wrap, pressed directly on top of the pastry cream to prevent a skin from forming. Refrigerate until cold, about 2 hours. The pastry cream can be stored up to 3 days in the refrigerator. Whisk the pastry cream until smooth before using.

Gluten-Free Sweet Pastry Crust

(EGG-FREE/LOW-CARB)

Use this light and flaky crust for any fruit or custard pie. For a savory crust, see the Variation, on the right.

MAKES 1 (9-INCH) PIE CRUST

¾ cup white rice flour

1 teaspoon sugar

½ teaspoon xanthan gum

¼ teaspoon salt

⅓ cup butter, in about 5 pieces

2 tablespoons cold water, plus additional, if necessary

1 egg white lightly beaten with 1 tablespoon water to make an egg wash (optional)

Preheat oven to 350F (175C).

In a food processor fitted with the knife blade, pulse the dry ingredients until thoroughly combined. Add the butter and pulse until the mixture resembles coarse meal. Add the cold water a little at a time, pulsing until a ball forms.

Form dough into a disk with your hands. Roll out the dough between 2 sheets of waxed paper or aluminum foil. The dough should be about 1½ inches larger in diameter than the pie plate. Peel 1 sheet of waxed paper away from the dough. Place the pie crust in an ungreased 9-inch pie plate. Remove the top sheet of waxed paper. Trim excess dough and crimp edges to form a decorative border. (At this point, proceed as directed in most recipes requiring an uncooked pastry crust.)

To prebake a crust to be further baked with a filling: Prick the bottom and sides of the dough with a fork and bake in the center of the oven for 10 to 12 minutes, or until very lightly browned. To safeguard against a soggy crust, brush the bottom and sides with the egg wash, if using. Return to oven and bake an additional 3 to 4 minutes, or until the egg wash is set. Set aside to cool before filling.

To completely cook a crust to be filled with fruit, chilled fillings, etc.: Prick the bottom and sides of the dough with a fork and bake in the center of the oven for about 15 minutes, or until lightly browned. To safeguard against a soggy crust, brush the bottom and sides with the egg wash, if using. Return to oven and bake an additional 3 to 4 minutes, or until the egg wash is set. Set aside to cool completely before filling.

Variation

To make Gluten-Free Savory Pastry Crust, follow the directions for Sweet Pastry Crust, omitting the sugar. Add ½ to 1½ teaspoons of mixed dried herbs (oregano, thyme, rosemary, etc.) or Italian seasoning to the dry ingredients before pulsing, if desired.

Italian Strawberry Ice

(VEGAN)

More rustic than sorbettos, Italian ices, also known as granitas, require no special equipment to make, save for a blender and a freezer. Raspberries or blackberries can be substituted for the strawberries, if desired.

MAKES 6 SERVINGS

1 cup sugar

½ cup water

2 pints (4 cups) fresh ripe strawberries, rinsed and hulled

3 tablespoons freshly squeezed orange juice

2 tablespoons fresh lemon juice

Fresh mint sprigs, for garnish (optional)

In a small saucepan, bring the sugar and water to a simmer over medium heat. Cook, stirring constantly, until the sugar is completely dissolved. Remove from heat and let cool to room temperature.

Place the strawberries in a food processor fitted with the knife blade, or in a blender; process or blend until smooth and pureed. Add the cooled sugar mixture, orange juice, and lemon juice; process or blend until thoroughly combined. Transfer to 2 (16-cube) plastic ice cube trays and freeze until solid, about 6 hours (frozen mixture can be stored in freezer in trays, covered with plastic wrap, up to 3 days).

About 45 minutes before serving, place ice cube trays in refrigerator to soften slightly. Spoon the strawberry ice into individual sorbet glasses or small serving bowls (if necessary, break up any hard ice crystals with a small metal spoon until fairly smooth) and serve at once, garnished with the fresh mint, if using.

PER SERVING: Calories 163; Protein 1g; Total Fat 0g; Sat Fat 0g; Cholesterol 0mg; Carbohydrate 41g; Dietary Fiber 2g; Sodium 1mg

METRIC CONVERSION CHARTS

COMPARISON TO METRIC MEASURE

When You Know	Symbol	Multiply By	To Find	Symbol
teaspoons	tsp	5.0	milliliters	ml
tablespoons	tbsp	15.0	milliliters	ml
fluid ounces	fl. oz.	30.0	milliliters	ml
cups	c	0.24	liters	l
pints	pt.	0.47	liters	l
quarts	qt.	0.95	liters	l
ounces	oz.	28.0	grams	g
pounds	lb.	0.45	kilograms	kg
Fahrenheit	F	5/9 (after subtracting 32)	Celsius	C

FAHRENHEIT TO CELSIUS

F	C
200–205	95
220–225	105
245–250	120
275	135
300–305	150
325–330	165
345–350	175
370–375	190
400–405	205
425–430	220
445–450	230
470–475	245
500	260

LIQUID MEASURE TO LITERS

¼ cup	=	0.06 liters
½ cup	=	0.12 liters
¾ cup	=	0.18 liters
1 cup	=	0.24 liters
1¼ cups	=	0.30 liters
1½ cups	=	0.36 liters
2 cups	=	0.48 liters
2½ cups	=	0.60 liters
3 cups	=	0.72 liters
3½ cups	=	0.84 liters
4 cups	=	0.96 liters
4½ cups	=	1.08 liters
5 cups	=	1.20 liters
5½ cups	=	1.32 liters

LIQUID MEASURE TO MILLILITERS

¼ teaspoon	=	1.25 milliliters
½ teaspoon	=	2.50 milliliters
¾ teaspoon	=	3.75 milliliters
1 teaspoon	=	5.00 milliliters
1¼ teaspoons	=	6.25 milliliters
1½ teaspoons	=	7.50 milliliters
1¾ teaspoons	=	8.75 milliliters
2 teaspoons	=	10.0 milliliters
1 tablespoon	=	15.0 milliliters
2 tablespoons	=	30.0 milliliters

INDEX

Page numbers in **bold** indicate charts; those followed by "n" indicate notes.